VERDICT ON JESUS

Leslie Badham (1908–75)

VERDICT ON JESUS

A New Statement of Evidence

Leslie Badham

with an Introduction by
Paul Badham
and new chapters by
Paul Badham and Gregory A. Barker

Originally published in Great Britain in 1950 Second edition published 1971 Third edition published 1983
Fourth edition published 1995 by IKON Productions Ltd
Fifth edition published in Great Britain in 2010 by SPCK

This edition published in Great Britain in 2020 by The Newson Trust

British Library Cataloguing-in-Publication Data
A catalogue record for this book is available from the British Library
ISBN 978-1-9163862-0-4

Image credit: “A fragment of a stone mosaic of Jesus Christ’s resurrection” by “giedrius_b” is used though a Shutterstock License.

Cover design: Laurence Hall and Emily Turvey

Contents

Contributors

The Revd Leslie Badham (1908–75) was a Senior Scholar at what was then known as St David's College Lampeter, before taking a second degree at Jesus College, Oxford. He served as an Air Force Chaplain during the Second World War, and afterwards was Rector of Rotherfield Peppard from 1946 to 1958, Vicar of Windsor from 1958 to 1973, and Chaplain to Her Majesty the Queen from 1964 to 1975. He combined his Church ministry with radio broadcasting, lecturing and writing. His other publications include *These Greatest Things* and *Love Speaks from the Cross*.

The Revd Professor Paul Badham is Emeritus Professor of Theology and Religious Studies at the University of Wales, Trinity Saint David. His publications include *Christian Beliefs about Life after Death, Immortality or Extinction?*, *The Contemporary Challenge of Modernist Theology* and *Is there a Christian Case for Assisted Dying?*

Dr Gregory A. Barker is a Fellow of the University of Winchester, an educational trainer and consultant, and writer. His books include *Jesus Beyond Christianity: The Classic Texts* and *Jesus in the World's Faiths: Leading Thinkers from Five Religions Reflect on His Meaning*.

Your Gift of Verdict on Jesus

You are being given this book under the terms of the Will of the Rev. Stanley Newson a former Vicar of St. Andrew's Chelsea. He found it valuable in discussion groups in his parish and wanted all future clergy of the Church of England to be sent a copy to help them in their ministry. The Newson Trust was established to fulfil his wishes and has extended this to all new Anglican clergy in Scotland, Wales and Ireland and more recently also to Methodist and United Reform Ministers.

Verdict on Jesus was written by the Rev. Leslie Badham, formerly Vicar of Windsor and Chaplain to the Queen. This sixth edition has been revised by his son, Paul Badham, Emeritus Professor of Theology, the University of Wales, Trinity Saint David and by the Rev. Dr. Gregory A. Barker, an educational consultant and former Head of the Department of Religious Studies at the University of Wales, Trinity Saint David. The Rev. S.G. Newson provided in his Will that, if funds permitted, clergy could also be given Henry Drummond's *The Greatest Thing in the World*. This is a classic religious meditation on St Paul's hymn to love in 1 Corinthians. The two books have been bound together in this edition for ease of access.

The Impact and Influence of Jesus

Verdict on Jesus offers a very distinctive approach to Jesus. It considers his impact and influence over the past two thousand years and asks what this tells us of his person and role. For almost all human beings, our biggest impact is during our lifetime. We may live on in the memories of our family, friends, and colleagues for a generation or two, and a tiny proportion of us will be remembered for centuries. But in the vast majority of cases our influence declines from our retirement onwards. It seems true of only a handful of religious figures that their influence continues to develop over the millennia. What is astounding about Jesus is the impact he has had on so many areas of life and for so long. Not only that, but his impact continues to grow.

In *Verdict on Jesus* Leslie Badham, covers not only the historical Jesus, but also the Jesus who has shaped subsequent history. He documents how much of western literature, art and music has been written in response to Jesus' life and work. He shows the social impact of Jesus' teaching on the formation of schools, hospitals, and universities. He explores the impact of Jesus' teaching on ethics, politics, philosophy, and science. No one in human history has had so profound and long lasting an influence on human history. It is an influence that continues to exert formidable power.

The Background to Verdict on Jesus

Verdict was written when Leslie Badham was Rector of Rotherfield Peppard, a small village in the Chilterns. This rectorship was a 'College living' which means that my father was appointed to the church by Jesus College Oxford and that the parish had always been served by scholarly priests. Leslie Badham continued in that tradition. For him the teaching role of the priesthood was its primary obligation. His sermons were always the product of long hours of work, both theological and literary. Sunday by Sunday the church was full for morning and evening worship, drawing his congregation from miles around as well as from the local village. The chapters in *Verdict on Jesus* and in his later work *Love Speaks from the Cross* all began life as sermons. They were then polished as broadcast talks and finally emerged in their published form in 1950. In 1958 Leslie Badham moved to Windsor Parish Church and subsequently became a Chaplain to the Queen. In that latter capacity, he greatly valued invitations to preach in the Queen's private chapel in Windsor Great Park.

This is the sixth edition, updated for the current generation of Anglican clergy and others. Its central argument is of permanent validity: the impact and influence of Jesus on European and global history. That influence is simply a fact of history, and it is good that new clergy and the wider public should have a continuing opportunity to read and ponder on these remarkable facts about Jesus highlighted by Leslie Badham. To help this, we have updated the language to accord with 21st century usage while retaining Leslie Badham's key messages and the quotations he cited.

His argument has been supplemented by considering the influence of Jesus' teaching on two of the most dramatic historical developments in the final quarter of the twentieth century: the fall of communism in Europe and of apartheid in South Africa. *Verdict* has also been supplemented to reflect revived controversies in science and religion in the twenty-first century, and to look at the impact and influence of Jesus beyond the Christian world.

Religion and the Fall of Communism

The two most dramatic events of the final quarter of the twentieth century were the sudden disintegration of atheistic communism in Eastern Europe and the former Soviet Union and the equally unexpected collapse of apartheid in South Africa. In both cases a very wide range of factors contributed, but one factor that should not be ignored is the continuing influence of Jesus' teaching in the hearts and minds of many of the people involved.

In Eastern Europe it should be beyond dispute that the strength of Catholic Christianity in Poland at that time played a key role in the events. Pope John Paul II's comment 'God has won in Eastern Europe' may be an oversimplification but Gorbachev's testimony at least supports the importance of the Pope's own role: 'What has happened in Eastern Europe in the last few years would not have happened without this Pope.'[1] The millions who flocked to his three papal pilgrimages in Poland demonstrated the undefeated spirit of a Christian heritage against which the tide of communism as an overall worldview faltered and died.

Poland was exceptional, but in other countries of Eastern Europe Christianity had continued to subsist as the one alternative ideology allowed to have any corporate existence. This enabled the churches to form a nucleus of dissent and to act as midwife to the change that occurred during the almost bloodless period from communist to democratic societies.[2] In the Baltic states of the former Soviet Union, in the Ukraine, Bulgaria, Georgia, and Armenia, a Christian heritage helped

---

1 Michael Bourdeaux, *The Role of Religion in the Fall of Soviet Communism* (London: Centre for Policy Studies, 1992), p. 16.

2 Paul Badham, 'Religion and the Fall of Communism' in John Esposito and Michael Watson, *Religion and Global Order* (Cardiff: University of Wales Press, 2000).

towards the revival of historic national feeling. Within Russia itself the revival of Christianity was a striking aspect of the new openness. The number of churches increased by 5,000 in the first three years of Gorbachev's rule, representing a doubling of their former number. Since then the revival has continued apace with the increasing restoration of church buildings, the revival of Christian music and culture, and the renaming of towns and villages back to their pre-revolutionary Christian identity. No wonder some speak of a new resurrection of Jesus in the hearts and minds of the Russian people.

Religion and the Collapse of Apartheid

In South Africa, opposition from the English speaking churches inside South Africa and from the World Council of Churches outside played a key role in alerting South Africans and the wider world to the evils of apartheid. Desmond Tutu was appointed General Secretary of the South African Council of Christian Churches, then Bishop of Johannesburg, and finally Archbishop of Cape Town and Primate of South Africa. His rise demonstrated the existential commitment of the Anglican Church to the principle that in Christ discrimination on grounds of race is unacceptable. In the end their arguments won over the theologians of the Dutch Reformed Church and thus spelt the end of any ideological justification for the 'separate development' of the peoples of South Africa. Once this had happened, apartheid came to a speedy end and a peaceful transfer of power to the Black majority was enabled to take place. This process was aided by Nelson Mandela's Methodist formation which led him to seek reconciliation and harmony among all the peoples of the new South Africa . To further this end Mandela appointed a truth and reconciliation commission chaired by Archbishop Tutu to aid understanding and peace .

Christianity in Relation to Science and Philosophy in the Twenty-first Century

One theme that runs through *Verdict on Jesus* is a conviction that the truth of Christianity depends on the rationality of belief in God. Leslie Badham was convinced that there could be no ultimate conflict between religion, science, and philosophy, for all that exists springs from the creative mind of God. He was always an enthusiast for Natural Theology and believed that reason could bring one to a well-evidenced conviction of God's reality. In the early years of the twenty-first century, this way of thinking became highly disputed. Richard Dawkins and a range of other writers who have come to be identified as 'the new atheists' have made a big impression on public opinion with their view that belief in God is both irrational and unscientific.[3] A number of Christian apologists have responded point by point to such arguments,[4] but these responses have as yet had nothing like the impact on the mind of the public that Dawkins has had. For this edition of *Verdict on Jesus,* Paul Badham has sought to address this challenge by adding a chapter on 'The Reasonableness of Belief in a Creator God in the Twenty-first Century'.

Jesus and the World Religions

The ongoing impact and influence of Jesus is the central thesis of *Verdict on Jesus* but, like nearly all his generation, Leslie Badham focused his attention almost entirely on the influence of Jesus within the Christian world. It is important however for us also to be aware of the influence Jesus has had on other world religions. This is the theme of an additional

---

[3] Richard Dawkins, *The God Delusion* (London: Bantam, 2006); Christopher Hitchens *God is not Great* (London: Atlantic Books, 2007).

[4] E.g. Alister and Joanna McGrath, *The Dawkins Delusion* (London: SPCK, 2007); Ian Markham, *Against Atheism: Why Dawkins, Hitchens and Harris are Fundamentally Wrong* (Chichester: Wiley Blackwell, 2010).

chapter by Gregory A. Barker editor of *Jesus in the World's Faiths*, and co-editor of *Jesus Beyond Christianity*.[5]

He shows that with the ending of the appalling anti-Semitism displayed over the centuries by the Christian churches, it is now possible for Jews and Christians seriously to engage together in the study of Jesus' life and teaching. We can see Jesus in his original context as a Jewish rabbi working within the life and thought world of first-century Judaism. Jesus himself, as well as the prophets before him, are part of our common Judaeo-Christian inheritance.

From the Islamic perspective Jesus is one of their greatest prophets. His name is always honoured by Muslims and traditionally they do not utter it without invoking a blessing. They believe in his virginal conception, miracle-working, ascension and second coming, though they reject his divinity and atoning death. Dr Barker gives a fascinating account of the Muslim understanding of Jesus and the influence Jesus' teaching and example has had on some developments within that religion, particularly within the Sufi tradition.

Within modern Hinduism, the person of Christ has had a fascination for many of its leading figures and reformers, including Ramakrishna,Vivekananda, and Mahatma Gandhi, all of whom have learnt from him. In Buddhism too Jesus has been much admired and some would even be willing to see him as one who fulfilled the Bodhisattva ideal. It is astonishing how great the impact of Jesus has been in these very different cultures, and Dr Barker's researches in the area can broaden our perspectives of Jesus and his role.

---

5 Gregory A. Barker, *Jesus in the World's Faiths: Scholars and Leaders from Five Religions Reflect on his Meaning* (Maryknoll: Orbis, 2007); Gregory A. Barker and Stephen E. Gregg, *Jesus Beyond Christianity: The Classic Texts* (Oxford: Oxford University Press, 2010).

However, the impact of Jesus goes even wider than the response to him of the great world religions. From 2004 to 2007 the Templeton Foundation funded a major survey of Chinese religious belief and practice. This survey found that only 2.8 per cent of Chinese professed Christianity and called themselves Christians, but that 11 per cent believed they 'should follow what was taught by the Christian God'.[6] This is a truly astonishing finding from a society that had been officially atheist for over sixty years, yet it testifies to the fascination with Jesus himself, which goes far beyond the boundaries of explicit Christianity. These further witnesses strengthen the awe and wonder that we feel in contemplating the life and work of the founder of Christianity, not only in his lifetime but in each of the succeeding millennia.

The Verdict on Jesus Website

To expand the usefulness of *Verdict on Jesus* the Newson Trust has created a website, www.verdictonjesus.com.

This includes video clips which can be used to stimulate discussion. The website also provides access to an article on '*Current trends in historical Jesus research*' by Professor Kathy Ehrensperger and video clips associated with that article. Those who are involved in church education, study groups, home Bible studies, and adult 'Sunday School' classes will find both this book and the accompanying videos helpful to explore the life and impact of Jesus.

---

6 XinzhongYao and Paul Badham, *Religious Experience in Contemporary China* (Cardiff: University of Wales Press, 2007), p. 32.

Foreword

This is a new and broad approach to a great subject. As a study of Jesus grounded on fact it is offered to those who are neither church-goers, nor professional theologians, nor yet convinced materialists.

It seems wrong that a great subject should be narrowly approached. In other ages the case for Jesus was frequently put with a fullness of thought that seems noticeably lacking in many narrowly angled books about Jesus today.

Some write of him devotionally as centring the worship of the churches, others study him academically, and use the New Testament either as a quarry for scholarly comment, or as a slip-way for academic theories. Others again, trim the Gospels to suit their materialistic or subjective assumptions. There is a point of view from which such studies appear as exercises in understatement.

Truth from many angles converges upon Jesus, and no study of him seems adequate that concentrates on one avenue of truth to the exclusion of other avenues of truth.

This book attempts, therefore, to take into view a mass and variety of evidence that is not normally to be found within the covers of one book.

As we seek today a new integration of religion and life some attempt at synthetic thinking becomes compulsory. Knowledge and experience of many kinds must be brought together. Studies which at first sight seem wide apart may have their own contribution to make.

The time is overdue for a wider assessment of the spiritual, and a new appraisal of its importance. The iron materialism of the nineteenth century has played itself out. Evidence is pointing to the need of a more spiritual view both of ourselves, and of the universe. The continual expansion of the whole horizon of knowledge brings us a better appreciation of the infinity of the unknown.

Truth is one, and the life must be seen in the round. No branch of human thinking is irrelevant. History and biography, sociology and psychology, philosophy and comparative religion, all have much to say. Religion has stimulated creative impulses in art and music. In all ages prayer and worship have evoked responses from humanity's inmost being.

At all intellectual levels there are millions today who casually dismiss the claims of historic Christianity. What they are dismissing is bigger than they think. The atrophy of the spiritual sense under the persuasions of current humanism, and the pressures of commercially stimulated materialism, may be as damaging to human progress as a decline in intelligence itself.

Our subject is the impact and influence of Jesus. What has it amounted to? What place should be his place in humanity's ongoing life? How is he to be assessed, and in what terms?

If the three brief years of Jesus' life and teaching, of which we have record, are unforgettable, so too is the expansion of his influence through the centuries and continents. If the building of an atomic stockpile, or a computer, are the outcome of the one sort of genius, the architecture, music, and literature of Christian civilisation, are the product of another. If the possibilities that technology opens up for modern society are important, so are the possibilities that Jesus opens up in terms of humanity's moral and spiritual advance. They are not, as we would emphasise, at variance, or to be supposed at variance, but grandly intended for the enlargement, and balanced development, of life as a whole.

Within the obvious limits of this book we take one line of inquiry after another, and in the way of the scientific inquirer, pile up evidence. Each fact is established with some fullness—even at the cost of some repetition, because each fact not only supplements the next, but carries with it suggestive further implications. The facts are not arranged to fit in with a preconceived view of Jesus, but rather to be interrogated, just as the facts of science are interrogated, in order to see which theory best makes sense of them.

Most of the facts are accessible to verification, but the word 'fact' is not interpreted to exclude those facts of experience that have played a part in shaping the story of humanity.

Some may feel that not enough weight has been given to much that is corrupt and unforgivable in the history of Christianity—its times of decadence, worldly preoccupation, persecution. But these have not lacked capable coverage in recent years, while the undoubted achievements of the Christian spirit have been notably played down. And if Basil Mitchell is right to insist that 'it can reasonably be demanded of any interpretation that it deal adequately with the phenomenon in its fullest and most impressive form',[7] it would seem appropriate to take a positive line. And just as it is customary to judge an artist by his finest works, a musician by his noblest compositions, a scientist by his greatest achievements, so it is merely reasonable to judge Jesus by the people and the movements that have represented him most worthily. Aristotle's view is accepted. 'The true nature of a thing is the highest that it can become.'

It is hoped that the book may interest those who are not normally attracted by religious writing, that it may provide material and ideas for those presenting Christianity to adult discussion groups and senior classes, and above all, that it may be of use to readers who are seeking a view of Jesus based on objective thinking.

---

[7] Basil Mitchell, *The Justification of Religious Belief*, p. 41.

PART ONE:

Thesis

The Foreword asks about the place of Jesus Christ. How is he to be assessed and in what terms?

We attempt a positive assessment in terms of Jesus' impact and influence. The inquiry is objective and based on the evidence of a sequence of tests ranging from his contemporary relevance to the scale and quality of his contribution to the highest life of humankind through the Christian centuries. We conclude with a comparison of Christianity with other religions.

CHAPTER ONE

What Can We Believe?
Jesus and the Modern Mind

The world's great spiritual voices have been few. Jesus stands out as unmistakably the greatest. What are the facts about his impact and influence? How far can reason take us in our quest for the truth about him?

What is at the back of our minds that prompts us to question one who has centred—and satisfied—the faith of the Christian centuries? Is it not that we are the products of our age and ask for evidence for what we believe, and before we believe?

Science has come and immeasurably added to the sum and certainty of modern knowledge. No subject remains where it was. New thinking and new attitudes of approach are the order of the day. We look at Jesus with the eyes of modern people.

We have been caught in one of the swiftest tides of history. Industrialisation, urbanisation, social upheaval, the pressure of a new morality—these strain old moorings. Spectacular scientific advances, and powers that no age has known before that confront us with the terrifying alternatives of progress, or recession—these divert our gaze from old landmarks. Has the compass long lost its magnetism?

There are changes in perspectives, value judgments, motivations, that are too big to go unrealised.

From the very nature of what they have to give, science and technology concentrate attention on material values. They spread the secular mind. Other values and other thinking tend to go by default, or to be virtually denied. 'Everywhere,' says Dr A. M. Ramsey, 'there is a rising belief in the omnicompetence of the technological sciences to explain man and to serve his needs.'[8]

To those who take this view, religion can easily seem irrelevant, no more than a left-over, a strangely tenacious survival from pre-scientific days.

This is no fault of science and technology. They have drawn on the best brains in the world, and the results in their own field have been magnificent. Not for the first time in history one aspect of human development has swept ahead, perhaps even ahead of itself. The challenge now is to balance material with spiritual values, and to keep alive the conscious and latent religious beliefs that have characterised humankind in all ages.

The challenge is sharper because it is becoming a particularity of the modern mind to be very much at home in a world that is bounded by birth and death.

To be in touch with the way many people think today is to realise that they have unusually little interest in the past, and even less interest in the possibility of any other life ahead. Their absorbed concern is for an interesting and vivid life *now*.

This colours any meaningful approach to Christianity, for Jesus may seem a figure from the past, and immortality wildly at variance with secular interests and assumptions.

It is a factor of real consequence in the build-up of people's minds today that some of the most spectacular strides in pure and applied science have been made. Those who have grown up since world war II have grown up with tremendous things—the television and computer, the acceleration of the population growth, the destruction of the natural environment, the problem of conserving it, the discovery of atomic fission and fusion, the biochemistry of the living cell, visits to the moon.

This gives rise to the exciting idea of a new world with new minds to match, and a tendency to disparage a past which never knew these things.

---

[8] *God, Christ and the World.*

Those who enjoyed a fair span of life before these things happened, stretch their minds to the changes, and see them not so much as making a break with the past as presenting in sharper terms the ongoing challenge of life itself.

There can be flattery and illusion in the phrase 'modern man'. In 600 bc Thales of Miletus divided the solar year into 365 days, using the learning of Egypt, just as he learnt how to foretell eclipses from the knowledge of Babylon. It was Democritus of Thrace (400–370 bc) who brought the natural sciences to astonishing heights and first postulated an atomic theory, but he too was a debtor to ancient Babylon and Egypt.

We have taken over from farthest antiquity more than we realise, and the surest way to bring a new Dark Age upon us might be to forget how earlier civilisations ran into theirs—various forms of the power game, engrossing sex, and a failure to balance material with spiritual need.

We hear much of 'the new morality' but a book by Bertrand Russell entitled The New Morality, raises the question of what in fact is 'new'? Is not the best conscience of modern society haunted on points such as war, racial relationships, economic justice, and purity of heart, by a morality preached in Galilee which we have not yet achieved?

To think of religion as irrelevant, a dated thing, with which we can dispense, is to forget that the most unchanging elements in human history are the deep experiences of the human spirit. All people were 'modern' once and it would be hard to establish that we are finer people because we are cocooned in a more complicated technological environment. We have to ask what sort of a showing we make when we are stripped of our accessories.

Like all who have crossed the stage of life before us we can turn the drama of life into comedy, tragedy, or even plain farce. We are as vulnerable as people have ever been to moral failure, loss of nerve, and to 'the slings and arrows of outrageous fortune ... the heartache and the thousand natural shocks that flesh is heir to … the dread of something after death—that undiscovered country from whose bourn no traveller returns'.

While material progress has been spectacular, moral progress has been fitful and uneven. Ours is an age that tops all others in the alleviation of pain. The triumphs of medicine and surgery exceed all praise. On a wide scale there is a blessed relief of drudgery through automation. Notable achievements of the welfare state have brought about a widening coverage of poverty, and diminished the woes of the sick and aged. Finer, and more open, educational opportunities, and the competent take-over of Christian social aims, have been brought about through the levelling of incomes and state subsidies.

Great enterprises like Christian Aid, Voluntary Service Overseas and other relief agencies have notably enlisted the support of youth. But youth itself in practically every land exhibits a new restiveness towards authority and tradition, and seems uncertain about former values and goals of life.

Comparative affluence, easy availability of the things money can buy, and the variety of commercialised entertainment, have not brought content. Peace of mind and happiness are not features of our day. Staggering numbers have need of psychiatric care. A rise in greed, dishonesty, violence, and crime, and a new permissiveness of lust and pornography, are hard to equate with progress. The secular city is a problem in itself. One has to come to a somewhat depressing conclusion that little that science has made available has helped modern humans to solve the dichotomy of their own nature. The trouble may lie in the God-shaped blank in their hearts.

HRH the Duke of Edinburgh, Prince Philip, who has travelled far and seen much, summed up our predicament as he saw it in his Commemoration Oration at King's College, London, in 1970:

> Material development alone cannot sustain civilisation. To make life tolerable, and indeed possible, for intelligent man, there must be some criterion of right and

wrong, some positive motivation, some vision of an ideal, some beckoning inspiration.

Without it we shall never get to grips with the population explosion, with race prejudice, with starvation, with the distribution of resources, with the conflicting demands of development and conservation, progress and pollution, or the control of the complex industrial communities, and the liberties of the individual.

Bishop Hugh Montefiore likewise insisted that the crisis facing people is fundamentally spiritual and that 'if man is not by his folly, frailty and ignorance to ruin his environment and with it his own future, then the most tremendous and unprecedented efforts to prevent this will be necessary'. Such motivation, Montefiore believed, can only come through a lively belief in God nourished through faith in the heroic figure of Jesus through whom God has disclosed himself to humankind.[9]

But are we today likely to gain that 'vision of the ideal, that beckoning inspiration, that higher motivation' which earlier generations have certainly found in Christ? For we are a part of all that we have met, and in modern life we have met a great deal that has not advanced us in moral sensitivity or spiritual insight. We have been exposed to the daunting doubts of humanists, and worst of all, to a version of Christianity without challenge and without power, associated with a wonderless worship and a questionable God. In so far as these may have played a part in our conditioning can we be expected to come to a right estimate of Jesus?

There are regions of the highest truth that may depend for their appreciation on the kind of moral beings we choose to be. 'Blessed are the pure in heart', said Jesus. 'They see God.' Aldous Huxley accumulated the evidence for this by the

---

[9] *Can Man Survive?*

scrutiny of many saintly lives. He shows that there are regions of spiritual understanding that are only accessible to those who have achieved love, purity of heart, humility of mind. But these are not virtues much to the forefront today.

Balzac, the eccentric genius, designed and built a house, omitting to leave room for a staircase. It had to be added on afterwards. In the building of the minds of many today, one can detect a parallel omission. Scanty attention has been paid to the construction of spiritual staircases. In some areas of modern education they are not taken into the plans. In others they are tolerated, but allowed to be frail and improvised structures, crowded into any corner not occupied by other more important interests.

So what does all this mean? As far back as Aristotle it was recognised that one could only understand a subject if one was familiar with a wide range of ideas and attendant considerations that gave the subject full significance and validity so that appreciation could begin. In the case of the Jesus it is very doubtful if many are acquainted with the broad facts and reasoned considerations that are essential for a right judgment of his significance. The tendency is to 'make do' with unrelated snippets of information, and to miss seeing the picture 'in the large'.

'Those who understand Christianity,' said a pilot, 'climb up to faith themselves, and then draw in the ladder after them.' His meaning is clear. Reason plays a necessary part in the achievement of faith, and when it is achieved it is easy to forget the steps that took us to it—steps of information, steps of experience, our own and other people's, and steps of spiritual growth.

This book aims at presenting some steps, and providing a ladder of reasoned thought that some have found useful.

We follow this glance we have taken at ourselves by a look at timeless elements in Jesus' teaching, and the depths in him to which some in all ages have responded. We note the durability of his influence, its expansion, and its striking fruitfulness and excellence. We check facts of historicity and the genuineness of the records. We see that the more we press forward our inquiry the more we become convinced that we are in touch with truth. We begin to understand the mysterious way in which he has revolutionised so many lives. We recognise how often he has established his influence in the face of difficulties and obstructive forces. Simply in terms of achievement his uniqueness is forced upon us, with the question arising, is a life and influence like his an accident or a revelation?

Could it be that as both science and religion seem to indicate, there is a Mind behind all things? We examine the centuries of Old Testament witness to God, and the way its teaching seemed to set the stage for a supreme revelation, and how this expectation of Christ's contemporaries was fulfilled in him. We face what Professor C. F. D. Moule calls *The Phenomenon of the New Testament* with its weighty evidence for the resurrection. Did these early reporters heighten their story, or is the basic truth of it borne out by what Jesus has meant in human history? Can we say with Professor John Hick that 'everything was for him within the context of God's presence and purpose'?[10]

This book takes its title from the Courtroom of the Sanhedrin at Jerusalem where the High Priest passed on Jesus the verdict of blasphemy which, the prisoner knew, carried the penalty of death.

We re-open the case, looking alike at the evidence as Caiaphas heard it, and at new evidence that has accumulated since, with the question facing us afresh, what are we to make of it?

---

10 *Christianity at the Centre*

CHAPTER TWO

The Test of Contemporary Importance

There are many who have scarcely made contact at all with Jesus of Nazareth. In so far as he has been presented to them, he has seemed irrelevant. We therefore suggest a direct approach.

If one has no religion as such, if he has closed his mind to all thoughts of the supernatural, if he regards the Churches as purveyors of outworn myths, there is still a place where Jesus may grip his attention. He stimulates curiosity.

Curiosity is a basic instinct, and agnostic as one may feel to be, one may still wish to know what has made Jesus the world's most unaccountable man. The answer is readily available in the world's most accessible book—the New Testament.

In a world teeming with the ordinary, here is one who has unquestionably made an extraordinary impact. He is unusual from practically any angle we look at him.

He has a mind that cannot be pigeon-holed, and a view of life that raises a question-mark over most current values and attitudes. As powerful opposing ideologies make their goals more apparent, the relevance of what he taught and stood for challenges contemporary thought.

If we could imagine him taking part in a television programme what an experience it would be! Any subject referred to him would at once be lifted to a new level. His replies would be incisive, and memorable, and be dealt with on a scale that would throw light on other subjects not then in view. The way he would acquit himself is not conjecture, for the Gospels are strewn with instances of the power and quality of his thinking, and the way cleverly framed questions got unanswerable replies. St Matthew (22: 15–46) shows how he freely exposed himself to public questioning, and the way he enlarged people's thinking.

The Pharisees and Herodians, for example, arrived together with a trap question about paying tribute to Caesar. We read 'the answer took them by surprise. They went away and left him alone. ' The Sadducees came next with a question about the reality of any life beyond this. The Sadducees had no belief in it. But his answer 'silenced them, but the people heard what he said and were astounded at his teaching.' Meanwhile the Pharisees had met to think up another question. It was on the matter of the greatest commandment in the Mosaic Law. Jesus combined two separate statements from that Law in a masterly reply that left no more to be said. He himself then asked them a question, to which 'Not a man could say a word in reply, and they shrank away from asking him any more questions.'

In a world like ours then, replete with questions but short of answers, should we not too hang on his word, for he could deal in the same breath with the particular and universal, the topical and the timeless? In short the Gospel statement, 'Never man spoke like this man,' is not so much a compliment, as a coolly discerning verdict.

On street corners Jesus met the questioners of his day, but he was never the mouthpiece of street-corner wisdom and repartee. Always he seemed to move from some passing incident to the disclosure of some truth that has only to be pondered to be found probing and profound.

The stories he told are among the world's literary masterpieces. Striking enough to catch the ear of the passer-by, they made his hearers realise the unexplained depths in him. Interesting enough at one level to win the attention in a

Galilean market place, they live on to challenge the moral and spiritual perception of those who have been the lights and leaders of successive generations.

To speak in parable, to illustrate truth on one plane by an illustration drawn from another plane is a difficult business. Felicitous illustrations, as every speaker knows, are usually the result of careful premeditation and anxious craftsmanship. But they sprang readily to the lips of Jesus, and they had the effectiveness of immediate appeal, and yet a relevance for all, always and everywhere.

The reception of most sermons in our time reminds us that things were dramatically different when Jesus preached. 'The common people heard him gladly … there was no room even about the doors … crowds followed him on foot out of the cities and villages.'

'They were astonished,' says the record, 'for he taught them as one who had authority, and not as the professional teachers.' As Jesus spoke people saw life taking new shape and meaning around great central truths. The 'authority' was that which people long to find, the authority that truth exercises over the mind, moral law over the conscience, spiritual insight over the soul.

Here then is the contemporary importance of Jesus. He said the highest things, and he said them with an authority that gives them finality.

Honest thinking that penetrates to any depth still takes us right in to the matters he talked about. Problem after problem today could be met by his answers. Economic justice, racial relationships, resorts to violence, and violence in its most tragic form—war—all show how far his thinking remains ahead of us. The facts of life call us to examine his teaching, freshly, objectively, as a pressing contemporary need.

It is plain that his parables deal with what we call 'situation ethics', drawn from the experience of life itself.

When the question, 'Who is my neighbour?' for instance, was brought to Jesus, he did not discuss it in a lawyer's way, citing current practice, levels of involvement and obligation.

He personifies the issue of the story of the Good Samaritan. He presents the situation of a man robbed, beaten up, left to die, and vividly contrasts a priest and Levite's utter detachment and indifference, with a Samaritan's readiness to be involved, to bind up the man's wounds, and make himself responsible for his care and rehabilitation. The appeal is direct to every one's conscience. If you would be a neighbour: 'Go and do the same.'

The story flows, as a good story should, as smooth as silk. But it is shot-silk with strong colours in it. The one who told the story is a Jew, the hero is a Samaritan. Neighbourliness rises above racial prejudices. Again, we know the race of the Samaritan, priest, and Levite. But of what race is the battered victim? We are not told. Social justice is not a matter of race, but of sheer human need.

The 'neighbour' problem faces our age. We face it in a world where collectivism is on top. But personal conscience, individual responsibility, cannot be ignored. Collective indifference is individual indifference writ large. The situation is brought home to us again in the parable of a man of affluence absorbed in his own selfish indulgence, while a man he should have neighboured dies destitute, starving, and with suppurating sores, at his gates.

Is life an entrustment? Is there moral accountability? Jesus taught it. To every individual the eventual and inexorable word is spoken, 'This night your soul is required of you.' Nor do we escape judgment here. How long can human society stand the tensions building up within it? Are the problems of social and racial justice to be solved volitionally, or compulsorily? Is freewill or force to decide the issues?

Many minds are stuck with the idea that the ethics of Jesus are perfectionist idealism, unsuited to this tough world. But the attitude of those who invert his teaching are the real problem, for we have come to the stage where the fortunes and fate of humankind are indivisible, 'We are members one of another.' None is safe unless all are safe. We need to hear the Gospel's ringing announcement, 'One is your Master, and you are brothers in the one great family of man,' and then to heed the ethic that alone can help us to meet the intolerable intimacy of proximity without community.

Is the ethic of 'everyone for him or herself abreast of the times? Or the barbarous creed that 'they should take who have the power, and they should keep who can'? Shortly before he was shot at Memphis, Dr Martin Luther King, the civil rights leader, posed what could be the choice before humankind in the near future: 'A world at peace or a world in pieces. Non-violence or non-existence.' This great man, like Gandhi in India before him, saw the urgent relevance to modern need of the saving ethic of Jesus, where sane discussion based on the moral law replaces violence and the outworn creed that might is right.

Does the ethical teaching of Jesus show a more realistic appraisal of the choice facing humankind today than we have been realising? Consider the solution he offered to the problem of evil and violence in the Sermon on the Mount; and in the determined teaching that evil should be overcome by good which he held to even on the cross.

What do you do when violence marches against you? It is a highly contemporary question when the trend towards attaining rights, real or imaginary, by force of one kind or another, is upon us.

The law of Moses put resistance, or reprisal, in terms of tit for tat. 'Life for life, an eye for an eye, wound for wound, stripe for stripe' (Ex. 21: 23–25). But Jesus brought new thinking to an old problem. He had watched people meeting evil with evil, force with force, and he saw the endlessness and viciousness of the proceedings. In a brief question he exposed its inadequacy, 'How can Satan cast out Satan?' How can you ever deal with any form of evil by matching it with equivalent evil? Somehow the vicious circle of evil answering evil had to be broken.

Jesus grounded his solution on the character of a God who was big enough to allow his sun to rise on the evil and the good, and the rain to fall impartially upon the just and unjust. Jesus counselled a new integrity. Be decent, ran his teaching, whether others are decent or not. Never let your own idea of what is ultimately right, be deflected by another's conduct. Be just in the face of injustice, bless even if cursed, love even if hated. Live life in terms of undiscourageable goodwill. In Simone Weil's splendid sentence, 'Never react to evil in a way that augments it.'

Has such a challenging ethic any place in a modern society reaching towards maturity? Is it a slice of realism? What does society gain by cynicism answering cynicism? What shall it profit a world if atomic bomb answers atomic bomb? Is this a viable solution to the problems of anarchy and war? Or is Jesus counselling a passivity that would result in evil striding ruthlessly on? But Jesus undergirds his bold ethic with a philosophy able to sustain it. He held out no promise that violence could be either checked or matched by a dispersed benevolence. He envisaged powerful unifications of humankind under the majesty of the moral law and that, in turn, supported by a common belief in the Fatherhood of God.

No age has fully realised the tremendous challenge such a teaching carries to the power structures on other lines that threaten humankind. But every step towards understanding and goodwill, towards justice in terms of moral rights, and towards the spread of faith, is a step towards that universal humanity which Christ proclaimed.

Profound motives of personal and public need call for a new scrutiny of the guidelines afforded by such teaching.

Jesus in his own person is a perennial challenge to thought. Ordinary portraiture has not coped with him. He expands the very stature of humanity. If there is truth in Plato's words that 'the noblest of all studies is what a man is, and how he should live,' then the personality of this man calls for fresh appraisal. He unites in his own life a number of qualities that in other lives seem wide apart. We find idealism and realism, humility and majesty, gaiety and gravity, love and justice. All of which are strange combinations. He united in his own life a granite-like strength with a disposition that attracted playful children. Powerful personalities in Church and State ceased to be powerful in his company, while we see in contrast, that ordinary people chose homelessness and persecution simply to be with him. He exhibits qualities of poise and balance that elsewhere we shall seek in vain to match.

A recent book carries a phrase 'living with mystery' which aptly describes humanity's situation. 'What is bad, what is good?' asks Pierre in Tolstoy's *War and Peace*. 'What should one love, what hate? What should one live for? What am I? What is life, what is death? What Power governs all?' These are everyone's questions. Since, liking it or not, we have to 'live with mystery', can we be indifferent to the replies that hitherto have been accepted as being most worthy of belief?

Such questions as Pierre's obviously demand an answer in terms of religious faith, 'believing where we cannot know'. They carry our gaze from the foreground of life to make us search for a spiritual background. Is this a universe blind to moral values? Is there an innate sense of right and wrong that corresponds to something ultimate? Is life a cul-de-sac ending in extinction? Are humans accidental intruders into a universe that never purposed them? Is there a Power that governs all that corresponds to the God that Jesus claimed to know and reveal? Life cannot be separated from such questioning, unless we are content to separate life from thought.

Here is not only the contemporary, but the timeless importance of Jesus. He claimed to reveal Reality, to put us in touch with the very Ground of all Being. In so far as such claims commend themselves to us, so we will not be averse to hearing what may be said for them.

The aim of this chapter, you remember, was primarily to stimulate interest. We have been scratching the surface in an initial inquiry. To go further may bring into fuller focus the most astonishing figure who has ever arrested the attention of humankind. More than we ever thought possible, we may find he is not in fact a man of the past at all, but our Contemporary.

CHAPTER THREE

The Test of Durability

An historian was asked: 'What single individual has left the most permanent impression on the world?' He at once named Jesus of Nazareth. 'It is interesting and significant,' he said, 'that an historian like myself, with no theological bias whatever, cannot portray the progress of humanity honestly without giving him foremost place.'[11]

In our last chapter we considered how relevant could be the solutions of this most significant man to some of the problems of today. But is it not startling to find one single individual so important? The date on the morning's paper shows how far humanity has come from his historic life.

Mohammed's flight to Medina sets the date by which the prophet's followers count time, but for the West, everything is dated from the time when Jesus was born, 'Nothing,' said Dr W. R. Matthews, 'has been the same since.' 'Life's but a walking shadow,' said Shakespeare, 'a poor player that struts and frets his hour upon the stage, and then is heard no more.' That holds true of the overwhelming majority. They cross the stage of life, and then get cried off, or clapped off, and then forgotten.

---

[11] H. G. Wells, author of A Short History of the World, 1940

A pathetic few fare better. Alexander, Caesar, Napoleon—they raised such a dust with their trampling armies that even yet the dust has not settled and hid their names. A few, like the Pharaohs, left monuments too big for the sands of time to cover, and a handful of choicer spirits linger in memory because of writings which remain like landmarks on the plains of thought. But these are exceptional. How few of all the computed millions of people now living will be remembered when the hearts that love them are still?

Jesus, of course, raised no army, left no monument, wrote no book, yet after two thousand years more people are interested in, familiar with, and influenced by, his life and teaching than by the career and writings of any other person alive or dead. Some may feel he has had more than his share of the world's time, but plainly others have not thought so.

Does such an enduring influence call for an explanation? At the very beginning of the Christian movement, the astonishing possibility was raised that in the course of time the durability of Jesus' influence might call for an explanation and at the highest level.

The occasion was when the success of the apostles' preaching alarmed the Senate of Israel, and one of their number, Gamaliel, a respected doctor of law, advised them to give it time. We have recently had a couple of popular movements, he said in effect, that have proved no more than a nine days' wonder. Leave these people alone. If this movement is of human origin, it will break up of its own accord. 'But,' he added, 'if this movement is of God you cannot stop it. You may actually find yourselves opposing God' (Acts 5: 38, 39).

Gamaliel may have known more than he was declaring, and was being cautious. In any case, is any test more demanding than durability?

Now, it is a striking thing that every fact about Christ gains, rather than loses, importance, the more it is considered. The permanence of his influence, for example, becomes still more amazing the more it is scrutinised.

An influence once given continues to exert itself. That is more true of Christ's influence than of any other. Normally, and for the generality of all, personal influence moves out from the individual to society in ever widening, and ever weakening, waves of power, until it is nothing more than an obscure undercurrent beneath society's thought and life. Naturally its relative durability depends on the strength of the original impulses, but as the wake of a vessel gets lost in the ocean, so there are few whose influence is not swiftly absorbed, and whose thoughts are not speedily assimilated and surpassed.

The influence of Jesus, however, has retained a perennial freshness and strength. It need not detain us here to examine what Christians believe to be the cause of that peculiar vitality. Rationalise it as we will, it is plain to see that the power of Christ has not diminished with the years, nor in fact does the weight of his impact, and the quality of his influence, bear any relationship to chronology at all.

If it is true that none of us can do more than lay their fullest capacities at the feet of their leader, then it is plain to see that Jesus has been as meaningful to General Booth as he was to St Bernard, as loved by Frances of Assisi as he was by the martyr Polycarp, as much a source of inspiration to C. S. Lewis as to John Bunyan, as central to the preaching of Billy Graham as to John Wesley.

This is not to say that people of such different types and backgrounds have found in Jesus precisely the same thing, still less that their wording of a great matter would be the same. The Christ of Mother Theresa may not be the Christ of John Donne, nor the Christ of Bernadette of Lourdes the Christ of a young Salvationist in London; the prayers of the ASB revisers are not those of Cranmer or Laud, but they would all agree with what Bonhoeffer wrote a few months before his death, 'All that we rightly expect from God and pray for is to be found in Jesus Christ.'

Each generation, and probably each human type, finds something personal in their relationship with Jesus, but all would join Peter in naming him 'the Prince of life'.

This repetition of Christian experience, this continuity of faith, explains why there have arisen from time to time burning souls who have recreated for their generation a sense of Pentecost. This explains the continual resurgence of the historic movement we call Christianity, and the number of times that the spirit of Christ has arisen, phoenix-like, from what seemed only the grey ashes of its former heat.

But let us anticipate an objection. Is it the Church—the visible extension of Christ's influence—which is responsible for this? Is it the movement that gives life to the founder, or the founder who gives life to the movement? At first sight the former seems the likeliest theory, but history disproves it.

Time and again, as a meteor for a moment brightens the sky and then falls back into the darkness, it has seemed probable that Christianity would share the mortality of other movements. But every decline has been answered by an unexpected resurgence of power, and every time that power has been attributable to a fresh hold on the original teaching of Jesus and a fresh consciousness of what is called 'his presence' in the Church.

Christianity was born in the Roman Empire, but it did not die with it. It drew to itself the best elements in the old culture, husbanded them, and lived on. The Dark Ages came, but the light of the Gospel was not extinguished. Islam rolled forward and it seemed unlikely that Christianity would survive its impact, but it did. Feudalism and Christianity were so interlocked that the failure of the one would seem inevitably to involve the other, but Christianity disentangled itself from feudalism and lived on. Before the many-coloured lights of the Renaissance one might have thought Christianity would have paled and died. But, contrary to expectations, the new learning lent it a wider background.

In most ages there have been some ready to write its epitaph. Celsus, for instance, did it in the early days, only to stir Christians to deeper thought. In 1736 Bishop Butler wrote his *Analogy of Religion*, directing it to those who 'regarded the faith not so much a subject for inquiry, as at length discovered to be fictitious'. How could they know that three years later John Wesley was to start preaching, that the Methodist and Evangelical Revivals were just round the corner, with the Oxford Movement to follow? On the Continent Voltaire declared that Christianity had only a few years to run. How could he foresee that his own spacious home was to be bought as a depot for the Bible Society?

Gloomy verdicts have increased since World War II, but even in the Soviet Union prolonged and calculated oppression has not killed the faith, and from the ablest Church historian of the twentieth century have come books called *The Unquenchable Light* and *Advance through Storm*. 'Twenty centuries of world history,' wrote Latourette, 'have confirmed in startling fashion, Christ's promise that the gates of hell should not prevail against his church.'[12]

These seem brave words. There are evidences of a hardening of human nature, and of a widespread indifference to Christian influence, and a powerful humanist dispute of its truth. The Church flags and fails in areas where once it was confident and strong. A shrewd observer, Quintin Hogg, observed at Coventry in 1970, 'What is at stake today is not religious orthodoxy or traditional piety, but the continued existence of Christianity and its influence on humankind.'

Is Christianity, then, like a leaky ship going to sink lower and lower in the water until it takes its final plunge? There are times when one might think so were it not for the philosophy that comes from a long view and we can see how time and again it has recovered confidence and found renewal.

---

[12] Prof. K. S. Latourette, *The Expansion of Christianity*, Vol. VI

There may be a salutary lesson in the present situation. When the German theologian Bonhoeffer was in prison awaiting death, he set down his reason for the weakness of the German Church as he was seeing it: 'Ecclesiastical interests well to the fore, but little interest in Christ. Jesus disappearing from view.' The same thing has been widely true of the Church generally. Everywhere the Church has been preoccupied with interests vastly less important than her proclamation of Christ to the world.

There are signs that a change is coming, and the reaffirmation that Jesus is not only the starting point of a viable faith, but as Teilhard de Chardin put it in *Hymn of the Universe*, 'the centre towards which all things move.'

After this excursion of thought we look again at the central figure of the Gospels, and ask what can be the secret of his continually renewed influence? He certainly makes no bid for easy popularity. At no time does he scale his teaching to flatter human weakness, or to countenance established prejudices. He demands life at new levels of genuineness, courage, purity, generosity, love, and faith. Those who accept his leadership must be prepared, like Saul on the road to Damascus, to remake the foundation of their lives.

Humility is as difficult to wear as a hair shirt, but Jesus puts it on his list of priorities. Forgiveness is so hard a virtue that few other religions mention it, but Jesus exalts it, and makes our own standing in God's sight depend on our willingness to exhibit it. Self-interest and self-indulgence have a freehold on most lives; who can evict them from their tenancy in the heart? But Jesus makes hard living a condition of discipleship, and only counts life well lived if it is spent in the service of others. Further, the road grows hard beneath our feet as we realise that he means by 'others' the very people whom we, with our limited sympathies, like to forget. Purity of motive, even in the best of people, is extraordinarily hard to achieve, but Jesus is interested in the corners of the heart. There is no escape from his insight.

And what shall we say about his call to forsake all and follow him, or about his repeated warning that the life of the wayfaring Christian should be shadowed by a cross? Recollect the terrible words in which he spoke of the cost of active discipleship, 'Whosoever follows me must be prepared to shoulder the gallows beam' (Mark 8: 34).

How was it, then, that ideas so uncongenial to much in human nature, and frequently so alien to much in the cultures they invaded, have been able to endure?

Plainly, if we are inclined to ascribe the durability of Christ's influence to the ease and magnetism of his programme, it is well to be reminded that he carried with him a lot of ideas which no ordinary person will consider magnetic at all, but disturbingly searching, difficult and revolutionary His hold on the centuries is not explained by any supposed ease or lightness in his challenge.

What then explains it? Why have people, to their own condemnation, retained the memory of a life that so vividly contrasts with their own? Why have they acknowledged as authoritative, ideals that have so demonstrably proved themselves to be beyond human reach? One could say with Wordsworth that it is 'man's most noble attribute'

To wish for something loftier . . . more adorned
Than is the daily garb of human life.

But such suggestions merely touch the fringe of the matter. Christ has not retained his hold because of the excellence of the moral code he brought to life. People have accepted his authority because they have believed him to be the revealer of the invisible God. The truth or falsity of such an amazing belief we shall be considering later. For the moment, we merely set it down, as a matter of fact, that the persistence of Christ's moral influence has been entirely due to the persistence of the theological beliefs held about him. It is the compulsion of those beliefs, and the assurance of the spiritual order that they imply, that has moved people to accept, and strain towards, the Christian virtues. The very difficulty of those virtues indicates how sure people have been about the supernatural authority of Jesus. No one uncertain about that authority would have ever attempted to stumble after such a demanding leader.

As we move forward now to another aspect of our subject, it may be well to recall some words that despite their strange audacity continue to challenge the future, 'Heaven and earth shall pass away, but my words shall never pass away.'

CHAPTER FOUR

The Test of Universality

The next fact we come to is even more suggestive. The influence of Jesus has not only been uniquely durable, but it has done an unusual thing. Instead of diminishing with the years it has increased.

One would have thought that the words of a man of Galilee would have had too provincial a sound for global repetition. One would have expected that in the course of centuries he would have been outstripped, surpassed, outmoded, but the opposite has been the case.

One enjoys the writing of a distinguished Chinese philosopher like Dr Lin Yutang, but one is conscious that the author, delightful and wise as he is, could not readily be naturalised among us. In tone and temper of thought he could not imperceptibly capture the West. But Jesus from Palestine has done it.

We may say 'East is East, and West is West, and never the twain shall meet', but Jesus combined the mysticism of the East with the hard-headed practicality of the West, and they meet in him. 'Christianity,' says Bouquet, 'is unique both in its ability to make converts in any latitude, and in its appeal to human beings of any racial group.'[13]

---

[13] *Phases of the Christian Church*, Chapter 11.

Astonishing as this may seem, Jesus has not only been a foremost influence in the West, he has his followers in every nation and every society throughout the world. 'That this has been achieved,' as Dr W. Temple put it, 'is one of the most astonishing facts of our time.'

The fact is more striking when we realise how often Christianity has been the first outside influence to enter many closed territories. It has been work fraught with difficulty, setback, and minimal human and material resources, but along with the faith have come gifts of education, medicine, social transformation. Other influences have been given a footing too, perhaps not wholly good as when trade opportunities have been exploited to the point of hurting the good name of Christian.

There is a natural holding power about traditional ways of life, and a natural reverence for old sanctities, that has made Christian influence slow to penetrate, slower to establish. Yet, given a chance, the life and teaching of Jesus has proved capable of awakening a response in every variety of human type.

In presenting Jesus to the ancient and higher religions there are difficulties all too seldom realised. There is a point at which all religious teachings, as Bishop Lesslie Newbigin puts it in *The Finality of Christ*, 'are gropings after a prodigious reality which they cannot compass'. There are specific difficulties, too, where Islam, Hinduism, and Buddhism are concerned.

It may be hard, for example, for Muslims to appreciate Christian teaching about the Sonship of Christ, if their concept of fatherhood does not mean a relationship of love and trust so much as the physical act of generation. Nor does their idea of divine providence allow them to believe God, mighty and merciful, entered into the suffering of the crucifixion. The specific denial in the Quran is well known. Yet typical Muslims have been converted.

Christianity comes to a crunch with Hinduism in the doctrine of Karma that pictures humanity as imprisoned by iron laws of cause and effect. The pessimistic Hindu expectation of endless re-incarnation is in direct conflict with Christian hope of a transformed and renewed life in eternity. Yet typical Hindus have been converted.

Theravada Buddhism is the creed most directly in collision with Jesus' teaching in so far as it teaches that there is no God, that human life is scarcely worth having, and that death means extinction.

It is a strange happening that Buddhism, which is much the farthest from Jesus, in that it denies God, is much the closest in its moral teaching to the Sermon on the Mount. With astonished eyes, therefore, the Buddhist looks at the West with its blatant pursuit of material gain, sensual indulgence, and the arts of 'getting on'.

It is expected, however, that as communication between the faiths of the world increases so direct acquaintance with what Jesus was and taught will see Christianity grow in influence, 'as a seed growing secretly', ever breaking new ground within the soul of the world.

As it is, those who profess and call themselves Christian are far and away more numerous than those who belong to any other living religion. Statistics are rightly suspect in dealing with spiritual loyalties, but nevertheless they may afford a rough guide to relative proportions.

Doubtless many 'Christians' are purely nominal in their acceptance of the faith, but who would suggest that the purely nominal adherents are to be found only in Christianity? Would they not, at least to an equal degree, be found among those credited to other faiths?

And how has Christ's Gospel managed to go out into all the world? It has depended on volunteers, few in number and many of them unpretentious in ability. 'The missionary movement of the nineteenth century,' writes Professor Latourette in *Missions Tomorrow*, 'has been the most notable out-pouring of life, in the main unselfish, in the service of alien peoples, that the world has known.'

But are we exaggerating the voluntary element? Have there not been times when the faith has been aided by coercion, privilege, by the blessing of political planners? But these have been precisely the times when the durability of Christian influence has been least marked, and when its rootage and power have been most shallow. It is when Christianity has been free from secular interference, and dependent solely on its own appeal, that its expansion has been most rapid and its impact greatest.

If we desire to see people enfranchised from superstition, ignorance, oppression, violence, and ill-will; if we think nobly of the soul, and recognise the unifying power of great religious beliefs, then we must face what Christ has done, is doing, and might, with reasonable expectation, further do, for the advancement and integration of humankind.

One form of words, the Lord's Prayer, grows with the growth of the individual's understanding. 'Say it slowly,' said an officer praying with a companion in a hut on a bleak spur of Iceland, 'Say it slowly, each sentence weighs a ton.' It has been translated into well over a thousand tongues and dialects. It centres the worship of the world-wide Church, but it is capable of still larger use. It is capable of universality. Dr H. D. J. Major, author of *Basic Religion*, used to call it 'the most unifying religious formula in the world. It could be said as it stands by Jews, Muslims, and Theistic Buddhists.'

Only with intelligence and imagination at their highest activity can we grasp what these great shafts of truth, if ever implemented by the heart's desire, could do for the religion of tomorrow.

But what, interjects the critic, has Christianity really done by its expansion? What practical results, if any, follow its numerical and territorial gains?

An answer to such questions would come appropriately from Chinese priests and doctors, from the three and a half million native Christians in India, from the blind in Burma, from the lepers in Nigeria, and from the native Christians, sons of former slaves, in Africa.

Missionaries have been the schoolmasters of whole races. They have carried with them ideas of justice and medical science. They have fought opium and prostitution, superstition and exploitation. They have set whole peoples on upward paths.

One of my distinguished predecessors at Windsor Parish Church, George Augustus Selwyn, became the first Bishop of New Zealand. For some years he worked among the Maoris at the Samuel Marsden Settlement. The judgment of Charles Darwin is impressive: 'The march of improvement consequent on the introduction of Christianity throughout the South Seas, probably stands by itself in the record of history.' Selwyn's method of evangelising his huge diocese was to visit every part of it in person, and for this purpose he used a steamer given him by his friends. He was often his own pilot navigating uncharted seas. His practice was to get the natives to lend him their sons to be taken to the College in Auckland, to be trained as either clergy or good servants of the Church. The Maoris would have been exterminated but for Christian influence.[14]

One cannot chart the working of wide and humanising ideas in all the corners of the earth, nor can one estimate what faith in Jesus, as the mediator of God's love, has meant to unnumbered multitudes newly released from the tyranny of superstition.

We cannot face facts like these without asking a searching question. Who inspired this religion that has gone round the world, who founded this fellowship that has proved so invincible? The answer is so amazing that the mind is humbled. A young man who grew up in a small town in a backward province nearly two thousand years ago. We stand in awe before the world-wide expansion and proven strength of the church that his words called into being.

---

14 Warre- Cornish, *History of the Church of England in the Reign of Victoria*.

It is almost disconcerting, therefore, to find that what has so strikingly come to pass was calmly anticipated by Jesus: 'You must go out into all the world and preach the Gospel: Go, therefore, and make all nations my disciples: The field is the world.'

What that command meant to the astonished provincials who heard it we shall never know. Even yet, when the literal fulfilment of Christ's command has in a measure taken place, many are content to leave out of their reckoning the one person who holds in his hands the map of the world.

We must not start, this early, to draw together the threads of the main argument, of which this is merely a strand. Later, we must consider what the fact of Christ's universality implies. No thinking mind would wish to evade such a consideration.

CHAPTER FIVE

The Test of Human Understanding

We have seen something of the significance of Jesus for our time. We have observed his hold on the centuries and noted how his influence has broadened out over the world.

It will be seen, too, that in no sense are we building up a case for Christ, any more than an historian builds up a case for the history he has to set down, or a geologist builds up a case for the strata that crops out before him. Facts and observable phenomena are being dealt with. We, too, in our study of Jesus are seeking to be objective, to be concerned not with creation but with observation, not with the adding to facts, but with the adding up of facts. We are recording observable truths.

We now move forward to inquire how it has been possible for Christianity to break through the dual frontiers of time and space. How has it been possible to transmit a basic Christianity to people of widely differing ages, races, mental level, and moral and spiritual apprehension? What is there in it that has awoken response in such varying hearts and heads? What accounts for it being capable of universal application?

Part of the answer is to be found in the way that Jesus presented his teaching. He clothed his thoughts in terms that made their world-wide diffusion a practical proposition.

'Most of our mental operations are inseparable from images or are produced by images. It is difficult to express thought clearly without images,' says Ernest Dimnet in *The Art of Thinking*. Recall, then, how the parables of Jesus fill the gallery of the mind with telling portraiture, how the moral lesson is animated and made graphic by human instances.

Morality in terms of abstract theory has a cold and limited interest. But Jesus made it vivid by showing it in action in people's lives. He sets the moral complacency of the Pharisee in contrast to the anguished penitence of the sinful tax-collector (Luke 18: 10); the unfeeling self-sufficiency of Dives against the pathetic needs of Lazarus (Luke 16: 19); the religious formalism of priest and Levite in contrast to the practical neighbourliness of the Good Samaritan (Luke 10: 30). He shows what the high-call can mean to a spiritual dilettante like the Rich Young Ruler (Matt. 19: 16) or to a morally earnest civil servant like Zacchaeus (Luke 19: 8).

Such images make their home in people's minds. They are transmissible from age to age, and from land to land.

Now ethics and theology, formally expressed, can be codified, and hardened into systems. Jesus has seen this happening. He had noted the people of his time keeping the letter of the Old Testament Law, and violating the whole spirit that lay behind the Law. In contrast, he cried out for living religion, for goodness springing out of the affections of the heart, for religion that revealed the positive engagement of the mind, the spirit, and the will, with purposes of God.

But how could he prevent formalism from sterilising his own message? He would make the hardening process as difficult as possible. He would invest his teaching with an inner life of its own.

True, being as they are, people would try to systematise his teaching, formulate it in legal definitions, but in themselves his ideals and principles would contrive to be distinct from the system, bigger than the formulation. Even if the system with which they were identified crumbled, his truths would retain their vitality and even contribute, when freshly handled, to the sweeping away of the system.

How often this has happened! History has justified the manner in which Jesus gave his teaching.

With changing circumstances, textbook definitions get left behind. But Jesus avoided textbook truths. 'The words I speak to you,' he said, 'are spirit and life.' They appeal not only to the intellect but to the understanding. They are capable of meeting the human mind at different levels of apprehension and discernment.

Stopford Brooke makes this plain by drawing a helpful analogy between Christ's words and music:

> Neither you nor I can say of an air of Mozart's that it means this or that, it means one thing to me, another to you. It leaves, however, a similar impression upon us both—a sense of exquisite melody, a love of a life that is in harmony with the impression received, and an affection for the one who so lifts us above ourselves. So it is with the words of Christ. The spirit receives them and each man receives them in accordance with the state of his spirit. To one, the words 'Blessed are the pure in heart' are solemn with warning, to another they are rich with comfort; to one they mean struggle, to another, peace.15

It is plain to see that of any characteristic saying of Jesus the same thing is true. Its meaning will challenge our apprehension. Yet amazingly enough, at whatever level we apprehend it, some high message will be conveyed.

Today, across the world, it is plain that this is happening. The Gospel is being interpreted in varying environments, and being applied to different circumstances. What the Gospel means in Labrador is not what it means in Lambeth. Yet in either place the pressure is upward, and the influence tending to

---

[15] *Christ in Modern Life*, p.4.

be unifying. That the Gospel is capable of universal application is being demonstrated.

Thus we face the flexibility and power of Christian principles, of something that is not so much a form as a spiritual force, not so much a small collection of aphorisms and parables as a creative power ever broadening out to meet growing apprehensions.

Perhaps we may suggest the Gospel's flexibility and power by a homely illustration. To mechanically minded car owners, a universal joint on a vehicle conveys a positive thrust in any desired direction. If the illustration is allowable, could we not say that the message of Christianity has a similar bearing, conveys a similar thrust to the whole of life? Without strain or torque, the words of Jesus line up with every circumstance. They have not to be strained to fit. They were delivered big enough to fit—to assimilate the best in Greek philosophy and Roman jurism, and yet to remain a central force conveying power and direction to every forward movement of the human spirit.

We have now noticed some reasons that help to explain the Gospel's universal appeal and continued vitality—its easily understood imagery, its freedom from form, its release of germinal ideas, its power to assimilate, and yet to remain true to itself, but we have not mentioned its main secret—the centrality of Christ's own personality.

Psychologists have familiarised us with the way mental processes are aided by the power of associated ideas, how life can be invigorated by associations that quicken the mind, kindle the emotions, and stir the will. To the Christian, however, there is little new in this. Church teaching has long anticipated in practice what psychology has recently expounded in theory.

From the beginning, Jesus called upon people to follow him and to find in his life and example guidance and inspiration for themselves. Nor has the Church forgotten the emphasis. In all ages it has stressed what Thomas a Kempis called *The Imitation of Christ*. Its teaching has centred on the way that the Jesus' life is interwoven with the common experiences of humankind.

For the Christian, where childhood is, there, too, is the associated thought of the child at Bethlehem. Where, again, the lips of love give pledge in marriage, there is the recollection of Jesus at the marriage at Cana of Galilee. Where the day labour of workers is in the harvest field, Christians can recollect the parable of the sower, the message of the wheat and the tares, and the thought of the day when the reapers are the angels. Or when the fishing fleets come home, there is before the disciple's mental eye the boats on the sea of Galilee, the recollection of Jesus preaching from the ship, and the reminder that he is to be, like Peter, 'a fisher of men.'

Naturally, none but the Christian, whose inward eye has been opened, can appreciate the emotional power of such associations. But the charge that all this is mere sentiment, heart-talk, weakens somewhat, when we note how intimately such associations are interwoven with a moral as well as an emotional significance.

When hot blood courses in argument, Christians are likely to be reminded of the way that Jesus lifted passing issues to the cool realm of absolute truth, as in his reply to the quarrelling brother about every kind of greed. When insidious wrong has established itself, they remember how Jesus set his face against compromise. When soft-footed temptation finds Christians in a wilderness of moral uncertainty, they draw strength from the memory of Christ's inner struggle from the outset of his ministry to its close with evil, and how he

...never sold the truth to serve the hour;
Nor paltered with eternal God for power.

There is moving testimony, also, of the way that the recollection of Jesus is able to fortify Christians in their own most intimate experiences. When Christians have to vigil alone, and no other heart seems to understand, there comes to his or her mind the memory of Jesus in Gethsemane, the moonlight falling on his strong, troubled face, and upon the sleeping forms of those who could not stay awake with him one hour. Or, finally, for the most poignant experiences come to everyone, where there is pain to be borne, or a dark river to be crossed, Christians turn to Calvary and to the hope that shines beyond.

Here, then, is the major reason why people in all ages and in all countries have responded to the Gospel. They have found it speaking to their condition.

The Christian Church has made the very circle of the year bring home to the believer the main doctrines of its faith. Advent brings to mind both the thought of Bethlehem and of the final coming of Christ as Judge. Christmas celebrates the divine birth, Epiphany the world-wide mission of the church, and Lent the need of self-scrutiny and self-discipline on the pattern of the forty days' sojourn in the wilderness. Holy Week recalls in detail the story of the passion, Good Friday the death on the Cross, Easter Day the immortal hope, Whit Sunday the coming of the Holy Spirit, and, finally, Trinity Sunday the wonder of God's three-fold revelation of himself to human experience.

Instructed Christians are in no danger of forgetting that they are living in a spiritual order, and that their own lives at every turn should be modelled on the one who left 'an example that we might follow in his steps.' And this is not without significance.

'The quality of one's images,' says Ernest Dimnet, 'largely determines the quality of one's thoughts.' If this is the case, who can estimate what it has meant to the evolution of humankind to have successive generations of Christians seeking to imitate the life and attitude of one who, on any estimate, was the holiest and wisest and greatest of all.

But how shall we speak of those further matters that touch the inner core of Christian experience?

Jesus knew the limits of human speech. Like Goethe, he would have said 'the highest cannot be spoken'. We find him, therefore, appealing to the mystic and emotional side of human nature, by conveying aspects of truth through symbolic and dramatic actions. Thus we find him, for example, teaching humility, not by verbal discourse only but by supplementing word by deed. While the disciples wrangled 'as to who should be the greatest', Jesus girded himself with a towel and performed the most menial task of the Oriental household. He washed the feet of his weary and fretful followers. Or again, proclaiming the importance of children, he crowned word with unforgettable gesture, 'He took them up in his arms, laid his hands on them, and blessed them.'

The most important of these mnemonic actions was the Last Supper. On a day, rich with past memory of the Passover, and replete with emotion for the morrow, Jesus desired to print upon the memory of his disciples the significance alike of his coming death and of his promised spiritual presence, so he took bread and wine, to invest them with such sacramental meaning that, wherever the Church has gone, the central service has been a re-enaction of that historic meal, the partaking, by faith, of the Bread of Life.

It is the witness of the world-wide Church, that such symbolism has everywhere proved of the highest spiritual worth, and one marvels afresh, at the one person in history, who has been able to stand before all with a message touching the whole of their lives and reaching the entirety of their nature. Who can fathom the mystery of an influence that, like a searchlight, turns in all directions and throws light upon every human path?

It will be noted that the deeper we inquire into the secret of Christian experience, the more we realise the complete centrality of Jesus in that experience. From him came the faith itself, and from him all those features that have made possible its world-wide extension. Dr Burkitt is factually correct: 'Christianity lives or dies with the personality of Jesus.'

CHAPTER SIX

The Test of Fruitfulness: The Church

A sure way of testing people's greatness is to ask, What did they leave to grow? Did they start people thinking along fresh lines with a vigour and boldness that persisted after him? Did they set up any new standards? Did they leave any mark on posterity worth calling indelible?

Such questions have only to be asked to make awe-inspiring the pre-eminence of Jesus over all who have ever lived.

Men and women of rare and distinguished abilities have competed for the elusive prize of fame after death. But they have failed in one way or another, to meet the test of fruitfulness. Strong and gracious spirits have over-topped their fellows in moral stature and spiritual insight, but when time brought them into judgment they were found to have made no lasting contribution.

One thinks, for example, of Marcus Aurelius, the author of *Meditations*, who, with the title of Emperor to lend him prestige, and with loftiness of personal vision, struck no chord that strongly vibrated in the conscience of those around him. The harsh candour of Renan is painful but hard to refute. 'Marcus Aurelius,' said Renan, 'left delightful books, an execrable son and an Empire in decay.' Then he draws a striking contrast, 'Jesus remains an inexhaustible principle of moral regeneration for humanity.'[16] What a strange disparity between relative opportunity on the one hand, and relative effectiveness on the other!

It is appropriate that we should judge Jesus by what he left grow, for he set up as the standard of human worth the test of fruitfulness. In words too plain to be misunderstood, he rebuked the empty life. How purposeless, he said, the hand to the plough if no furrow was to be cut! How pointless the long prayer if the life contradicted it! How futile the nurture of trees if they brought no fruit to perfection! With hard- headed realism he looked for positive results. 'You shall recognise men by their fruits.'

Many an idealist have dreaded being weighed in their own scales, but not so Jesus. No life compares with his when measured by the test of fruitfulness.

Jesus left to grow a massive movement that has seen empires rise and fall, that has survived political frameworks and seen social orders crumble, that has been transplanted far from its native soil, and that has succeeded everywhere, in producing spiritual and moral growth.

One thing is certain, the more we know of the influence of Jesus, as it has impinged on history and shaped it, the more we shall appreciate what it has meant to humankind. His stature is such that it can only be seen in its true dimensions when it is thrown into its true perspective against the life of the race as a whole.

* * * *

We are not averse to a fresh approach, but where Christianity is concerned where can we begin? Let us begin with ourselves as we took our first glimpse of Christianity.

---

[16] *Vie de Jesus*, p.289.

We found the Church in working order when we were born. In a world that contained pubs and clubs, schools and universities, law courts and hospitals, and all the varied amenities of a civilised community, we found also an institution called the Church. Doubtless we took it for granted and judged it either by hearsay or by its local embodiment. In short, we took it out of its impressive context.

But the Church was immeasurably older than anything else we faced. It had retained a recognisable shape for twenty centuries. It had been attacked by enemies without and betrayed by foes within.

It had become the mother of all kinds of offspring. Some of its offspring, by the time we saw them, had reached such a vigorous maturity that we barely connected them with the Church at all. But the Church had known them in their cradle days and had held them up until they could stand up. Many of the ideals and values we accept today would not have been ours at all if the Church had not cherished them and kept them alive when no one else cared.

To do the Church justice, then, and to get an idea of what it has done for humankind, let us turn our attention to a movement that has shaped the pattern of much of our thinking and that, despite many grievous failures, has not ceased to hold before successive generations, the message of Jesus.

* * * *

We have greatly over-simplified the picture of life in New Testament times. Palestine was then heavily timbered, fruitful, beautiful. It had a population of between five and six million. Galilee was a choice area, and the most populated.

When in Luke's account of the ministry we read 'he went through the cities and villages of the Decapolis, preaching and teaching and bringing the good news of the Kingdom' (Luke 8: 1) we do well to remember that those ten cities included Gerasa, Sebaste, and Caesarea Philippi, magnificently built with wide streets, colonnades, race-courses, amphitheatres. There was sophistication and worldly glory in the world Jesus knew. There was also tension, political unrest, and the spirit of insurrection between Jew and Roman. In ad 70 the armies of Titus laid Jerusalem level with the ground. While the Gospels were being written some two and a half million people were probably killed.

Humankind was old, deeply entrenched in evil, when the Church was born. Passages in Herodotus, or a glimpse at the Epistle to the Romans, show us the sort of world it faced. Could some 'time machine' take us back to the days of the Caesars, we should feel lost and alien, with many of our accepted standards outraged and many of our ideals not even granted a hearing.

We would be surprised not only at the material competence of Rome—its fine roads, amphitheatres, its far- flung systems of justice and administration, but we would note the lack of reverence for life, the callousness that enjoyed the butchery in the arenas, the cheap estimates of womanhood, the strange excesses and perversions of sex.

We would notice how bewilderingly varied were the ideas that jostled each other throughout the empire. Old gods and goddesses stood in the Pantheon, Greek and Roman mixed, the left-overs of a mythology that was empty of further significance, yet superstition was widespread and no one was free from it. A noble and ennobling minority turned for comfort to the worthwhile philosophy of the Greeks, and the austere moral code of the Stoics. But there was a general feeling that life was played out. The winds of pessimism cut through the once proud togas of the Stoics. 'What mortal,' they said, 'achieves more of happiness than the mere appearance of it? Short as life is, no man is so happy that he would not wish many times to be dead.' It was an age suffering from failure of nerve.

Into this world there broke, as the incontestable result of the life, death, and resurrection of Jesus, a small minority with a new hope, dauntless spirit, and a great faith.

In the New Testament we have the actual documents of what these first Christians believed and taught. The writings cover from about ad 50 to the era of persecution.[17]

They believe themselves to be the new people of God, more than fulfilling the hopes of the Old Testament Church. They make, for their number, an extraordinary impact. Their enemies credit them with 'turning the world upside down.'

We see happenings remarkable for the time. Widows, for example, get practical care (Acts 6). Greeks in Macedonia raise funds for hunger-stricken Jews in Jerusalem. Corinthian dissolutes get so changed that Paul can 'never stop thanking God for all the graces they have received through Jesus Christ' (1 Cor. 1: 4). There is a caring and a sharing previously unknown. 'Ideals of virtue,' wrote Augustine of Hippo, 'once considered attainable only by a few philosophers, are now attained by innumerable ordinary men.'[18]

Yet in this promising field there are tares among the wheat. From the start we witness the paradoxical character of the Church. It is God's agency in the world, but it is also an assortment of fallible humans. The widows who are receiving help, grumble. Leaders argue who is to be top. There can be a contentious party spirit. But there is evidence of a lively conscience. Ananias and Sapphira are so scared at being caught lying and cheating that they both get seizures. People accept rebukes, try to do better, and love their teacher. There is convincing preaching and the faith spreads.

As early as ad 195 the historian Tertullian can report that 'places of the Britons unreached by the Romans are

---

[17] Dr. C. H. Dodd, *History and the Gospels*, pp. 47-74.

[18] *De Vera Religione*, 111. 5. The second century pagan physician Galen says much the same thing. Harnack, *Expansion*, p. 266.

nevertheless obedient to the laws of Christ.'[19] In ad 314 three British bishops, a priest and a deacon are signatories at the council of Arles. The evidence is striking that the faith brought to Britain when she was a Roman province was still strong when Augustine made his famous landing in Kent in ad 597.[20] By ad 350 Christianity had spread to Arabia, Abyssinia, Afghanistan, and Ceylon.

The first three centuries suffered capricious and cruel persecution. Even an unyielding stand for the faith was to risk it, while Tertullian says any affliction could cause a mob to cry 'Christians to the lions'. But a change came in ad 312 when Constantine the Emperor adopted the cross with the monogram of Christ as his imperial standard. A year later, with the Edict of Milan, Christianity was not only tolerated but some of the property filched from Christians was returned to them. The incredible had happened. The Empire was professedly Christian.

But the great Empire itself was not long to survive. A series of invasions by Teutonic tribes brought down the weakening giant, and the very ground which the Church had won in the Empire menaced its life, but the Church disentangled itself to survive.

In adverse environments Christians created little social islands where Christian ideals could be lived out. Gregory the Great devoted the whole of his inherited wealth, for example, to the poor and to the subsidy of the famous monk missionaries who came to Britain. Benedict was the founder of Western monasticism and his noble rule is one of the sanest products of the human mind. When the Kentish Princess Ethelburga went to Northumbria to marry King Edwin she took the scholarly Paulinus with her and the court was converted. Columba founded Iona and a centre of Celtic Christianity for four

---

[19] Adv. Jud., c.vii.

[20] *The Christian Island*, Beram Saklavala, 1970.

centuries. Christianity kept Western civilisation alive. Bede of Jarrow knew Latin, and then learnt Greek because Theodore of Tarsus was a Greek. An African, Hadrian, came here with Theodore who brought a library with him making the Benedictine monastery at Canterbury a centre of Greek and Latin studies. Boniface turned his back on ecclesiastical preferment in England to create and organise the Church in the Rhine valley. In the early days Denmark, Norway, Sweden, and France all drew on English teachers.

* * * *

But another picture comes to mind. Not only invasion and barbarism broke in on the faith. The Arab invasion of the sixth and seventh centuries was of a different kind. Islam, with its particular appeal in some lands, strode over some half of the territory that the Church had won.

The history of the Church has been one of advance and recession, with 'each recession', as Latourette points out, 'tending to be less deadly and of shorter duration than the last'. So it happened now. By ad 950 Christianity was established over a wider area than before the Muslim advance.

Monasticism was a force to be reckoned with from the sixth century. Houses dedicated to Benedict's rule of work and worship were hives of wholesome influence over Europe for centuries. 'It was chiefly through the Church and its monasteries,' writes Latourette in *The Unquenchable Light*, 'that such education and learning as survived was handed down to later generations, that the poor were succoured, that the marriage tie was given sanctity, that the sick were cared for, that travellers were sheltered, and that morality was inculcated.' In long ages of violence and unrest, the bishops stood for law and order and were the protectors of the weak.

The two Great Orders of Preaching Friars—the Dominican and the Franciscan—were somewhat complementary in their activities, the one characterised by high thinking and the other by kindly service to the sick and poor. As we see an outstanding Dominican, like Thomas Aquinas for example, takes his place in the long line of Christian thinkers who from the Apostolic Fathers to luminaries of our own day, have given God their brains.

The Franciscans, on the other hand, have a secure place among those who have taken upon themselves 'for Christ's sake' something of the burden of the world's pain, poverty, and hardship. They shared to the full the grim conditions of those among whom they worked, and in their lives of simplicity and single-hearted service the spirit of Jesus lived again before their eyes. For such as Francis not one gesture of Jesus could be overlooked. Had he laid compassionate hands upon a leper? Then Francis, too, must kneel in the dust beside one and do him service, even as nameless medical missionaries since, in Nigeria, China, Africa, and India, have sought to staunch some of the world's sore pain.

Long after the sun has gone down, its reflection remains in the sky, and for centuries from religious houses the inspiration and rule of Benedict, Francis, and Dominic, shone over Europe.

* * * *

By 1350 the faith that Jesus left grow was spread over more of the earth's surface than any faith had conquered before.

Christians were to be found from Greenland to China, from Iceland to Ethiopia, while every aspect of European life felt its influence.

Frequently Christians had to be content with partial successes. We find them mitigating evils they could not remove, curtailing things that they could not cure, realising with Gregory that 'one must ascend step by step to a height, and that everything cannot be cut off at once from rough natures'. All the same their successes were not insignificant.

Educating peoples that delighted in war, some monks gave themselves to the arts of peace. They drained fens, cleared forests, encouraged agriculture, fostered craftsmanship, developed architecture. The monks, nuns and Church leaders of the Dark and Middle Ages had no knowledge of the false distinction that time has drawn between secular and sacred affairs, so we find them very logically attempting to quicken and uplift every aspect of life—to fix and enforce, for example, a just price in business, and to forbid the exploitation of the poor by usury.

With skill and ingenuity the Church tried to keep outbreaking wars within bounds by imposing on countries that professed the faith 'the Truce of God', forbidding fighting on such days as could be called the fasts, vigils, and feasts of the Church. Where possible, tribal warriors were groomed into knights, and fighting passions were sublimated by codes of chivalry. Brotherhoods and guilds were formed, and a deepening sense of a common community in Christ was preparing the way for what later became International Law.

* * * *

Many times in history it has seemed as if the Church was likely to go down in ignominious decay. But never did the danger seem so close as in the period from the middle of the fourteenth to the close of the fifteenth century. Christianity was both feeling the pressure of an aggressive Islam and torn internally by scandal and papal schism. Nor was this all. A new movement, the Renaissance, to which the Church had greatly contributed, had awakened people's minds and made it restive of the Church's authority and intellectual leadership. Was what Jesus left to grow able to survive these three-fold perils?

The answer is a surprising 'Yes'. Territorial losses in some places were offset by gains elsewhere. Geographical discoveries were opening up the world. Within Europe new movements were stirring. Expansion and revival lay ahead.

In Europe, hasty and impulsive surgeons were preparing to deal with anything that they considered outgrown or diseased in the organisation and faith of the Church. In England, Wycliffe, the morning star of the Reformation, agitated for reforms, and handed the country its first full translation of the Bible.

To take the place perhaps of the monastic orders of the Middle Ages, numerous Protestant bodies began to grow. There was too much vitality in the faith of Jesus for his followers to be content with one traditional mode of faith and life.

* * * *

The period from the beginning of the sixteenth to the middle of the seventeenth century was one of enormous geographic expansion. The mariner's compass unlocked fast-closed seas. Settlers and their descendants established Christianity in the Western Hemisphere. The faith passed swiftly to many Native and African Americans. There were Christians, too, along the shores of Africa, in India and Sri Lanka, in Burma and Thailand, in Indo-China and in the East Indies.

Everywhere it exerted its characteristic power to change conditions and to shape culture. It advanced education and stimulated care for the sick, the poor, the orphaned, and the aged. Practically all the education which existed in colonial America was the result of Christian effort, while the faith of the early settlers did much to mould the ideals of the future United States.

In this period Christianity inspired some of the greatest sculpture, painting, architecture, and music that has ever enriched humankind.

Many leading minds, like Newton, were Christian, while writers of genius, like Milton and Bunyan, took from the Bible their themes and inspiration.

* * * *

The eighteenth century saw a surge of material and industrial expansion that aided the advance of rationalism. Wars and revolutions in America and France upset the political and social scene. Writers like Voltaire and Rousseau captured human thought. For a brief time Christianity was 'abolished' in France, and the attitude of the time expressed itself in the enthronement of the 'goddess of Reason'. Bishop Godet and a number of clergymen were forced to join in a procession that marched to Notre Dame Cathedral to place a harlot from the Paris theatre on the high altar.

Church-going was strong in England during the Tudor and Stuart period, but the industrial revolution took multitudes from rural life into the monstrous growth of unplanned factory towns where the workers were exploited by greed in an industrial system divorced from ethics, and where there was scarcely a church to indicate a Christian presence. As a rough generalisation one can say that new churches and parishes were not provided for the urban areas of industrial Britain until approximately two generations after the communities had established themselves and a tradition of non-churchgoing had become a seemingly irreversible part of their inherited culture pattern.

Ironically enough outstanding theologians like Bishop Butler and Paley were writing brilliantly in support of the faith, but they knew nothing of the factory workers, and the factory workers knew nothing of them. The Christian social conscience was slow to awake, but there was not lacking boldness and vision in other directions.

While Holland was under the French heel the Netherlands Missionary Society was formed. New vigour had arisen among the Protestants of Germany, Bohemia, and Moravia since the end of the Thirty Years War. While Napoleon threatened Egypt, the London Missionary Society was formed. While he waited to invade England, the British and Foreign Bible Society was launched. In the middle of the war with France, the slave trade was abolished.

* * * *

The Methodist and Evangelical Revivals and the Oxford Movement all had large-scale effect. The revival associated with Wesley created a profound impression in the British Isles, the British West Indies, and in the United States. In Britain, thanks to Wesley, and the Evangelical party in the Church of England, there was a resurgence of the national conscience that led to no less than five major applications of Christian principles to current evils—the abolition of the slave trade, the reform of the prison system, the passing of the humane Factory Acts, the beginning of the ideas that led to trade unionism, and last, but not least, the marshalling of Christian opinion to the wider support of missionary endeavour, 'to make the best reparation in our power for the manifold wrong inflicted by the slave trade'.

At home awakening after awakening stirred Protestant Christianity, and many new denominations and literally hundreds of societies with Christian aims were born. More than at any other time in its history, impulses deriving from Jesus were being transmitted to humankind as a whole.

These impulses poured through varied channels and touched human well-being at many points. It was due to Christian intervention, for instance, that modern education reached China and the outcaste of India, that scientific medicine was introduced to many nations and tribes, that protest was made against the debauchery resulting from the sale of liquor and against the introduction of firearms.

Much of the Christian effort was not so much aimed at conversion as to the application of Gospel principles to the whole society, and in this work sectarianism did not intrude. 'High Churchmen and Low Churchmen, Nonconformists and Roman Catholics,' says Walpole in his *History of England*, 'have all made such an effort as was never before made to infuse religious activity into national life.'

Once more the faith of Jesus shattered rationalist calculations.

In formative times of settlement it had been built into the rising communities in the United States, Australia, New Zealand, and North and South Africa. The Church was established in Hawaii and Madagascar, in Indo-China and Burma.

From the Battle of Waterloo to 1914 Christianity surpassed all previous records in the extent of its geographical spread.

* * * *

The Victorian age was by no means as complacent as it is sometimes supposed to be. Large-scale movements of thought and feeling were changing England. 'Under the pressure of money-making,' declared Sir Arthur Bryant, 'the character of the English middle-class was changing. They were growing sterner and narrower in sympathy.'[21]

Eloquent and informed speakers, like Disraeli, realised that the Church, and the traditions she carried forward, represented all that was best in our heritage. He spoke of the Church as 'broadly and deeply planted in our land, mixed with our manners and customs, one of the prime securities of our common liberties'. He laughed at a society which, having mastered a few scientific principles, mistook material competence for civilisation, and left out of account a Church that was 'part of our history, part of our life, part of England itself'.[22]

The great historian, Lecky, wrote in 1865, about the Church:

> What institution is there on earth which is doing so much to furnish ideals and motives for the individual life by its moral appeal; to guide and purify the emotions through its well-appointed worship; to promote those habits of

---

21 English Saga, p. 157.

22 Moneypenny and Buckle, 11, 96

thought and desire which rise above the things of earth; to bestow comfort in old age, in sorrow, in disappointment; to keep alive a sense of that higher and further world to which we go, as is the Christian Church?

Being a Christian became much more a matter of individual choice and spiritual experience, and a very diverse picture emerges.

On one hand, we see grinding economic theories coming to power and giving rise to what Froude described as 'miles and miles of squalid lanes, each house the duplicate of its neighbour; the dirty street in front, the dirty yard behind, the ill-made sewers, the public house on the corner'. On the other hand we find the sweater and the slum landlord being met by the Christian socialist. We see the Oxford Movement deepening the spiritual life of thousands. We mark the impact of Jesus mediated through a galaxy of gifted and indignant Christians.

In literature the novels of Dickens, Charles Kingsley, the pamphlets of Carlyle, the essays of Ruskin, the poems of Elizabeth Barrett Browning, all stirred the reading classes to various aspects of reform. In education Dr Arnold, dreading a secular state, built strong Christian principles into the Public Schools. In social action the Reverend F. D. Maurice's 'Working Men's College' endeavoured to equip the working person with a sufficiency of knowledge to state the case for social betterment. In philanthropy, men like Lord Shaftesbury and Dr Barnardo fought apathy, prejudice, and avarice, to provide some answer to 'the cry that rose with ever-increasing urgency from bewildered and unhappy people and from destitute children.' Meanwhile, two women of profound Christian conviction were doing great work: Florence Nightingale, in the mud and blood of the shamble-hospitals of Scutari, was revolutionising medical nursing; while Elizabeth Fry was influencing prison reform on an international scale. Nothing is more remarkable than the religiousness of the early leaders of the Labour Movement. Professor Owen Chadwick tells us in *The Victorian Crisis of Faith* that when the TUC met at Norwich in 1894 Keir Hardie led the Congress into the Cathedral for Evensong.

If religion was given a small place in the new State-aided schools, it underlay every ragged school and orphanage. If there was widespread ignorance of the worth and relevance of the Christian heritage, the Oxford Movement fought for better education for the clergy, achieved closer co-operation with the universities, and built more schools.

* * * *

In the latter half of the nineteenth century, Christian thinking received a number of severe jolts—from developments in Biblical criticism in Germany; from the controversy about evolution which followed the publication of Darwin's *The Origin of Species*, and from the fresh approach to traditional doctrine typified by such works as *Essays and Reviews* and *Lux Mundi*. However, although at the time many found these developments hard to accept, subsequent Christian understanding has found its faith in Christ enhanced rather than diminished by the new learning, provided of course that this learning continues to be interpreted within a spiritual rather than a secular framework of thinking. For as Dr William Temple argued:

> Our task with the world is not to explain it, but to convert it. Its need can be met not by the discovery of its own immanent principle in signal manifestation through Jesus Christ, but only by the shattering impact upon its self-sufficiency and arrogance of the Son of God, crucified and risen and ascended, pouring forth that explosive and disruptive energy of the Holy Spirit.

He stressed the need for a deeper awareness of the Church as an historic institution and the scandal of its divided state. He urged a better equipment in social studies, so that the Church might play its proper role in shaping society. 'One day,' said Temple, 'theology will take up again its larger and serener task, and offer to a new Christendom its Christian map of life, its Christ-centred theology.' It was to be a longer, tougher road than Temple foresaw; and all the longer, perhaps, because he died prematurely.

Both world wars brought padres from different Churches who were serving with the armed forces. They had learnt to achieve an easy relationship, too, with men of different denominations, and of none. It boosted the new ecumenical spirit.

Commissioning some five hundred padres recalled for the great RAF Mission of 1953, Archbishop Fisher declared: 'It will give you strength before men, as Church of England and Free Church missioners, stand shoulder to shoulder, in proclaiming your agreements in a common faith.'

What timidly began in the first World Conference of Churches in 1910, and in successive Conferences since, has now become the great feature of this century, with adventures in understanding, freedom of dialogue, and warmth of spirit, that would not have been credible even a few years ago. Here in manifest form is evidence of the activity of the Holy Spirit.

The same Spirit is undoubtedly inspiring the international scholarship that is cutting across ecclesiastical and geographical frontiers in the study of the Bible. A succession of fine translations are now readily available.

But a counter attack commenced in the mid–1960s. A new alliance between agnostics and humanists commenced a vigorous campaign to 'liberate' society from religious beliefs.

Since the mid-sixties, particularly in Europe, a widening gap has opened between religion and culture, causing a falling away from the churches. They have been able to take advantage also of the literature of protest that has been provided even from within the Church.

The Church itself has been much preoccupied with its own maintenance, organisation, legislation, and liturgical experiments, but it has also given generously of its energies to meet the rightful challenge of the social gospel. Christology has been subordinated to sociology. Dr Moorman, one time Bishop of Ripon said: 'The Church is becoming so occupied with secondary matters that it has neither the time nor the energy to preach the gospel, to teach people about God, to persuade them to love him, and to inspire them to do his will.'

But the Church does not live for itself alone. It is called to be a leaven at work in all parts of our society. As Prince Philip the Duke of Edinburgh said in an address to the General Assembly of the Church of Scotland in 1970:

> For over a thousand years every aspect of our national, family, and individual lives, has been influenced by the Christian Gospel, and all the major institutions are based upon, at least nominally, the Christian ethic.
> Christianity has provided the inspiration for all that is best in our achievements and institutions, and I believe that most thinking people would like this inspiration to continue into the future. Either way, whether people like it or not, the influence of the Churches, positive or negative, in this process of reform, is absolutely crucial.

CHAPTER SEVEN

The Test of Positive Achievement: Jesus and Morality

> Let intellectual and spiritual culture progress and the human mind expand as it will, beyond the grandeur and moral elevation of Christianity, as it sparkles and shines in the Gospels, humankind will not advance.
>
> Goethe

'Only those are to be enshrined in the pantheon of heroes,' declared Rafael Sabatini in *Heroic Lives*, 'whose achievements influence posterity by the inspiration they supply, the traditions they have created, and the standards they have set.'

The mere mention of such criteria brings to our minds the incomparable pre-eminence of Jesus over all other claimants in history. So emphatically is this the case, that one notes that in any discussion of the world's greatest people, it is customary to take for granted the surpassing eminence of Jesus, and to pass on at once to people of more measurable achievement. No competent mind questions that Jesus stands alone. Yet, is not this very fact more, and not less, reason for discussing him?

In our last chapter we were concerned with the historic march of Christianity as it has expressed itself through the agency of the Church. We now turn to the influence of Jesus as it has affected human attitudes towards the person.

As we set the Gospel against the background of history, a few general ideas about it arrest our attention. We see, for instance, that the teaching that Jesus gave to a handful of very ordinary people has been profound enough to bear the scrutiny of the world's brightest minds, and that it has been flexible enough to stand application in a thousand ways that were plainly beyond the immediate horizon of those who were his contemporaries.

In the brief compass of the Gospels, large parts of which contain duplications of both sayings and incidents, we have practically all that is available of Christ's life and teaching. Who would imagine that the most influential moral code, the most far-ranging philosophy, and the sublimest religious insights, could be contained in such slender records?

Anyone who has attained a mental grasp of the smallest facet of truth in science, ethics, philosophy, or religion, knows the difficulties of simplification, the pitfalls of over-simplification. Yet Jesus had the ability to pass the width of his wisdom through people of humble scholarship and limited perspective, so that what they were able to record, has remained an inexhaustible treasury for thought and application for two thousand years.

Jesus knew how far his teaching was ahead of his time. He realised that many ages must pass before the intelligence and conscience of people would be able to rise to it. In the imagery of the seed growing secretly, and especially in the parable of the mustard seed, we are permitted to see his long-term patience. The mustard seed is small. It is liable to be overlooked, yet when it is grown to maturity, it is large and spreads out with generous branches. He implied that it was precisely the same with the seed of thought. For a time his words might be overlooked, but they would grow secretly and eventually become immensely fruitful.

The simile was brilliantly precise. The apprehension of the truth of Christ's words has been painfully slow. People have taken long centuries to rise to the thoughts of Jesus, yet when they have done so the results have been tremendously rewarding. When put to the test, no thought from the mind of Jesus has been found to lack the potency of life. Every saying has been germinal. Every principle he announced has proved capable of branching out into wide applications. Look where you will in the field of ideas and something of Jesus' sowing will meet the eye.

'From Jesus,' says Professor Latourette, 'have issued impulses that have helped to shape every phase of civilisation.' The word 'impulse' is well chosen, for the influence of Jesus, like the impulses from a beating heart, shows alternate periods of pause and pulsation with periods of quiescence followed by the periods of effective activity.

We pick up a few of those impulses as they have made themselves felt at different periods of history and we find them with the passage of time exerting an ever-growing pressure. The teaching of Jesus came to a world where ruthlessness and inequality were accepted, and where children, women, and slaves counted for little. He brought a change.

One of the most revolting features of the world when Jesus was a boy was child murder. In a letter written in the twenty-ninth year of Caesar Augustus a worker, Hilarion, advises his wife, Alis, who was shortly to be confined, to throw the baby on the midden if she did not want it. He did not expect anyone to demur. In the cities of the Empire you could always pick up abandoned children and bring them up as slaves; or if girls, as worse than slaves. Some people made a living by trafficking in children. Among the Jews, higher estimates prevailed, but children were heavily subordinated to paternal rule, and often, as we gather from Paul (Col. 3: 21) harassed and broken in spirit.

In such an age, then, we understand the disciples' astonishment when Jesus took up children in his arms and blessed them. He was opening up a new era in which children were to be esteemed, not as chattels or so much livestock, but for their own sake, and as the heirs of Heaven.

But the changed attitude came slowly. Falls have been frequent. All the same, if we look back across history and imagine the course of it as an ascending spiral, we would find the ideals of Jesus tending to meet each circuit, as it were, at higher and wider levels.

The new view was in the mind of Gregory when he declared, as he watched the little children from Britain arriving as slaves in Rome, that 'they should be called not Angles but angels'. The monasteries gave practical expression to Christian estimates throughout the Dark and Middle Ages. And as the centuries move on, we see Christian ideals getting ever wider and more efficient expression. Robert Raikes and Hannah More start village schools. Protests are heard against child- labour in field and factory. A barbarous practice of employing children as chimney sweeps gets abolished. Factory Acts are passed. People of deep Christian convictions like Charles Dickens and Kingsley plead the cause of children, or like Shaftesbury and Barnardo directly alleviate their lot.

Today, Christian estimates are taken for granted, even by those who themselves have no specific Christian theology, and the teaching first given in Galilee colours beneficent legislation, promotes clinical and educational facilities, and expresses itself in a general attitude of mind that is imaginable only in a country long nurtured in Christian traditions.

We turn now, to give a rapid glance at the elevation that Jesus had brought to the status of womanhood. Until the coming of Christian culture few knew what it was to be free, or to be treated of equal status with men. When Jesus confided in women some of the choicest truths of the Gospel, his disciples 'marvelled' that he talked with them. It was a novelty to see ordinary women sharing the higher thoughts of men. They were the lower species, so that even Socrates counted it a particular blessing, for which he thanked God three times a day, that he was a man and not a woman.

One has only to look at the present status and influence of women in countries that have known Christian influence, to see that to half the human race Jesus has brought new life, distinction, and opportunity.

Proceeding naturally from the higher conceptions of manhood and womanhood, there has come into being an entirely new relationship between the sexes that has lifted the whole tone of human life. Mere force is seen as a sign of moral inferiority, while coarseness, brutality, and callousness, are revealed in their true colours.

Turn now to a third momentous change that Jesus has effected in human relationships.

Surprising as it may seem, neither the indifference to childhood nor the contemptuous view of womanhood, constituted the gravest blot on ancient civilisation, but rather the institution of slavery. Slavery offended the moral sensibilities of none. It was taken for granted. True, the Stoics taught a certain theoretical equality, but it was left entirely to the coming of the Christian spirit to put it into practice.

It is incredible to recall that the slave population of Rome greatly exceeded that of those who were free. Nor were slaves merely hewers of wood and drawers of water. They were sometimes educated people —tutors, philosophers, physicians, and state servants. Some managed to save enough to purchase their freedom, but the teeming majority had to remain among a class counted scarcely human. Cicero declared slaves to be 'the excrement of humankind'.

But these were the people who from the first were admitted into the fellowship of the Church, 'brothers' as Paul put it, 'for whom Christ had died'. Christian ideas began at once to cut the ground from beneath a system bound up with self-interest and immemorial custom. Before the New Testament closes we find Paul carrying the teaching of Jesus from the implicit to the explicit. He writes to a slave-owner, laying down that the law of Christian brotherhood must determine his attitude to his run-away slave (Epistle to Philemon). He goes further. He announces the principle that 'In Christ there is neither bond nor free' (Gal 3: 28).

Slaves and prisoners were counted fair sport in the Roman arenas, but by the time of Telemachus a new reverence for human life was becoming general, so that when the monk gave his life to protest against men being butchered to provide a Roman holiday, public opinion was such that the gladiatorial shows were abolished.

The new reverence for life caused other changes. It humanised the slave laws in general and promoted a new sense of justice and moral responsibility.

About ad 360 the Emperor Theodosius allowed some seven thousand people to be massacred in Salonica without a trial. By this time Christian influence was of sufficient strength to enable Ambrose, Bishop of Milan, to impose an eight month's discipline on the Emperor, and only allow him readmission to the Church on condition that he passed a decree that no capital sentence was to be carried out henceforth, without it being under consideration for a whole month. Theodosius agreed, and 'with tears entreated pardon'.

Wherever Christ's Gospel went, a new attitude to the 'underdog' became apparent. In turbulent Northumbria, for instance, Aidan the monk (d. 651) used the money he received from the rich to redeem captives, many of whom became his disciples and were ordained by him. When Oswin rebuked him for giving away a horse that he had been given from the royal stables, Aidan's reply, while strange to modern ears, indicated the fervour with which many of the old saints insisted on Christian estimates. 'Is the son of a mare,' he blazed out, 'of more value in your eyes than a child of God?'[23]

---

[23] *Dictionary of Church History*, Ollard and Crosse.

Such affirmations kept alive, and spread in rough days, the conscience that was, when come to maturity, to abolish the slave trade of modern times. It is hard to imagine today how monstrous was that traffic in human flesh and blood. British shipping alone conveyed over fifty thousand slaves a year from Africa to America—great numbers of whom died in transit. In 1727, however, the Quakers protested against the

Merchants rich in cargoes of despair ;
Who drive a loathsome traffic gauge and span
And buy; the muscles and the bones of man.

Their denunciations were taken up by the Evangelicals who with burning eloquence reminded people of the laws of Christ. When in 1833, Parliament indemnified the slave owners to the tune of twenty million pounds, the long maturing ideas of Jesus had brought forth fruit.

Many in our day are reluctant to face the piety of their forebears, but the minds of such as Wilberforce and Buxton were fired by Christianity and Christianity alone. They fought against something which Christ had taught them was a sin against humanity, and a denial of God's revealed will, and the slaves, too, knew under what inspiration their release had been effected.

'As the hour of the slaves' liberation struck,' says Walpole in his History of England, 'in every place of worship in the West Indian Colonies, a hymn of praise was raised to the God of the white man, the God of the black man, the God of the free.'

'The unwearying, the unostentatious and glorious crusade against slavery,' says Sadler, 'may be regarded as among the three or four perfectly virtuous pages in the history of nations.'

Almost equally spectacular was the effort of Christian men and women to reform the prison system.

It is hard for us to envisage the horrors of gaol fever, the gross and demoralising conditions that John Howard and

Elizabeth Fry combated. Prisoners who had already served their sentences had to bribe their gaolers to be released. Female prisoners, condemned to transportation, were hounded in chains across England, and then immured in the poisonous holds of ships on a nine months' voyage to Botany Bay In England male prisoners were let into the women's quarters at night. In Botany Bay nothing awaited the unfortunate women but to be seized as mistresses, or as beasts of burden, by the roughs who boarded the boats.

'The saints everywhere have made their dents upon the world,' said Evelyn Underhill, and the impact of a great Christian like Elizabeth Fry is a notable instance. She shook the conscience of the world with her remedial measures, her prison libraries, working parties, educational classes; her reform of transport conditions, her provision for helpful activities for criminals at home and in Australia; and above all else, her personal influence, 'patterned,' as she said, 'on the great Jesus —the exquisite tenderness of His ministrations, His tone and manner to sinners.'[24]

We have now indicated, in concrete terms, something of what Jesus has done for children, women, and the slave, but such bald instances by no means do justice to the range and fineness of his work.

We are not attempting to pin-point the story of an ecclesiastical organisation but rather something of what has resulted from Jesus' teaching entering the human conscience, for the real work of the Church is not the shaping of itself but rather the permeation of life and civilisation with the Christian conscience and spirit.

In order to get anywhere, we have to take a positive line. In presenting a thesis no scientist would concentrate on exasperating experiments that failed. They have to go to those that succeeded. Similarly, while we could deal with the tragic

---

24 Quoted by Janet Witney, *Elizabeth Fry*.

occasions when Christians have outraged the Christian spirit—as in the hideous third degree trials and burnings of the Inquisition—it seems right in a short sketch to treat these as experiments that failed in understanding, tolerance, and pity, and concentrate on the individuals and occasions when a spirit shone out that could fairly be identified as 'the real thing'.

We turn therefore to indicate some individuals, and groups in which 'the real thing' can unmistakably be identified. One thinks of the spirit of the social and philanthropic work that commenced in the Apostolic Church when deacons were appointed to care for the widows and poverty-stricken (Acts 6). Wonderful again was the spirit that fell on those building Chartres Cathedral in 1144, when lords and ladies came from all over France to harness themselves alongside the masons and workers to pull the carts dragging stones from the quarry.[25] Daily, we are told, the wealthier folk came burdened with provisions that they all shared together, and all the hearts beat as one, and none had grudges or held back from the roughest work. Many hundreds of priests perished in the mid-fourteenth century in ministering to their plague- ridden parishioners; and heroic are the efforts of Christian doctors, teachers, and evangelists, both at home and in the mission fields of today.

Only in imagination, too, can we have any idea of the leavening of society that has been achieved by those noble individuals who, in contrast to the rank and file, have brought the spirit of Christ into daily life. Chaucer's picture of the saintliness of the 'poor parson of the town' would scarcely have been drawn if there had not been others like him in the fourteenth century, and a life like George Herbert's in the seventeenth century must have had a persuasive influence hard to estimate. 'He lived and died a saint,' wrote George Walton, 'unspotted from the world, full of alms-deeds, full of humility.' Or again, there comes to mind the inscription on Wilberforce's

---

[25] Sir Kenneth Clark, *Civilization*.

tomb in Westminster Abbey, 'There remains, and ever will remain, the abiding eloquence of his Christian life.'

Granted, of course, that only a sprinkling of Christ's followers have ever approximated to such excellences, yet, that a few in all ages have done so must be of significance, if only because they have set a standard, widely known and accepted as authentic, by which the remainder of Christ's followers have been judged. Only a resolute cynicism would make light of the steadfast courage of both Catholic and Protestant martyrs at the Reformation, or of the love for their fellows that distinguished Father Damien or General Booth, or of the effective evangelism of individuals as distinct as Hannah More, Wesley, the Studd brothers and Billy Graham, and Studdert Kennedy, as varied in spiritual technique as the Quakers, the Oxford Movement, or of the Churches of South India, or as united in essential purpose as the mediaeval guilds, and the Industrial Christian Fellowship. Yet plainly it is the same Lord they seek to proclaim and serve.

No thinking person can question the quality of Jesus' influence upon the human conscience. It is no exaggeration to say that as the warm Atlantic Drift mixes with icy waters and infuses them with life-giving warmth, so the quality of the Christian outlook has entered, at some time or another, most of the channels of human life. The Stream affects the temperature and climate in which millions live who know little of its hidden course. In the same way the consciences that Jesus has enlivened, have produced an atmosphere which affects the relationships, attitudes, and judgments of millions who personally never enter a church.

Loisy could say in *La Morale Humaine* that 'the best thing in present-day society is the feeling for humanity that has come to us from the Gospels and that we owe to Christ'.

This 'feeling for humanity' has condemned purely utilitarian ideas, so that sickness and age, weakness and poverty, ignorance and injustice, have ceased to be matters of indifference, but have become challenges to amelioration and practical effort.

What this has meant on the scale on which Christianity has operated, no one can estimate, save to agree that Lecky tells part of the story in *History of European Morals*:

> The simple record of Christ's short years has done more to soften and regenerate the heart of humanity than all the exhortations of moralists and all the disquisitions of philosophers. Christianity has covered the world with countless institutions of mercy utterly unknown in heathen lands.

In so far as there exists this feeling for humanity, we must see it as a consequence of the moral discipline and spiritual culture that past generations have voluntarily accepted. Inspired by Christianity, there have been those who have not been content to live haphazardly. They have taken themselves in hand directionally. They have shaped themselves by conscious evolution nearer the humanity and closer to the ideals of Jesus. By our time the results are embedded in standards and assumptions, in attitudes and institutions, that only years of insulation from Christianity could wholly efface.

Meanwhile, based on the Christian estimate of personality, democratic attitudes and ideals have seen the light of day, safeguarding under democratic ways of life, the individual's place, rights, liberties, and responsibilities, in the scheme of things. There has been a sense of public and private duty; an ideal of wealth and power being a trust; a sense of responsibility towards backward peoples. People and societies being what they are, there have been lamentable breakdowns that have shamed the ideal, but a knowledge of the ideal has been widespread enough.

If today we are achieving fairer opportunities for all, better working conditions, and more equitable rewards, we are moving towards something that has always been implicit in the teaching of Jesus.

Or if, again, the fear of war is forcing us more and more to consider what is involved in human brotherhood and if that ideal of brotherhood can ever win political expression, Christians will have nothing new to put on their agenda. It has always stood there, and always offered itself for implementation.

Christ's thought spans the tardy centuries and is abreast, nay ahead, of the most realistic thinking of our day.

When Jesus released into the world the simple but profound idea of the individual's importance as a child of God, having a place here, and hereafter, in his Kingdom, and then made it unforgettable by dying for all on the Cross, the world began to be a different place. If now we think that concern for the person is no more than good humanitarian sociology, and needs no religion to support it, we may find that concern growing less personal and more loveless, when the faith that originated it ceases to supplement 'natural' kindness.

The moral elevation of Christian thought would stand out in much bolder relief if we had not had, directly and indirectly, long familiarity with it. More than is realised, we have been conditioned by the momentum that Christianity has gathered in its unobtrusive passage from age to age.

An influence once given, a field of ideas once opened up, may become the property of people not directly in touch with the original inspiration, and they may underrate it, miss the source of it, mistake the end of it.

When Jesus gave to the world his conception of the Kingdom of God, he was sharing a comprehensive vision of the divine purpose, age-old, heaven-high, embracing every individual and the whole destiny of all, embracing all existence and the fulfilment of all being.

In Norse mythology we find life pictured as a tree, Yggdrasil, the Tree of Existence. Its roots are deep down. Its trunk reaches up heaven-high. Its boughs spread over the whole universe.

This image of the Northern mind, has achieved reality if we apply the illustration to Christianity. Recall Carlyle's words about Yggdrasil in *Heroes and Hero-Worship*:

> Its roots are watered from the Sacred Well. Its boughs, with their buddings, dis-leafings—things suffered, things done—stretches through all lands and times. Is not every leaf of it a biography, every fibre an act or word? Its boughs are histories of nations. The rustle of it is the noise of human existence, onwards from the old. It grows there the breath of human passion rustling through it; or storm tossed, the storm wind blinding through it like the voice of all the gods. It is the Tree of Existence. It is the past, present, and the future; what was done, what is doing, and what will be done...

Jesus has refreshed, as from a perennial spring, the very roots of human compassion and self-sacrifice. He has inspired, as has none other, a love that is ever branching out for the good of others. We may speak of promising boughs, hopeful twigs, innumerable leaves, a veritable Tree of Life, whose wood is in his cross, 'deep down, heaven-high'.

Is this what the Norse myth meant in its elemental way, about Yggdrasil, Tree of Existence, and what the Cross means positively, with its compassion, and its caring, and its call to care?

CHAPTER EIGHT

The Test of Excellence: Jesus and Culture

> In the end civilisation depends on man extending his powers of mind and spirit to the uttermost.
>
> Sir Kenneth Clark

As an avalanche gathers weight as it proceeds, our argument moves forward to consider a further fact about Jesus. The whole argument is cumulative, and what we say now presupposes what has gone before, and adheres to what we shall say later.

We now ask, 'What has been the nature of his contribution to human life?' The answer has already been foreshadowed. It has been of unmatched quality.

Some such general statement is likely to meet with ready approval. You can fool some of the people all of the time and all of the people some of the time, but only intrinsic quality can explain Jesus' central and continued place in history.

But how can we make real the full nature of that achievement? Or realise the width and worth of what has happened? When Christianity moved out into the Roman Empire it must have seemed a thing of no possible lasting consequence. Small, scattered, persecuted, Christian groups looked very unlike being the torch-bearers of a new culture. Who could imagine they were holding the bridgeheads over which a faith would pass that would outlast the mighty Empire, survive the Dark Ages, and press forward the creative energies of a new civilisation?

But the incredible happened. We have to credit Christianity as the major shaping force in our culture and civilisation, with an excellence of influence hard to dispute.

The average person is inclined to believe that religion is one thing, and culture generally is another. It is striking to see how intimately they are related and interwoven. The vitality and character of a society is shaped by its religion.[26]

'Throughout the greater part of humankind's history,' says Christopher Dawson, 'in all ages and states of society, religion has been the great central unifying force in culture. We cannot understand the inner force of a society unless we understand its religion.'

Buddhism tamed the Mongols—look at the peaceful inhabitants of Tibet. Islam has influenced and transformed countless millions of people. Judaism has made distinctive a whole race. Christianity has given Western civilisation its characteristic features, and it is easy to agree with T. S. Eliot's opinion that 'the culture of Europe could not survive the complete disappearance of the Christian faith.'[27]

As far as our own culture is concerned it has certainly been religion that has extended human powers of mind and spirit to the uttermost.

In architecture, for example, the master-builders, craftsmen, and artists have been superb interpreters of Christianity.

The Church of St Sophia in Constantinople was one of the most outstanding works of humankind. It was built about ad

---

[26] Christopher Dawson, *Religion and Culture*

[27] T. S. Eliot, *Notes Towards a Definition of Culture*

537. In the days of its glory the doors were of gilt bronze, the windows of bronze grille, or translucent marble, the screen of silver, and the altar of enamelled gold. Nothing was too good for the glory of God.

The massive Norman style of Durham, Gloucester, and Southwell cathedrals suggests assurance. The vaulted roofs, the great piers, and the mighty towers, all speak confidence in the divine.

The soaring lines of Gothic must surely be one of humanity's most satisfying spiritual achievements. The columned shafts of Winchester, Salisbury, and the like, pass effortlessly into spanning vaults and poised and pointed arches. The very stone seems weightless, and stretches the mind to the infinite. Add now the spire and the bell-towers and the welcoming porches, the mullioned tracery filled with storied glass, and roofs 'where music dwells, fingering and wandering on as loth to die', and you have something so excellent that mind, spirit, and senses are all invited to respond.

Obviously it was the Church that provided the creative artists with their themes, and gave them the fullest scope for accessory carving, for tapestries, for the jewelled brilliance of glass as in Chartres, for glories of sculpture like the Pieta of Michelangelo in St Peter's, Rome.

It is a long ascent from the simple drawings in the catacombs to the elaborate frescoes of the Renaissance like *The Creation of Man* or *The Last Judgment* of Michelangelo in the Sistine Chapel; there is a long way between Salvador Dali's *Last Supper* in Washington and Leonardo da Vinci's in Milan, but the same faith tutored them all.

There is the obvious right of the doctrine 'Art for art's sake' but obviously Rembrandt's *Christ Preaching of Forgiveness*, and Giotto's *Kiss of Judas* will gain appreciation in depth if we understand their religious significance.

Some of us again, may be swift in our response to music, and give it a high place in our cultural heritage. From childhood, perhaps, we have responded to Bach's 'Jesu Joy of

Man's Desiring', or Gounod's 'Ave Maria', or we may have been thrilled as Handel's 'Halleluiah Chorus' tried to 'Bring all heaven before our eyes'. Or, perhaps, as members of a choral society, we may have noted how large a proportion of works, chosen primarily on musical merit, works that bear the emphatic stamp of greatness, have been the products of religious inspiration, like the *St Matthew Passion,* or *The Dream of Gerontius*. So music has done the work of an evangelist, and in the completion of our appreciation, has given us something more than music.

No matter, it seems, what medium expresses the highest life, that highest life owes something to one, whom the author of the Fourth Gospel called 'The Light of the World'. What a leap of faith that title entailed at the end of the first century. From some points of view it is more easily understood in the twentieth!

A walk round the oldest Universities provides some of the evidence. The very names of the colleges proclaim their Christian origin—-Jesus, Corpus Christi, Trinity, Magdalen, All Souls, St John's.

Similarly, the inspiration that founded the great hospitals is embedded in their titles—St Bartholomew's, St Thomas's, St Mary's, St Luke's. And who would suggest that the influence that saturates the age-old traditions of such temples of learning and healing, requires any lengthy argument to establish its excellence?

Less well known, perhaps, is the contribution of Christianity to our legal constitution. Christian principles were introduced by the early Code of Justinian; by the laws of King Alfred who inscribed at the head of them the Ten Commandments; by Magna Carta with its introductory assertion that 'The Church shall be free and shall keep its laws'; by the Puritans pressing home The Declaration of Rights, and, as Christian principles penetrated more and more consciences, through countless reform bills and factory acts, and through numberless precedent laws, that owed their tone and excellence to successive judges who were themselves people of deep Christian conviction.

The influence of Christian principles penetrates to the very roots of our constitution. Despotism, arbitrary power, the stifling of individual liberty—these have been held in check by the doctrines of the Church that 'there is a higher authority, a divine authority, to which all men owe allegiance'.[28] Definitions of guilt—that an action must be proved morally blameworthy; the axiom that people are innocent until proved guilty; forms of punishment—that they must not be so much vengeful as remedial—these are but a few of the conceptions that have come from Christianity.

Even less known than its influence on law, is the impetus Christianity has given to science. Modern science, it can be observed, has arisen entirely within the borders of Christendom. Its rise was not accidental. It drew on both Palestine and Greece.

Nothing, indeed, was further from the mind of the early and mediaeval Christian than that they were preparing the way for the rise of natural science; but they laid some of the foundations which made it possible. Jesus' promise that 'The Spirit of Truth will guide you into all truth' in itself implied search and industry. The spirit of charity aided a democratic attitude, and anticipated what is best in humanism. Belief in God's universal sovereignty carried with it a belief in the general rationality and order of the natural world that expressed itself in the mediaeval conception of an Order of Nature.

Granted, of course, that eras of intense bigotry, cruel persecution, clericalist rule, and the suppression of new thought, have powerfully worked against science, yet when the Renaissance came and the Reformation burst the fetters, conceptions of immense significance from the earlier periods were released and bore fruit. As Dr Whitehead points out, 'the mediaeval insistence on the rationality of God' carried with it

---

[28] Lord Denning, *Church of England Newspaper*

'the inexpungable belief that every detailed occurrence could be correlated with its antecedents'.[29]

'The one creative achievement of the Reformation,' says Professor John Macmurray in *Reason and Emotion,* 'was science and the scientific spirit. Science is the legitimate child of a great religious movement, and its genealogy goes back to Jesus.'

So, science, the outstanding feature of the modern world, the gift that all non-Christians accept with unanimous enthusiasm, has its roots in what Jesus left grow.

Turn now, momentarily, to Christ's influence on language and literature. In well over a thousand languages and dialects, the thoughts of Jesus now travel the globe, not only to awaken people spiritually, but even to lift some races to literacy itself. Complete Bibles or New Testaments are available in no less than 578 tongues, while portions of the Scriptures are available in 853 more, so a total of 1,431 languages or dialects carry at least a portion of the Scriptures. Therefore, no less than 96 per cent of the world's population may be said to be in range of the Christian message. *The Greatest Book in the World*, by Dr Darlow, describes how several hundred languages have been reduced to written form, and provided for the first time with an alphabet and grammar, simply and solely that afterwards they might become vehicles for conveying the message of the Bible.

But the Bible has not only brought light to the simple, it has been a star of innumerable rays to the world's most sophisticated minds.

Is it not remarkable that the writings of Dante, Tolstoy, Emerson, Goethe, Shakespeare (to mention only a few) are saturated with the metaphors of a Jewish carpenter, and that the literary giants of Italy, Russia, America, Germany, and England, echo the ideas of Galilee? And the influence does not wane. The

---

[29] *Science and the Modern World*, See also John Bailie and M. M. Foster

journalist, the dramatist, the statesman, the moral reformer, and, indeed, all of us in our day by day speech, stand under the eminence of Christ.

As one reads the brave books that house the hopes and insights, the wisdom and the gentleness, the moral passion and the greatness of our literary tradition, one realises the debt to him who 'spake as never man spake'—writings of devotion as distinct as Caedmon's 'Song of Creation', and Francis Lyte's 'Abide with Me'; of mysticism as varied as Blake's, Donne's, and Evelyn Underhill's; of moral force as influential as Langland's *Piers Plowman* and Cranmer's Book of Common Prayer. Or what shall we say of the impress on our thought of Tyndale and Coverdale's Bible, The Authorised Version, Bunyan's *Pilgrim's Progress* and Milton's *Paradise Lost?*

Indeed, the influence does not end with specific inspirations. Christianity has contributed also to the background of all whose writings have used, or presupposed, Christian values and ideals and morality. Has not Norman Nicholson pointed out that without a Christian context of faith and morality, literature in general, even in competent hands, tends to become arid and joyless, unlit and purposeless?[30]

Deep in the Arctic Circle I have seen the Aurora Borealis slashing the midnight sky with scimitars of steel-blue light, but even as one watched, the metaphor became inappropriate. The light softened and changed into ribbons of gold, crimson, and jade, flying out over the ice-caps and the ebony of the sea. Then again, its form would change, and the strange light would shape itself into a triumphal archway, spanning all that was visible in that cold world, and being magically reflected in it.

So one would describe the quality of Christ's influence as it has shone across the dark centuries; as in the many phases, changes, and spheres through which it has passed, men and movements have reflected its light and colour.

---

30 *Man and Literature.*

The mere mention, then, of what Jesus has meant to the highest life of the human race is likely to make one sensitive of their own limitations, to see with keener eyes the narrowness of his appreciations, the pathetic width of his ignorance! It may rightly be said that 'Christianity is a religion that educates'.

CHAPTER NINE

The Test of Historical Truth

> I must understand in order to believe, and by doubting come to questioning and by questioning perceive the truth.
>
> Abelard

> I take sides decidedly with those who emphasise that Christianity is an historical religion and against those who say that the quest of the historical Jesus is irrelevant. I therefore unashamedly address myself to those who are prepared to allow to historical evidence a place in the considerations leading up to faith...
>
> C. F. D. Moule, The Phenomenon of the New Testament

We owe a great deal to biblical criticism. It is an ongoing search for truth with scholars able to check and, where necessary, correct each other's work.

It began in German universities in the eighteenth century and spread generally in the nineteenth. Literary and historical methods of research were applied to the discovery of the sources, authorships, dates, and historical setting of biblical writings. We shall see, in Chapter 16—Faith's Radical Testing—that what at first appeared wholly destructive, has stimulated deeper study, and better understanding.

We now know that the Hebrews were the first ancient people to practise continuous, objective, historical writing, and that we are dealing with substantially reliable records. It is clear gain to be able to place biblical writings in a fairly agreed chronological order. This in turn enables us to see the story of the Hebrew people leading up to the Christian Gospel as intelligible history. In so far as archaeological, linguistic, and historical checks have been applied it has been found that there is a basis of fact underlying the main pattern of Bible events.

This is of first importance, because it was within the framework of this historical record that the Hebrews had their vivid experiences of God. Similarly, we have carefully documented records of the life, death, and resurrection of Jesus, of his historical impact, and of the rise of Christianity.

At the beginning of the twentieth century, Karl Barth initiated a deeper inquiry. He 'threw a bombshell', as he described it in *The Epistle to the Romans* 'into the playground of the theologians', by insisting that they looked not only at the Bible as history, but concerned themselves with what made it worth looking at—its theological content, as the Word of God. His call led to a revival of biblical theology.

'That which makes the Bible intelligible as a whole,' wrote Dr A. G. Herbert in *The Authority of the Bible*, 'is the connection that runs through it of a purpose of God in history.'

The call of Abraham, the Exodus under Moses, the giving of the Law, the kingdom of David, the Captivity in Babylon, the experiences of the Exile—were all steps in the Hebrews' developing religious experience.

Within this framework we meet that remarkable succession of inspired writers who saw truths for their time big enough to be truths of all time. Stage by stage ideas of God are enlarged and moral understanding advanced, as though, like a cantilever bridge, it was spanning forward to meet the teaching of Jesus.

To the prophets we owe the phenomenon of the Messianic hope, which in actual fact brightened up to the time when Jesus came.

As in *A Light to the Nations* Professor N. K. Gottwald rightly says, 'One might as well attempt to evaluate the Greeks without considering their philosophy or art, or the Romans without regard for law or engineering, as understand the history of the Hebrews without regard to religious convictions.'

One of the strangest of these convictions is that God's love and power would be made manifest to the nations through Israel, or some supreme figure in Israel who, even at the cost of limitless suffering, would bring in a new relationship with God.

But the Old Testament, and the apocryphal literature, leave us with the Messianic hope unrealised. 'He who should come' does not come. The figure in whom the whole story of revealed religion was to culminate, fails to arrive.

The New Testament, however, rings with the proclamation of his arrival. 'The time is fulfilled.' John the Baptist, last of the prophets, is privileged to be the greatest, for he heralds the Messiah, identifying him as Jesus of Nazareth. The figure pointed to in the Old Testament is central in the New. He, too, is a fact of history, the Christ-event is the climactic happening in which God's hand is seen.

Here, therefore, the message of the Old Testament finds fulfilment in the New. There is a striking continuity. It suggests nothing less than an historical revelation.

Grotesque as it may appear, the idea is sometimes put about that the Jesus-story is something of a myth. Such an idea raises more problems for the serious historian than to accept the essential features of the Gospels as facts. The pendulum swings too far that emphasises that the Gospels are religious and not also historical documents, and tends to decry 'mere facts of history'. 'It belongs to the specific character of Christianity,' says Dr C. H. Dodd in *History and the Gospels,* 'that it is an historical religion, and cannot be separated from the actual truth of the events described and interpreted.'

Those who would loosen the bolts that hold Christianity to its massive implacement in history would make it dependent on their own subjective ideas, and part company even with the noteworthy evidences of Christianity in Jewish and Roman writings.[31]

The Gospels give the picture of a definite, potent awe-inspiring personality. They carry a conviction of reality. Of course there are difficulties and obscurities, and some irreconcilable differences in detail between one Gospel and another. There was no on-the-spot reporter. Stories, teaching passed from lip to lip. Jesus spoke in Aramaic, and the Gospels are in Greek. Before the invention of printing texts suffered from copyists who made mistakes. But in the main we may have confidence in the teaching ascribed to Jesus. He was frequently addressed as Rabbi, and we now know that it was the custom of the Jewish Rabbis to encourage their disciples to memorise their teaching. Jesus made this easy, since much of his teaching can be translated back into Hebraic verse forms, as Dr Burney points out in *The Poetry of the Gospels*.

Eyewitnesses saw his mighty works. He was actually seized in their presence in the Garden of Gethsemane and, before the eyes of those he loved most, he was actually crucified. To the same people he appeared again in recognisable form, and 'was seen of many'. Paul refers, as to a fact of unquestioned and general knowledge, to 'over five hundred brethren' who had seen the risen Jesus for themselves, and who were alive, and presumably ready to be questioned, at the time he wrote (1 Cor. 15).

There is no evidence that those who had the strongest motives for denying the Resurrection were able to do so. The

---

[31] The Talmud *Sanhedrin*, 43a. Josephus, *Antiquities*, 18. 3. 3., 20. 9. 1.; Tacitus, *Annals,* XV. 44; Pliny's *Letter to the Trajan*; Suetonius, *Life of Claudius*. See Prof. J. N. D. Anderson, *Christianity; the Witness of History*.

historical perspective of Peter's first speech in the Acts (Chapter 2) is generally accepted. But it was delivered in the very city where the memory of Jesus was most vivid, and before an audience to whom the recollection of the crucifixion must have been most painful. Nevertheless, Peter unhesitatingly appeals to their sensitive memories:

> Men of Israel, listen to me: I speak of Jesus of Nazareth, a man singled out by God and made known to you through miracles, portents, and signs, which God worked among you through him as you well know. When he had been given up to you, by the deliberate will and plan of God, you used heathen men to crucify and kill him. But God raised him to life again, setting him free from the pangs of death, because it could not be that death should keep him in its grip (Acts 2: 22–24)

and there is no evidence that they howled Peter down for being preposterous. On the contrary, 'They were smitten to the heart,' cowed, we must assume, by the unassailable truth of Peter's words, and were baptised in their thousands.

On such facts as these Christianity is based. 'These things' said Paul to King Agrippa, 'were not done in a corner.' Obedient to these facts the doctrines of the Church were fashioned. The Creeds are not complicated exercises in metaphysical speculation. They are attempts to grapple with and to state, certain facts that were real and vivid in historical experience.

'The theological interpretation which sees the life of Jesus as an act of God, is not something arbitrarily added to the bare facts,' writes Dr C. B. Caird in *Jesus and God*. He continues:

> There never were any bare facts. The life of Jesus was experienced at the time by those who knew him as an act of God. More than that, the religious interpretation was present to the mind of Jesus before even the events

happened, and thus was built into the very structure of the events, and in no place is this more obvious than in the account of the supreme event of the Resurrection.

The Resurrection resulted without question in Jesus being decisively recognised as the Messiah. The disciples were absolutely convinced that the cross on which he died had not terminated the pattern and purpose of his God-given life, and as Dr Ramsey put it:

> It is not too much to say that without the Resurrection the phenomenon of Christianity in the Apostolic Age, and since, is scientifically unaccountable. It is also true to say that without the Resurrection, Christianity would not be itself, as its distinctiveness is not its adherence to a teacher who lived long ago, but to its belief that 'Jesus is Lord' for every generation throughout the centuries.[32]

We may dislike these facts, and may wish to shape Christianity apart from them but what would result would not be Christianity, it would be speculative, man-made, and without authority. Those who gave their lives 'to bear witness to the truth' were not at liberty to teach what they liked about Christ. They were pinioned down by the historical and well- known happenings of his life, death, and resurrection.

It should be apparent, therefore, that it was not the Church that created the facts but the facts which created the Church. 'This thing we are declaring unto you,' said John, 'this Word of life, we heard it, gazed upon it, yes, our own hands handled it.' If the Church were dealing with theories of fine spun fancies, it could retract or modify its doctrines at will, it could prune its beliefs to suit the turn and twist of criticism and popular taste, but as it is dealing with facts of history, its doctrines are ready

---

[32] *God, Christ and the World*, pp. 77, 78

made, and it has to forgo a heady desire to be popular for a hard-headed effort to be accurate. It remembers how Peter in his Epistle broke out hotly, 'It is no cunningly devised fable we are giving you, for we were eyewitnesses.'

It is tempting to scale down the records of historic Christianity, to cut out or explain away passages that challenge the dominant assumptions of a secular age. But it is also an age that claims to be objective in its search for reality. We have, therefore, to present it with the phenomenon of the New Testament. We cannot present it as other than it is. We certainly cannot say that the portrait of Christ is hidden from history.

Professor D. Nineham is no easy believer, but his summing up in *St Mark* is impressive:

> Our basic picture of Christ is carried back to a point only a quarter of a century or so after his death; and when we bear in mind the wonderfully retentive memory of the Oriental it will not seem surprising that we can often be virtually sure that what the tradition is offering us are the authentic deeds, and especially the authentic words of the historic Jesus.

Similarly Howard Marshall argues in *I Believe in the Historical Jesus* that 'there could be no Christian faith in Jesus if it could be shown that he never existed or that he never rose from the dead or that his career was substantially different from that recorded in the Gospels'. Marshall believes that 'historical study confirms that Jesus lived and ministered and taught in a way that is substantially reproduced in the Gospels'. Yet he insists that the 'Jesus of the historians is not enough'. We need also to experience Christ as the risen Lord who continues to illuminate the mind of the believer. Stephen Neill in T*he Interpretation of the New Testament* makes the point neatly. 'The New Testament/ he writes, 'bears witness to one historical figure, unlike any other that has ever walked this earth, and although much about him must remain unknown, and even more, must remain mysterious ... he is not so much the unknown, the problem, as the one who to the believer is well known/ In the words of Alice Meynell, 'he is the one we know by heart'.

The second reason is that Christianity not only allows, but demands progress, by the germinal nature of Christ's teaching, and by the doctrine of the activity of the Holy Spirit, 'that works unceasingly to lead us into all truth'.

We shall not here enter into that weighty doctrine save to say that at an historical date in history that doctrine began to be a decisive factor in Christian experience (Acts 3).

In the light of much evidence then, we understand the missionaries, who tell us of the joy and conviction with which people turn from religions of speculative opinion, to greet the solid grandeur of a faith that meets them with a mass of documentary and factual evidence of its truth and relevance. They face an historical person, the testimony of an historical community, the impressive witness of an unbroken historical spiritual experience, and the challenge of a religion that continues to awaken an ever-deepening perception.

CHAPTER TEN

The Test of Intimate Inquiry

> There is something unique, continuing, self-vindicating, in the Christian experience itself.
>
> Professor Grensted

It is probably already becoming apparent to us that the more closely the life of Jesus is considered, the deeper one senses the greatness of it, and the higher one reaches for terms in which to describe it.

But a moment's reflection will remind us that this point in itself is suggestive. It is an unhappy fact of experience that the majority of human beings pale off a little on closer acquaintance. More intimate knowledge of their character and idiosyncrasies may not mean heightened admiration.

Nor, indeed, are the great ones of the earth always better for closer knowledge. Press agency reports may leave nothing to be desired, but behind the facade of outer appearance, within the circle of intimacy, how hard to miss the human weakness, the edges of limitation. The sad business of 'debunking' thrives on the uncharitable disclosures of those in the inner circle who claim to know 'the real man or woman'. The incorrigible cynicism of the world would have us believe that to keep one's heroes one must keep them at arm's length.

With Jesus, however, the contrary is true—the fuller the knowledge, the more penetrating the study, the greater is likely to be our homage and devotion.

This was the case with those who were privileged to know the historic Jesus. They found discipleship an increasingly uplifting experience. Simply to share his company, men and women gladly embraced lives of hardship and sacrifice. Matthew gave up that most retaining of callings, the civil service, Peter and Andrew, James and John, abandoned their fishing smacks. Mary forsook Magdala, women like Salome and Mary Cleopas broke up their homes and, with their sons and breadwinners, faced a perilous future, and, humanly speaking, what had they to gain? Jesus was frankly realistic. He gave them clear warning that the same brutal things might happen to them as he foresaw might happen to him.

We must needs see how supremely great must have been the personality that drew out such devotion, how surpassingly rewarding must have been the near view of his personality and ministry.

But were they just simply folk, readily impressed by a fascinating and charismatic personality? Why, then, do we catch glimpses of men of the ruling class like Nicodemus and Joseph of Arimathea, members of Herod's household, and a woman like Claudia Procula, grand-daughter of Caesar Augustus, among his followers?

Let us keep the historical perspective. In his earthly ministry Jesus 'chose twelve that they might be with him', and with him on every possible occasion, and, as far as we can ascertain, these, and the women who accompanied Jesus, were the very people who came to the sober conclusion that no human language was fit to do him honour. They bowed before him as before one who was in the very counsels of God, and who had command of seemingly limitless resources.

While those on the outer fringe of discipleship were prepared to acclaim Jesus as 'John the Baptist returned from the dead, or as one of the prophets', those who heard and watched Jesus daily were not content. They felt that the estimate was inadequate. A momentous conviction, barely expressible, grew in their hearts. They saw in him a manifestation of the power of God and the wisdom of God. They came to the stupendous conclusion that a life so exemplary and awe-inspiring was of cosmic and eternal significance. 'A zone of silence,' says B. S. Easton in *The Gospel Before the Gospel,* 'separated Him from all other men. Even in his lifetime his disciples were personal believers.'

At Caesarea Philippi, Peter, the spokesman of the Twelve, made the biggest guess in human spiritual history, saying with all the awe and wonder the identification would have for a generation familiar with the Messianic hope, 'Thou art the Messiah' (Mark 8: 29).

This heightening of conviction, following on close personal knowledge, was true of all who had any part in the three years' ministry. Indeed, not to have shared as an eyewitness and a follower in those remarkable years was to be lacking in prestige and authority in the early Church. One finds, for example, that when a successor had to be elected to take the place of Judas, no one was counted eligible unless he had followed Jesus 'from the time of his baptism to the day of his ascension' (Acts 1: 21). Even a man as zealous and spiritually mighty as Paul laboured always under the handicap that he had not had a part in the earthly ministry of Jesus.

What must be our conclusion, therefore, about the effect of intimate knowledge of Jesus upon the first disciples? It was 'those who lived most intimately with him who stood most in mingled love and wonder in his presence, gave him the highest name they knew to express transcendent greatness, Messiah, and after his Resurrection, triumphantly and with utmost courage proclaimed him as "The Prince of Life"'.[33]

The affirmations about Jesus in the Epistles and Gospels have been re-echoed in all centuries, and always most emphatically by those who have sought most earnestly, inquired most deeply, and witnessed most sacrificially.

Unfortunately, one of the oldest and most repetitive of heresies is that the fundamental beliefs of Christianity disintegrate under the impact of vigorous thinking or probing research. But the contrary is most generally true.

Granted that Jesus has been loved and worshipped as Lord and Saviour by unnumbered multitudes of believers who have neither been able to understand subtleties of doctrine, nor cared for the credal formulations of the great Councils. Yet always there has been a minority—and those vitally influential—whose faith has been grounded on reason, and these have been the ones who have looked most searchingly at the documents, most steadily at the Gospel portrait.

Consider the verdict of one of our soundest theologians: 'The more critical our study of the New Testament,' said Dr C. H. Dodd, 'the more sure we become that here is a real person in history challenging us all by a unique outlook on life. We discover that Christ is in some way identical with that inner light, that indwelling spirit, or whatever it is, that we live by at our best.'

Even honest doubt has been to many people a blessing in disguise, for it has stimulated a deeper inquiry, and that inquiry, like fire tempering steel, has produced a quality of conviction that the less thoughtful have never known.

Dr John Mott was a source of strength to great numbers. But it was the result of strenuous wrestling with doubt, and all the more worthwhile for the encounter. 'I gave myself,' he says, 'to hard honest study of the original documents of the faith, and I

---

[33] Dr. H. E. Fosdick, *The Man from Nazareth*, p. 187.

shall never forget the moment when, with my notes spread out on the desk and on the faded red carpet, I was able, like Thomas, to say, "My Lord and my God".'

Such was the result of intimate inquiry in the life of the man who made an unequalled contribution to the spiritual life of the youth of the world through the Student Christian Movement. If testimony is anything to go by, there is a slick and easy way of arriving at spiritual experience, but there are surer ways, and one of them is certainly through thought and study that brings our better self to consciousness, and allows the Holy Spirit to speak. 'It has certainly been my experience,' writes Profesor H. D. Lewis in *We Believe in God*, 'to have arrived at great certainty in proportion to my thought about the Faith, and I am profoundly concerned to give a true impression to others of what may be gained in this way.'

Another sure road to Christian experience seems along the road of self-denying ministry to human need, for as a right faith results in service, so a life of service seems to result in faith. People feel called, even counted on, until they echo Theresa's famous words, 'Christ has no hands but our hands to do his work today,' or come to realise like Albert Schweitzer in the steaming primeval jungle that we minister to sickness and disease in a higher name than our own. 'He puts us to the tasks which He has to carry out in our age. He commands, and to those who obey Him, whether they be wise or simple, He will reveal Himself in the toils, the conflicts, the sufferings which they shall pass through to His Fellowship, and, as in an ineffable mystery, they shall learn in their own experience who He is.'

But how can the validity of such personal conclusions be established? How far does wishful thinking or self-deception play a part in the phenomenon of 'Christian experience'?

Such questions may be answered along two lines of reasoning. First, what abler test of any truth have we than that people of probity and high intelligence and spirituality have testified to it? And, secondly, is it not true that evidence which may be called subjective when it comes in the shape of an isolated individual's experience takes on an objective value when a vast number of corresponding experiences, and a weight of unanimous testimony, confirms it?

If this is the case then, how impressive is the evidence for the Christian view of Christ! What high experience has been more general, more common to all sorts and conditions, than the inner response to the divine in Christ! Moreover, how varied are the ways in which people have been led to make it! Let us glance at a few.

Some, as we have seen, have come, like the disciples of old, drawn irresistibly by 'the light of the glory of God in his face'. Others have come by way of the intellect, head first. To them, Christianity is life's noblest hypothesis. Others have come by way of mysticism and to them Jesus intuitively appeals. Others, again, have come with broken lives, and to them the Gospel is restoration and revived incentive. Others, again, have felt that call of the social Gospel. They have heard Christ's summons to practical tasks. But such clear-cut divisions are arbitrary and unreal, for in practice several roads may be used by the pilgrim, and the call 'Follow thou me' has many accents.

This is the explanation why individual experiences are not readily communicable—as Crean said to Shackleton in the polar wastes of South Georgia—there is a feeling of 'the dearth of human language, the roughness of human speech'. There is naturally a shrinkage too, from any form of claim or hint of exhibitionism, in referring to the deepest and most intimate thing in life.

However, some are willing to testify on the basis of their own experience. For example, Lord Hailsham declared at Coventry Cathedral:

> I am left with the necessity of an avowal of my own faith, with the inevitable consequence that you will note my inability to live up to it, rather than the strength which it has given me. For more than thirty years, Christ

> has been the light of my life. Many times have I betrayed, neglected, denied the light. But never has the light deserted or betrayed me. Of course I think of Christ as an historical character born and died two thousand years ago. Of course I look for guidance and knowledge about him in the Gospels, in the historical context of the ancient world, in the tradition of the Christian community. But more and more I have come to realise that this is not the essence of what I mean when I say, I believe in Christ. I think of him as alive. I think of him as here and present, as now, as within, and not outside the field of my own consciousness, and not as remote in time and space.

It may be argued that if you have not the gift of faith, there the matter ends, and nothing can give it to you. You must go on without even an opinion about it. This is a world where the blind do not judge art, nor the deaf adjudicate on music, and where the gift of faith must be estimated by those who have the necessary sensibilities.

Is there then something rare, reserved for the few, and from others barred, about Christian experience? Hardly so, for there is no discernible religious 'type'. People of all types, and of all walks of life and age-groups, were among the first disciples, and very varied have been the multitude who have followed them in every generation—peasant girls like Bernadette of Lourdes, heroines like Nurse Cavell, evangelists like Catherine Booth, tinkers like Bunyan, schoolmasters like William Carey, young athletes like the Studd brothers, priest- scientists like Teilhard de Chardin, priests who have stood in the last ditch with their fellow-men like Studdert Kennedy, and sophisticated intellectuals like Dag Hammarskjold.

If it is the aim of the scientific mind to include the whole of the observable, then widely observable are the lives and endeavours of those who have, in one way or another, undertaken an intimate inquiry into the meanings of Christianity.

Their experience, with a unanimity that proclaims its genuineness, is made articulate in their lives, in the devotional writings and hymns of the Christian centuries, in the affirmations and insights of the saints, in the earnestness of preaching, and in the clear witness of the world-wide Church.

It is, indeed, hard to believe that from the dross of illusion there could come such an amount of testimony, that, after all sifting and allowance have been made, leaves a deposit that demands recognition as gold.

We do not aim at enlarging further on so great a matter, save to say that the point is established that intimate inquiry into Christianity tends to result in personal awareness of the divine in Christ, so that millions who have undertaken it have ventured on his promises, rejoiced in him as Saviour, and have looked beyond the veil to see his face.

CHAPTER ELEVEN

The Test of Revolutionised Lives

> Jesus remains the very heart and soul of the Christian movement, still controlling men, still capturing men—against their wills very often—changing men's lives and using them for ends they never dreamed of. So much is plain to the candid observer whatever the explanation.
>
> Dr T. R. Glover, The Jesus of History

We now come to a rather startling fact, namely that in the history of Christianity, there is much evidence that if anyone has no wish to become a disciple, would be well advised to keep all thought, both of Jesus and of his ideals, at arm's length. Closer acquaintance may result in unexpected and overwhelming results.

To the early Church, for example, who seemed more immune than Saul to the fascination of Jesus? Schooled in the straitest sect of the Pharisees, an unswerving monotheist, the very claims made on Christ's behalf by his followers were blasphemous to him. Little about early Christianity could have fitted into his scheme of things. He could never have thought it possible that Christ would shatter his scheme. He approved the murder of Stephen. He even held the clothes of those who grew hot with the grim exercise of stoning him. He counted it a stern duty to deal out threatenings and slaughter among Christians, and generally to 'make havoc of the Church'.

It seems unthinkable that Saul himself would be converted. But it happened. Intelligent man that he was, he felt that he could not persecute Christianity effectively without understanding it, but the outcome overwhelmed him. The high-handed persecutor became Christ's devoted bond- servant. The Pharisee became the greatest Christ-mystic of the ages.

Nor has Saul's conversion been an isolated instance. The record of the faith is weighty with evidences of almost similar dramatic changes.

How often, where Christ has been concerned, wholly unexpected things have happened—particularly perhaps to those whose subsequent influence has proved to be of outstanding value to the Christian cause. One thinks of the classic instance of St Augustine, one-time libertine, busily employed in breaking the heart of Monica, his mother, and yet, a few years later, the consecrated Bishop of Hippo and one of the most influential names in Western theology.

There was that day of spiritual struggle and change in the life of John Wesley that began at five in the morning with him opening his New Testament on the words 'There are given unto us exceedingly great and precious promises', and later in the morning reading again at the passage 'Thou art not far from the Kingdom of God'. In the afternoon he was asked to go to St Paul's and was moved by the anthem, 'Out of the deep have I called unto thee, O God'. Finally the climacteric experience when in the evening 'I went very unwillingly to a meeting in Aldersgate and about quarter to nine heard the speaker describing the change which God works in the heart through faith in Christ. I felt my heart,' says Wesley, 'strangely warmed. I felt I did trust in Christ, Christ alone... I began to pray with all my might.'

Here was an experience decisive in Wesley's life and, through it, of immense consequence for so many other lives.

Or there comes to mind the name of Toyohiko Kagawa of Japan. How incredible it would have seemed to those who knew him, that he would ever be a humble Christian worker in the wretched slums of Shinkawa, or that his liberated mind and dedicated abilities would have lifted him to a position of national influence in Japan far exceeding anything that he would have experienced had he not given himself to Christ. Perhaps no story brings the reality of the Christian Gospel right into the mid-twentieth century more than *Miracle on the River Kwai* where Captain Gordon of the Argyll and Sutherland Highlanders describes how the reality of Christian experience was discovered in the hell of unspeakable prisoner of war conditions and the agonising wretchedness of the building of the bridge over the river. Here, sinking into degradation, with countless prisoners dying, or ruthlessly cut down by their captors, life itself was bereft of elementary decency. Then came the virtual resurrection to a new life through the rediscovery of religion:

> Through our readings and discussions we gradually came to know Jesus. What he did, what he was, made all sense to us. We understood that the love expressed so supremely in Jesus was God's love— the same love that we were experiencing for ourselves. The doctrines we worked out were meaningful to us. We arrived at our understanding of it, not one by one, but together. We found unity. We stopped complaining about our plight. Faith would not save us from it, but it would take us through it.

Later as Dean of the Chapel at Princeton University, Captain Gordon continued his testimony: 'Jesus had spoken to me. He had opened me to life, and life to me. The grace we had experienced is the same in every generation and must be received afresh in every age. The Great Debate continues, and the answers depend on the quality of response we are prepared to make.'

Very naturally, perhaps, in view of the change that came to their lives, people like Paul, Augustine, Kagawa, Wesley, the prisoners on the River Kwai, have seen the matter, not so much in terms of their finding Christ, as of Christ finding them. They have looked back on their lives and come to the amazing conclusion that long before they themselves were aware of it, the path to their conversion was being cut.

For many, it seems that faith is incompatible with informed thinking. Yet we find very able people who come to faith in spite of doubt. It would be hard to think of a brighter mind than Dag Hammarskjold's. He was a man of the world, a sophisticate, a friend of avant-garde intellectuals in the arts, literature, and philosophy, mercilessly honest with himself, and he knew the torturing loss of early faith. His book *Markings* is a sensitive exposure of his inner experiences to the time when as Secretary General of the United Nations he lost his life in an air crash.

At what was the turning point he writes: 'At some moment I answered "Yes" to Someone—or Something—and from that hour I was certain that existence was meaningful, and that therefore, my life in self-surrender had a goal.' Through Schweitzer's teaching and example of 'reverence for life' he found the key to the world of the Gospels, and to One almost too wonderful for him to name. 'I don't ask Who the Lord is,' he said, 'so much as what His Will is. He asks service of me, not comprehension.'

Through years of mounting strain and public service it was Scripture that guided him and steadied him. 'He who puts himself into the hands of God,' he said, 'how strong he is!' Certainly this strength none could mistake, nor his steel-like devotion to duty. His *Road Marks*, like his life, speak for themselves... 'that a living relationship to God is the necessary pre-condition which enables us to follow a straight path, and yield character fit for leadership in this tortured, frantic, unhappy age'.

Sometimes tremendous inner conflict is set up before long-established prejudices, or cherished pride of mind or will, have allowed a man or woman to surrender to Christ. One thinks of the Sikh aristocrat, Sundar Singh, who before he became known as 'The St Francis of India', was so torn between his New Testament and his old associations, that he laid his head on a railway line, only to determine, at the last moment, to be a Christian Sadhu, a friend of the poor, the leprous, the outcast.

To be sure, Paul on the road to Damascus, felt very sorry for himself. Another personality had cut across his own. But later, from the vantage point of his great apostleship, he looked back on his conversion, not as the end of his career but as its radiant beginning, not as one thwarted in a conflict, but as one immeasurably enlarged and completed by it.

Nothing in Christianity encourages contentment with some spiritual experience already attained. Rather it challenges us to surpass all customary criteria of effort and excellence, that a fuller experience and more fruitful forms of service might grace the future. 'Not as though I had already attained, or were already made perfect,' cries Paul, 'but this one thing I do, I press on to the prize of the high calling which I have in Christ Jesus' (Phil. 3: 12).

'Let every sincere man remember well his whole life,' said Tolstoy in *What I Believe*, 'and he will see that never once has he suffered from obeying the teaching of Christ, but that most of the misfortunes of his life have come about because he has followed the world's teaching.'

What Jesus left to grow, then, in the souls of those who have sought the truth of things, has been a knowledge of himself. A knowledge that has brought its own persuasions and that has resulted not in mere intellectual assent only, but in the entire and joyous commitment of the whole personality. A knowledge that, for those who have attained it, has seemed to grow more and not less cogent, with passage of time and the accumulation of experience.

PART TWO:

Antithesis

Resistance the faith has encountered – persecution – partial thinking – opposing systems of thought – materialism – secularism – radical criticism – pertinacity of outworn ideas – resilience of the faith – Christocentric nature of its vitality and renewal.

CHAPTER TWELVE

Advance Through Storm

I know of no study which is so unutterably saddening as the evolution of humankind as it is set forth in the annals of history.

Thomas Huxley

O smitten mouth! O forehead crowned with thorn!
O chalice of all common mysteries!
Thou for our sakes who loved thee not, hast borne
An agony of endless centuries;
But we were vain and ignorant, nor knew
That when we stabbed thy heart, it was our own
Real hearts we slew.

Oscar Wilde

Any victory rises in our estimation if it happens to have been won in defiance of difficulty. The Fifth Symphony of Beethoven, remarkable enough in itself, is heard with enhanced wonder when we remember that the composer was deaf when he set it down.

The Battle of Britain, again, will have a timeless place in our annals, because it was won by pilots outnumbered but undaunted, who snatched victory from seemingly certain defeat.

Similarly, does not the growth and splendour of Christ's influence gain in impressiveness when we remember the appalling odds that it has encountered, and the varied stubborn resistance it has worn down?

With an accuracy that time has vindicated, Jesus described himself as a sower of seed (Matt. 13: 3), facing not only clean and fertile tilth, but stony ground, superficial soils, and land overrun with ancient growths. Elsewhere, too (Matt. 13: 24), he anticipated the sinister hand of the Evil One, busily engaged in sowing tares among the wholesome wheat. The whole story of the faith offers a running commentary on the realism of those parables.

If we cry out impatiently, 'Christianity has been two thousand years in the world, and what has it done?' we must appraise realistically the opposition, the evasive action, the deeply entrenched evils with which it has had to deal.

This is a world where the victory of all ideals is partial, where even the bare survival of truth, justice, and beauty is precarious, and where they must fight afresh for recognition in every age. What would we expect, then, to be the prospects of a massive movement of the spirit, like Christianity, that seeks to establish all the known virtues in their highest form?

Let us glance, therefore, at a few of the difficulties that Christianity has encountered.

The path of reformers is notoriously rough. 'In the country of the blind they kill the man who "sees".' Outside the city walls they hammered in the nails. But the disciples took up the challenge. In Jerusalem, in the most intractable of all places, they commenced preaching the very truths for which Jesus had been crucified.

Opposition came swiftly, and from powerful quarters. Judaism, the cradle of Christianity, nearly provided its grave.

For two thousand years Jewish faith had spoken of an exclusive covenant between God and his chosen people Israel. Yet now Christianity spoke of a new covenant between God and all humankind and claimed that ‘God has no favourites, but in every nation the man who is God-fearing and does what is right is acceptable to him’ (Acts 10: 34). Even worse, Christianity ventured to supplement and even supersede the long-venerated and hallowed Law given by God through Moses. The very Sabbath day itself was to be overshadowed by the day of Christ’s resurrection ‘the first day of the week’. An imaginative appreciation of first-century Judaism makes us marvel that any of them became converts. But conversions were made, and despite intense hostility Christianity was able to build on its Jewish foundations and yet universalise its message of God’s loving concern for humankind.

Opposition came even more bitterly from the pagan world. It came from trade. The silversmiths of Ephesus, for example, saw their trade in idols threatened and eventually brought to nothing. It came from the State. It was tantamount to treason to refuse, as the Christians did, a formal recognition of the Emperor’s ‘divinity’. It came from Roman Law. Were not secret and closed societies suspect and forbidden? Obviously, too, opposition came from all who stood for ‘broad-mindedness’. The Graeco-Roman world thought that Christian intolerance of other religions was itself a crime.

A long line of emperors with varying severity sought to uproot the faith, and for three hundred years to be a Christian was to run the risk of martyrdom. The Emperors Nero, Domitian, Trajan, Hadrian, Antoninus Pius, Marcus Aurelius, Decius, and Diocletian, all shed the blood of the martyrs, and yet there were probably thousands to whom loyalty to Christ was worth the sword, the woodpile, the lions, stoning, and crucifixion.

But surely, we feel, the Christians must have merited in some way their heavy lot. So thought Pliny, historian and proconsul in Asia. Yet having examined Christians by torture, he affirmed to Trajan, the Emperor, that 'the whole of their error lay in this, that they were wont to meet together on a certain day, before it was light, and sing among themselves a hymn to Christ as God, and to bind themselves by an oath (*sacramentum*) not to commit any wickedness, nor to be guilty of theft, robbery, or adultery, and never to falsify their word or deny a pledge.' Then he adds, 'great numbers must be involved in these persecutions, which have already extended, and are likely to extend, to persons of all ranks and ages, and of both sexes.'[34]

With candour Jesus had spoken of the danger of pursuing ideals like his in a world like this. 'If they have persecuted me,' he said, 'they will also persecute you.'

Let us hear what the persecution could amount to. 'Nero,' writes Tacitus the Roman historian in his *Annals*, 'punished with the most exquisite tortures those who called themselves Christians. They were covered with hides of wild beasts, and worried by dogs, or nailed to crosses and set fire to, and when day declined burnt to serve for nocturnal illumination.' Yet despite persecutions, the faith of Jesus persisted and, in numbers and weight of influence, the Church grew.

The example of the first witnesses, their dauntless faith, standing as they did in the near light of the first evidences, has been a steadying power to the Church in all subsequent ages. However, much of compromise and caricature, feebleness and shamefulness have figured in the story since, those of whom Cyprian speaks have a fame that cannot be effaced:

The glorious company of apostles,
the noble fellowship of prophets,
the white-robed army of martyrs...

---

[34] *Plinii et Trajani Epistulae*, 96, 97.

We have mentioned the centuries of crimson malice, but what of the persistent obstruction that has come from grey negligence? In all ages this has impeded the work of Jesus. Inertia, apathy, slovenliness of thinking, conscienceless caricature, sheer indifference—what can survive these damnable things? Great is the farce of much that has passed in the world for the faith of Jesus.

Direct opposition can be invigorating. While the faith was struggling to find its feet, for example, various heresies arose. Christian thinking was incisively challenged. But the conflict was creative. It forced the Church to clarify its thinking. It drew out the intellectual implications of the Gospel. It imposed upon Christians the wholesome discipline of closer study.

Similarly, even persecution served a salutary purpose. It sifted the wheat from the chaff, it closed loose ranks. In a sense, as Tertullian said, 'the blood of the martyrs was the seed of the Church.'

But what good ever came from dumb apathy, from professing but listless followers? They debilitate. They destroy a cause from within. Teachers of all creeds and in all lands have spoken down the ages, and humanity has answered not with defiance but with that serene, intractable negligence that in the end defeats all higher law.

Even high-minded appreciation of a great cause may not be enough to move one to follow it without deviation. Paul knew the difficulty: 'I cordially agree with God's law, so far as my inner self is concerned, but then I find quite another law that resides in my members, and that makes me a prisoner of sin. Miserable man that I am!' (Rom. 7: 23–24).

If one wonders why, after two thousand years, Christianity has not conquered the world, you can find part of the answer here—in the shirking of allegiance, the refusal of costly commitment, the 'quite different law' that resides in one's mortal nature. When we bemoan the failure of the Church we must take this fact into account, together with the charitable realisation that how costly the good life is, only those understand who have attempted to pay the price.

Pilate washing his hands of responsibility; the Rich Young Ruler going sorrowfully away; Peter weeping at cockcrow when it was too late; Demas loving this present world— such types are by no means only to be found in the New Testament. They have, in all ages, taken a large and tragic place in the history of the Church.

So far, then, we have seen Christianity clashing with things long established. We have found it opposed by individual and State. We have seen it weakened by apathy and inertia, and, in one guise or another, these factors have always been recurring. But the list is by no means complete.

Christianity has lost momentum—as when Rome fell. It has experienced set-backs—as when Muslim invasion severed its path. It has lost intellectual prestige—as when seemingly rival fields of ideas have been opened up, or when writers like Shelley have written *On the Necessity of Atheism* protesting against lifeless religions. Nor is such damage undone when, as in Shelley's case, his own soul testified to:

The light whose smile kindles the Universe
That Beauty in which all things work and move.

Christianity, too, has been sorely wounded by the rapacity, intolerance, and bloody-mindedness of some of its followers, and who can say that the case is relieved when over-anxious apologists have tried to extenuate things like the bitter spirit of schism, or the horrors of the Inquisition?

Plainly one cannot compress such matters into a light resume like this, particularly as there is interplay between one factor and another. We will make brief reference, however, to a few further matters that have deflected some from Christianity in modern times.

In the early centuries some Christians wholly repudiated war. It belonged to the realms of Caesar. Compromises began to enter in when 'Caesar' professed himself to be converted, when right and wrong could be presented as overlapping, when war, in certain instances, could be called 'holy'. Relativity in ethics long anticipated the enunciation of it in physics.

In the twentieth century many Christians have been forced to choose war as the lesser of two evils, but its moral 'rightness' has not minimised the wholesale material waste and destruction, the diversion of thought and energy from constructive and peaceful ends, nor made less tragic the loss of thousands, who were, on any assessment, the choicest of human stock.

One item of war's expenditure people are slow to appreciate —what Shakespeare called 'expense of spirit'. This has come from the conditioning of millions, in formative periods of their lives, to sub-Christian standards of thought and conduct. It has come from the break-up of home life, the weakening of married loyalties, the loosening of parental control.

We have now had generations of industrial employment, with people's hearts and heads becoming increasingly conditioned by technical and material preoccupations, by the secularity of the media, and by commercialised entertainment. Such things, while not necessarily evil in themselves, combine together to produce an atmosphere not conducive to spiritual development. Then, almost inevitably, the facile logic of the materialist becomes more compelling than the high witness of the saint, and the deep argument of the theologian. The superficial is always more easy to grasp than the profound.

Does material competence then, and the artificiality of modern life, explain the spiritual dryness that increasingly obstructs the faith of Jesus? Assuredly, not completely. Material competence itself might have been an unmitigated blessing, had moral and spiritual competence kept pace with it. Why this has not happened we shall be discussing in Chapters 14 and 15, when we speak of the turning and twisting theories that have made people doubt the basic truth of their historic faith.

As we link up this brief sketch with what has gone before, and with what follows, the old question reasserts itself: Why has the Church not succumbed to all this? Why has it had the vitality and resilience not only to survive, but to see in each recessive factor, not the grounds of defeat, but the call to greater endeavour? Why is it, that after measuring all that has obstructed Christianity, and then assessing its present position, Professor Latourette is able to entitle his last volume on the expansion of Christianity, *Advance through Storm*?

CHAPTER THIRTEEN

Partial Thinking

> We imagine that we are initiated into Nature's mysteries; we are as yet but hanging round her outer court.
>
> Seneca

Human knowledge has become a jig-saw of countless separate pieces, with few knowing enough to fit the pieces together. Specialisation, that has brought humankind so much of worth and excellence, has often resulted in people losing touch with subjects other than their own. It becomes increasingly difficult to 'see life steadily and see it whole'. We consider this as a possible factor that may contribute to the popular fallacy, for such it surely is, that religion and science are at variance.

'I have taken all knowledge to be my province,' wrote Francis Bacon. He was a man of extraordinary achievements and capacity of mind. As author of the *Novum Organum* he is often considered the originator of the modern school of experimental science.

But since the sixteenth century the scope of knowledge has widened. Detail has accumulated. 'The province of knowledge,' even of a single subject, has to be broken up, and shared out among department specialists. The day of the computer has now come.

The result is not reassuring. 'We have become,' said Dr A. S. Russell, 'increasingly lop-sided in our knowledge. Whole tracts of fertile country are left strangely unexplored, while nearly all of us concentrate, like beavers, on one small part of the field.'

Intensity of focus, specialisation, has resulted in discoveries like those of Jenner, Pasteur, Lister, Alexander Fleming, and Simpson, that will forever bless humanity. The mere mention of names like Darwin, Mendel, Marconi, Einstein and Rutherford, indicate the range and excellence of what specialised science has achieved. What Bacon advocated — 'a true and patient understanding and interrogation of nature through phenomena and facts'—has had immense rewards.

But concentration on a particular line of study may often be paid for by a narrowing down, or even the total exclusion, of other studies. Individually, few now see more than a tiny aspect of truth, understand more than a little of knowledge in the round.

Consider the absorbed attention that scientific specialisation demands. Science learnt from Christianity the love of truth and order, and that sense of the rationality of the universe that underlies scientific research. It learnt from Aristotle that truth along certain lines could be reached by the accumulation and interrogation of facts. These facts would suggest general laws. We see the method at work in Darwin's tireless accumulation of the data for his *The Origin of Species*, and in Mendel, probing the secret of hereditary trends by the elaborate classification of varieties of peas. The method was impersonal, factual, detached.

The scientist piles up facts, as the worker piles up stones, in the hope of building something out of them, and the scientist, like the worker, can only build within the limits of the material they have got together. They may have omitted valuable material, or be using material inadequately sorted out, but they raise their building. Whether that building—in the case of the scientist—is a pleasant or habitable home for people does not concern them.

Scientists, by the very nature of their assumptions, have to leave aside a whole world of values, and even to proceed as if they never existed. But how will men and women fare if they leave aside human values as in history and literature, or aesthetic values as in art and music, spiritual values as in philosophy and religion?

People have seized with enthusiasm the idea of evolution with its happy suggestion that life tends ever to move upwards to the higher and better. But what of Darwin's other theory that under specialisation life may not so much open up as narrow down? What of the law of recession, the dreadful threat of spiritual atrophy, that Darwin also enunciated? Who can read unmoved Darwin's poignant account of how he himself was aware of the working of this chilling law?

'My mind,' he records, 'has become a kind of machine for grinding general laws out of large collections of facts.' He speaks of powers perishing for lack of employment, of his waning taste for art, music, and literature, of the 'atrophy of that part of the brain on which the higher tastes depend'.

'The loss of these tastes,' he continues, 'is a loss of happiness, and may possibly be injurious to the intellect, and, more particularly, to the moral character, by enfeebling the emotional part of one's nature.'[35]

Readers will recall the equally well-known supporting statement in the *Autobiography* of John Stuart Mill: 'For I now saw, what I had always before received with incredulity—that the habit of analysis has a tendency to wear away the feelings when no other mental habit is cultivated, and the analysing spirit remains without its natural complements and correctives.'

---

[35] *Life and Letters of Charles Darwin*, p. 100.

These are intimate revelations from people of true greatness, who were themselves deeply conscious of the validity of spiritual values, and of the reality of the spiritual side of humankind's nature. But are there not some who have followed such scholars in the path of specialisation, who have little or no awareness of the existence and worth of those things, the loss of which Darwin and Mill so movingly regretted? Science for science's sake can be so immensely absorbing, that it may even obscure consideration of humankind's welfare, safety and happiness.

Some years ago Sir William Dampier could say, 'The pure scientist should always stick to pure science, however dull their work may seem to others, let them pile up results regardless of their use.' But could it be said that science should pile up results, say of atomic fission, and be morally regardless of the consequences?

Robert Jungk recounts in *Brighter than a Thousand Suns* how the atom bomb was made as a work of pure research. But then came the awful realisation of the possibilities of its use and the desperate, and futile, attempts made to banish it from use.

'Bigger and better scientific laboratories,' wrote Professor C. A. Coulson in a letter to *The Times*, 'do not necessarily make for world peace, or a more balanced, harmonious life; a more extensive knowledge of metallurgical technique does not necessarily mean a mature judgment, or a satisfying personality.' But in indicating the limitations that may beset one approach to reality, the scientific, are we not forgetting that efficiency in any work involves specialisation? The works-foreman, architect, businessman, doctor, minister of religion, all have to say:

My nature is subdued
To what it works in, like the dyer's hand.

Theology itself is a highly specialist sphere, and as capable as any of producing the closed mind. Who, for instance, did more than Bishop Wilberforce to give colour to the idea that religion and science were at variance, when in argument with Thomas Huxley he declared that 'evolution is absolutely incompatible with the word of God in Genesis'? The irony of the whole situation was that the good Bishop was not only out of touch with science, but out of touch with liberal thought in some contemporary Christian journals, and the very early ideas of St Gregory of Nyssa who lived from ad 330 to ad 395. 'God in the beginning,' said Gregory, 'only created the germs of life, or causes of the forms of life, which were afterwards developed in natural course.'

Negatively, such an instance is a warning against the closed mind wherever it is found. Positively, it is an invitation to be hospitable to truth from wherever it may speak, confident that God is honoured wherever truth is perceived. We are in a world where all our faculties should be enlisted, and truth from all quarters be freely exchanged and heeded.

It is not within the province of science to vindicate Christianity, the herald of values and insights that are beyond either mere sense perception, or scientific explanation. All the same, as can be easily realised, there are some basic attitudes on the part of science that are more congenial to the acceptance of Christian truths than are others.

Today the nineteenth century idea that science could explain all mysteries has gone. There is a new awareness of the spiritual sense. 'You will hardly find one among the profounder sort of scientific minds,' said Albert Einstein, 'without peculiar religious feelings of their own. Their religious feeling takes the form of rapturous amazement at the harmony of the natural law. It is beyond question akin to that which has possessed religious geniuses in all ages.'

The harmony of the natural law is a great theme. Alone on the steep slopes of knowledge, glimpsing what Darwin called 'the laws impressed on matter by the Creator', the scientists can become aware that their picture of the physical world is far from being the product of their own mind. They face a harmony that is 'given', that is inherent, that is humbling, so the physicists realise that their formulae and equations are at best but approximations and imperfect representations of what they find. Or the cosmologists may admit with astonished wonder that their inquiries into the nature of the universe bring them answers finer in concept and grander in design than anything they could have imagined.

Nor are there lacking parallel situations in all other approaches to reality. So there are the unwavering laws of mathematics, systems of balances and checks in the order of nature, ultra-microscopic genes and their companions the chromosomes, that are the absolute keys to all human, animal, and vegetable characteristics, permanent factors in the working out of the modern law, even a givenness about the harmonies of music and a 'golden mean' in the constitution of art.

Overarching all partial thinking there are these great beautifying and immutable realities that cry out for religious interpretation.

Professor C. A. Coulson in *Science and Christian Belief* is surely right. 'Religion is the total response of man to all his environment. Living the good life is not an endless struggle to balance the conflicting claims of science, art, poetry, philosophy, and worship, as though they warred together, like the tribes in Anglo-Saxon Britain. Living the good life means receiving these partial revelations, reflecting upon them, and responding to them.'

Unfortunately, there is a painful, even dangerous time- lag between the views of leading thinkers, and the mental attitude persisting strongly in some quarters. Intellectual systems have a knack of surviving their own death. In the next two chapters we comment on the resistance Christianity encounters from the tenacity of old ideas.

CHAPTER FOURTEEN

Materialism

Graceless Western man has turned against the religion that found him a barbarian and that has promoted him to the lordship of the world.

Arnold Toynbee

Religion and natural science are fighting a joint battle against scepticism, against dogmatism, against disbelief and against superstition, and the rallying cry has been, and always will be, 'On to God'.

Max Planck

The attitude of the prisoner who refused to be released from the Bastille is not unique. It has its counterpart in those who display a similar attachment to some narrow ideas that responsible science has discarded.

Ideas have a peculiar knack of hardening around us. We become accustomed to them. They govern our world. Like the prisoner long accustomed to their cell, and long unfamiliar with any other world, we refuse almost subconsciously, to desire the wider air.

This explains the resistance that Christianity encounters in some quarters today. Minds have settled down into frameworks of thought, built some time ago by scientific materialists. True, modern physicists have abandoned the old sites and are building more airy structures elsewhere, but people are refusing to move.

In *Meaning and Purpose* Kenneth Walker writes:

> Looking back, I have clearly seen that at different periods of my life my mind became incarcerated within the narrow limits of some doctrine—such as the scientific materialism of the last century, the idea that evolution occurred through the action of blind mechanical forces, or the equally pessimistic systems of psychology sponsored by Pavlov or Freud—and what is particularly apparent to me, now that I have escaped from these mental prisons, is that while confined in them, I was completely satisfied with my surroundings... It is only now that I realise that I mistook tentative theories for absolute truths, and temporary resting places of thought for permanent residences.

It is a helpful exercise at any time to consider the parentage of ideas. Consider, therefore, a few old ideas that although refuted by later thought, continue to hold people's minds today.

Many of our underlying mental attitudes and assumptions today can be traced back three centuries to the scientific materialism that derived from the physics of Sir Isaac Newton (1642–1727).

It did not appear to dawn on Newton, who was a devout Christian, that his system of mechanics and his theory of gravitation carried with them two powerful suggestions, which, when taken into philosophy, would violently conflict with Christian beliefs.

In the light of Newton's theories, Nature seemed to appear to human beings as a vast machine with people merely insignificant cogs in it. The implications of his theories were anticipated by Hobbes, a writer of fluent pen. Hobbes gave scientific materialism that place in human thinking which it seems never to have lost.

Nor indeed is this surprising. The idea of the Universe as a super-machine was obviously congenial to generations whose own lives were to be increasingly linked with machinery.

Hobbes taught that matter was the only reality, that events of every kind were simply due to the motion of water, that humans were only a lively material body whose thoughts and emotions were due to the activity of the atoms inside them. Everything was open to mechanical explanation, and the future was set by 'mechanical determinism'.

But here was a theory that seemed supported by the great name of Newton that cut the nerve of the Church's teaching on free-will. 'On his imagined freedom,' said Sir James Jeans in *Physics and Philosophy*; 'had built up his social system and his ethical code. It formed the cornerstone of religion ... but if human conduct was only a matter of the push and pull of atoms, all this became meaningless. Exhorting men to be moral or useful was as foolish as telling a clock to keep good time when it was pathetically dependent on its works.'

Human beings who had thought themselves the heirs of two worlds— the material and the spiritual—now choose to find what pleasure and profit they could in one: the material. Life had narrowed down with a vengeance.

But Hobbes was wrong. His philosophy is on the scrap-heap—and put there by responsible modern science. 'The scientific bases of the older discussions,' says Jeans, 'have been washed away, and with their disappearance have gone all the arguments, such as they were, that seemed to require the acceptance of materialism and the renunciation of human free-will.'

If the arguments have gone, powerful ideas that they promoted have continued. Released into the mainstream of the world's thinking the ideas of scientific materialism soon became influential. Scientists, for instance, soon spoke with a new assurance and dogmatism. 'One day,' said Tindal, addressing the British Association, 'science will be able to explain everything in terms of the movement of atoms—everything from the evolution of worlds to the proceedings of the British Association itself.' 'Let the Church,' declared Comte, 'take a subsidiary place, and hand over the leadership of humankind to science.'

Philosophers, too, big and little, became more sceptical. In the first thirty years of the eighteenth century the 'Deists', such as Toland, Collins, and Tindal, were allowed to print their views without the opposition they would have encountered earlier. In France, under the influence of Voltaire, 'Deism' became more uncompromising and more anti-Christian. The road was being cut to the moral scepticism of our day. In France the seeds that were to grow into Existentialism were being sown.

More influential in advancing scepticism in philosophy was David Hume (1711–1776). He envied the seeming finality of Newton's work. He wanted to establish a moral science, to discover the 'Laws' that govern our internal impressions, just as Newton had established the general laws that govern the movement of material particles. Religion and free-will were denied validity. Human beings were wholly parts of nature.

Hume was answered by Kant's great work, *Critique of Pure Reason*, just as the 'Deists' were out-matched in argument by Bishop Butler, Bishop Berkeley, Bentley, and William Law, but patterns of thought were started that were increasingly to grip minds, and send them out on those grey seas of scepticism.

Today there is little comfort, and much that is ironical, in realising the confidence with which the natural philosophers set out, and how inconceivable it would have been to them to imagine that their rigid materialistic concepts, would, in our time, be looked on warily by responsible scientists, if not actually discounted.

Scientific materialism certainly increased the popularity of nineteenth-century Darwinism, the one seeming to lend colour to the other.

It is notable that both Darwin and Wallace took pains to say that *The Origin of Species* (1859) was not irreligious in its implications. Darwin told Wordsworth personally that his theory 'in no way interfered with Christianity'; while Wallace averred that 'the Darwinian theory, even when carried to its extreme logical conclusion, not only does not oppose, but actually lends support to, the belief in the spiritual nature of man'.

But minds steeped in materialistic assumptions thought otherwise, Darwinism in a crude form became 'popular'. The colourful idea of humans descending from the ape was taken with vivid literalism. It became increasingly common to minimise the specifically human qualities of *homo sapiens*. The grandeur of life's age-long ascent, the diverse branches of the tree of evolution, the awe-inspiring mystery of life itself, the wonder of its strange mutations, the scholarly correctiveness to a harsh literalism in Darwin's writings—all these were left out of account by lesser minds.

Numerous writers seemed to delight in narrowing, or in ignoring altogether, the gap between human beings and other creatures. The uniqueness of human evolutionary history, the continual nature of the human sex response (as distinct from the discontinuous sex life of the animal world), our biological dominance and variability, our almost infinite capacity for adjustment to environment—these were passed over, while our capacity for conceptual and abstract thought, together with our moral sensibilities and spiritual appreciations, seemed deliberately set aside.[36]

Now, when you get a pseudo-scientific materialism leaving out God, ignoring the validity of ideals, questioning morality, and giving a purely biological account of the place of human beings in the universe, two things are bound to result—people stand defenceless and disinherited in a world that has lost its sanctities, while predatory forces, unchecked by higher law, exploit and strip away their right and liberties.

Phrases from the scientists, like 'the survival of the fittest', could suggest to Bernhardi, and then to the Nazi mind, the cult of a girded and aggressive might, while in industry it could condone a profitable sweating of the lower classes. Similarly, the phrase 'natural selection' was suggestive to the political ideologist, and lent encouragement to class, national and racial claims, and vanities.

Human's mental life is a flowing stream into which a variety of currents are continually pouring. As ideas mingle, they tend to lose their identity and to become anonymous in the general thought of an age, and, when this has happened, it is almost invidious to specify the original sources.

It is doubtful, therefore, if many of those who accept Freudianism or Behaviourism in psychology, are aware that beneath these theories are the assumptions of scientific determinism—that we are 'conditioned', that we must act in accord with 'nature', and so forth. Similarly, many who are impressed with the simplicity of Marx's teaching about the iron law of economic struggle, may not see that underlying it is a transference into the economic sphere of that idea of conflict, 'red in tooth and claw', that evolutionists first found in the jungle. Still more important, many who from motives of social idealism embrace Marxist communism, may not perceive that

---

[36] See G. K. Chesterton, *The Everlasting Man; Julian Huxley, The Uniqueness of Man.*

underlying the Marxist philosophy are the old concepts of scientific materialism and determinism.

Let us therefore glance at the tremendous social-political movement that, with social justice in the forefront of its programme, is in reality but the rigorous working out in history of the ideas and assumptions of the scientific materialist.

Marx's celebrated 'Manifesto' saw all past history in terms of class-war—masters and slaves in the ancient world, lords and serfs in the mediaeval period, and capitalists and wage earners in the modern period, and the clash between them determined by remorseless economic law.

Very properly Marx drew attention to the important part played in history by competing economic interests, but in emphasising this, he overlooked the causes, other than economic, that have also played a part in engendering bitterness and conflict—for example, the clashes between King and Parliament, or between Church and State, and the numerous ideals, other than economic, that have occasionally actuated society—as when the British taxpayers laid aside their self-interest to meet a bill of twenty million pounds to free the slaves.

But Marx's great motto, 'From everyone according to his gifts, to everyone according to his needs', is one that every Christian would endorse, echoing, as it does, Christ's own words, 'Unto whomsoever much is given, of him shall much be required; and to whom men have committed much, of him they will ask the more' (Luke 12: 48). But the Christian would not interpret it exclusively in an economic sense.

This distinction explains part of the clash between Christianity and Marxist communism, for communism has the essential nature of a heresy. It takes one value—the economic—and exalts it at the expense of other, and more specifically 'Christian', values.

The Marxist communist acts on the assumption that the Throne of the Universe is vacant, and that religion is a word of no meaning. Material facts alone have relevance. Everything is determined by material laws. In the place of God stands the Process of History. For faith in ideals is substituted confidence in an economic drift. For the Kingdom of God is substituted the utopian goal of a classless society. Before the eyes of a secularised world, men and women are presented, not as children of God, but as virtual slaves of the state. With no belief in anything transcendent in the world of values, truth is regarded as relative and utilitarian, while morality is subordinated to expediency.

The secular mind with its complete submission to materialism seems everywhere to threaten the human spirit, but it is not producing a larger life but a narrower one; not a safe, happier world but one demonstrably more dangerous and unsatisfying. What W. B. Yeats wrote fifty years ago, in *The Second Coming*, is increasingly true:

Things fall apart; the centre cannot hold;
Mere anarchy is loosed upon the world,
The blood-dimmed tide is loosed and everywhere
The ceremony of innocence is drowned;
The best lack all conviction, whilst the worst
Are full of passionate intensity.

We have sketched in swift generalisations some of the fruits that have grown out of the root ideas of Newtonian physics.

What of the future? The philosophy of any period tends, to some degree, to be related to the science of the period, so that any fundamental changes in science are likely to produce reactions in philosophy, and this must be particularly true at a time when the changes in scientific thought have a distinctly philosophical hue.

With the discovery of quanta, relativity, and the electron, the defects of the older physics have become so obvious that much of it is no longer serviceable to science. Yet nothing except the authority of science, insisting on this fact, can clear people's minds of what the older physics embedded in human thinking.

Sir James Jeans spelt out what he saw as the implications of the new learning in his *Physics and Philosophy*:

> Direct questioning of nature by experiment has shown that the philosophical background hitherto assumed by physics, to have been faulty. Determinism and free-will, matter and materialism, need to be re-defined in the light of our new scientific knowledge. We come to conclusions very different from the full-blooded matter, and forbidding materialism, of the Victorian scientist. His objective material Universe is proved to consist of little more than constructs of our own minds. In this, and in other ways, modern physics has moved in the direction of mentalism.

Many scholars would feel that Jeans overstates the case. But it remains true that, as William Temple put it, 'much in the scientific and philosophical thinking of our time provides a climate more favourable to faith than has existed for generations'. Since Temple wrote those words the situation has grown still more favourable. In the field of philosophy the acceptability of religious discourse has been greatly assisted by the demise of logical positivism; philosophers have simply found it impossible to maintain the principle that for a statement to be meaningful it must be capable of empirical verification. And this of course opens the door to speaking about God, which cannot in principle be subject to the kind of tests which are possible in the natural sciences. At the same time, observations in astronomy which suggest that the universe may have had an absolute beginning, literally from nothing, also encourage a religious perspective. It is important not to overstate the case at this point; science can never vindicate a religious proposition. On the other hand if the scientific community were to arrive at a general consensus that the universe did indeed have an absolute beginning, this scientific conclusion would at least be very easy to combine with the religious doctrine of an *ex nihilo* divine creation.

These developments challenge the Church to proclaim its faith more adequately, to show that changes in modern science and philosophy encourage rather than discourage a reappraisal of the spiritual view of human beings.

CHAPTER FIFTEEN

Faith's Radical Testing

> If the story of Jesus was at all parallel with the story of other great men of the past, we should have no hesitation in saying on strictly historical grounds that the Gospels have every right to be treated as a substantially reliable record … The manuscript evidence for the reconstruction of the New Testament text is older, more plentiful, and more reliable than for any other ancient writing.
>
> Dr G. B. Caird Jesus and God

Jesus Christ has been brought to trial many times in different courts and on different charges. In the nineteenth century there were a number of scholars heavily influenced by the ideas and assumptions of scientific materialism. They brought Christianity to trial on the charge that its records were untrue.

Lutheran Germany produced critics like Baur and Strauss, who are well described by Browning:

They could not believe, not statedly that is, and fixedly
In any revelation called divine.

Accordingly, they excised or explained away, the supernatural elements in the Gospels. They believed that Christianity had borrowed heavily from the superstitious rites and beliefs of the Mystery Cults that had been imported into the Roman Empire. They sought parallels for Christ's sayings in other sacred and classical writings. They assumed that the New Testament writers were avid for miracles, and that these had been grafted wholesale onto the simple life of Jesus. By one theory or another, they sought to reduce him to manageable size, and this led inevitably to an all-round attack on the integrity and historicity of the New Testament as a whole.

However, the early critics did pioneering work of the first importance. They saved Christianity from being sheltered from scholarly scrutiny. They stimulated deeper inquiry. Thanks to the research they initiated we now see the Bible as a progressive revelation, and can place its writings in their approximate chronological order. If the early criticism seemed entirely destructive, the later scholarship has gone on to restore confidence both in the unity and the authority of the Bible.

Had the radical critics not been met, religion would not have been able to hold up its head, for as Erasmus trenchantly put it, 'To equate new learning with heresy, is to identify orthodoxy with ignorance.'

On the other hand, there were losses as well as gains, for the early critics brought to a subject formerly considered sacred, a scepticism of attitude, and a ruthlessness of method, that was new. Consequently it attracted a publicity not given to the scholarship that answered it. Doubt, of course, breeds doubt. It gains ground under the adage 'no smoke without fire', and returns in slightly different shape. For this reason we recall the nineteenth-century attack on the Gospels, as having a family likeness to the twentieth century attack on their historical value.

We now know that the earlier critics were prejudiced against traditional beliefs, and that their handling of the evidence was partial, and therefore unscholarly. They tended to theorise first and to search for the supporting evidence afterwards. Theorising, for example, that the entire supernatural element in the Gospels had been superimposed on what had been originally the simple narrative of an ethical teacher, they spoke of a 'heightening process'. But this presupposed an interval of time long enough for legend to accumulate. They sought to prove, therefore, that the Gospels were written long after the events they purported to describe. They placed them somewhere in the second century, implied that they were full of interpolations, and generally the work of unknown and unreliable hands.

Of the Epistles ascribed to Paul, only four—Romans, Corinthians 1 and 2, and Galatians—were allowed to stand, the remainder were ruled out. The Acts were regarded as of little or no historical value.

In short, we were invited to believe that Christianity arose, not on the rock of fact, but on the sand of credulity; that it was not the work of great first-century personalities, but of unknown second-century compilers. We were asked to believe that the noblest ethics were put together, and an intelligible faith fashioned, out of bits and pieces of otherwise unrelated material, by a scissors and paste mentality. Even more incredible, it was suggested that the sublime and utterly self-consistent portrait of Jesus was a matter not so much of historical fact as of devout invention.

The turn of the tide came with the verdict of Harnack, one of the greatest of the German critics, that:

> In all main points, and in most details, the earliest literature of the Church is, from the literary-historical point of view, trustworthy and dependable. One can almost say that the assumptions of the extremist school are now wholly abandoned... The chronological framework in which tradition has arranged the documents is, in all the principal points, from the Pauline Epistles to Irenaeus (i.e. from ad 50 to the last quarter of

> the second century) correct, and compels the historian to abandon all theories with relation to the historical course of things, that are inconsistent with this framework.[37]

The vogue of the extremist criticism was drawing to its close. It was a time in which theological science learnt much, and after which it had much to forget.

A number of scholars, by a typically English combination of common sense with sound scholarship, were to establish the trustworthiness of the early records of the faith, and their successors were to confirm their work.

They confirmed Paul's authorship of the bulk of the Epistles that bear his name. They placed the Gospels in the first century, Mark about ad 65, Luke and Matthew between ad 80 and ad 90, both employing earlier material, and the Fourth Gospel ad 100. By exhaustive analysis of the Third Gospel and the Acts they showed that both were written by St Luke, the physician, and for sixteen years the friend of Paul, his companion on the second and third missionary journeys. He was an historian of the first rank, and his chronological, geographical, and medical references carry an assurance of his integrity and care as a writer.

The long interval that was conjectured to intervene between the death of Jesus and the setting down of the record is now known to have no basis in truth. The supposed 'heightening of the portrait of Jesus' is the product of nothing more than heightened imagination on the part of the theorists.

The supposed 'reading back' into the days of the ministry of the faith and doctrines of a later time, together with the general infiltration of the Gospels with material from pagan sources, has not survived investigation. 'The historical perspective of the Gospels is genuine,' writes B. S. Easton in *The Gospel*

[37] *Chronologie der Altchristlichen Litteratur*, 1897, pp. viii-x.

Before the Gospels. 'The writers of the Gospels were profoundly respectful of the primitive testimonies.'

It is being widely recognised that the New Testament is wholly congruous with itself. Like the robe that Jesus wore it is 'all of one piece'. The supernatural elements are by no means separable from the rest of the material. The phenomenal is inextricably interwoven with the ethical teaching. It is an integral feature of the whole portrait of Jesus. Cut it out and what is left is incoherent, and in no way capable of giving rise to a movement like apostolic Christianity.

Early attempts to show that Paul and the Fourth Gospel give us a view of Jesus that is out of keeping with what is implied in the primitive sources, have not proved convincing. Jesus' claim to be the Messiah belongs to the earliest and most authentic traditions. The tremendous conception of him as the Son of God is embedded in the primitive testimony of Mark.

But what is the implication of these facts? That the one person that cannot be traced in the New Testament sources is the Jesus who was a mere ethical teacher, who did no mighty works, and made no disquieting theological claims, and who got pathetically crucified because he had the temerity to preach a kindly humanism and to go about doing good. What we discover is the towering figure of the Son of God invested with power, accompanied by mighty works, speaking parables of terrific implication, claiming nothing less than divine Sonship, the sceptre of judgment and the power of saviourhood.

We are not far from the 'earliest eyewitnesses and ministers of the word'. They alone were responsible for the kindling of the faith that dazzled and exalted the Apostolic Church. Here is the explanation of the place and authority accorded to them in the Church. They alone could testify to the historic evidence on which an enduring Church could stand.

We now know that the limits in which the earlier critics moved were inadequate. Obsessed with historical and textual problems, they lost their sense of proportion. They almost wholly ignored the religious importance of their work. Looking back on their omissions, Adolf Deissmann says in *The New Testament in the Light of Modern Research*: 'I can only confess the guilt of my own science. We have followed one- sided doctrinaire interests, strained our eyes with doctrinaire matters, until, unfortunately, we have become, too often, religion-blind... so we dealt with secondary derivative aspects, instead of with powerful, living, primary facts.'

* * * *

Were these 'assured results' to last? What more could we wish, for example, than to know that Mark had taken down his Gospel from the very lips of Peter? Just as Papias had said he had done. Peter's recollections were of photographic clarity. What could be better?

Starting from the time of the First World War, however, German scholars like Dibelius, Schmidt, Rudolf Bultmann and others, used the Gospel traditions first of all as evidence of what was taught in the early Christian communities. Then came the question if a Gospel taken down from the lips of people was strictly history? Had not several decades passed before there was a written record? Here was a time when the traditions about Jesus could have hardened into forms. Here was a likely interval, they thought, when the needs and convictions of the earliest Christian groups could have influenced the form, selection, and transmission of what was set down in the Gospels.

This is arguing in a circle. It looks to the Gospels to find what was taught on their authority in the first Christian communities, then it alleges that the Gospels are poor history since they only contain matters taught in the first Christian communities. This idea meets with increasing incredulity.

Some of the negative judgments of Form Criticism have been astonishing. Bultmann, for instance, stated in *Jesus and the World* that 'we can now know almost nothing concerning the life and personality of Jesus, since the early Christian sources show no interest in either.' True, he goes on to say, 'that Jesus is the one in whom God's word encounters man.' But what, if we 'know almost nothing about Jesus,' can 'the encounter' amount to? Something very different from the effect it has undoubtedly had on the Christian mind.

Anyone who knows communities, knows too how limited are their creative powers. Could the life and personality of Jesus that the Gospels present have been the composite work of a community? Or have been 'made up' at all? 'Who among the disciples,' asked John Stuart Mill, 'was capable of inventing the sayings ascribed to Jesus, or of imagining his life and character?'

One can imagine Peter recalling, for Mark to take down, actual Aramaic words that Jesus had used like, '*Talitha cumi*—Get up, my child', '*Eli, Eli, lama sabachthani*—My God, my God, why have you deserted me.' Peter still had the sound of the words in his ears; and he told Mark that Jesus had held a small child 'in the crook of his arm'. He could still see it. But the later Christian community would not have known Aramaic anyhow, and could never have imagined the captivating human detail about the child. What the later Christian community worried about was Baptism, the Holy Spirit, the Gentile mission, and these are not the things the Synoptic Gospels emphasise.

No one would deny that stories passed on by word of mouth might vary a little. But that is far from saying that the Christian community invented, or read back, into the life of Jesus things that he had never said, and never done. Their main concern was for the truth, and they had plenty of access to the truth through the presence among them until the Synoptic Gospels were safely in writing, of eyewitnesses and first preachers of the word.

Far from casting doubt on the records, the facts of oral transmission made the record of Jesus' teaching and life, and the details of his death and Resurrection, an affair of the whole community, and everything shows that they were anxious to sift the truth as much as they could, and for as long as they could.

Here is a careful man like Papias, writing sometime before ad 135:

> I shall be willing to put down along with my own interpretations whatever instructions I received with care from the elders and stored up in my memory, assuring you at the same time of their truth. If then, anyone who has attended on the elders came, I asked minutely after their sayings, what Andrew or Peter said, or what was said by Philip, or by Thomas, or by James, or by John, or by Matthew, or by any other of the Lord's disciples; what things Ariston and the Presbyter John, the disciples of the Lord say For I imagined what was to be got from books was not so profitable to me as what came from the living and abiding voice of the Lord's disciples.[38]

It is clear that it is not what is believed in the Christian groups around him that he thinks authoritative, but what single detail he may yet learn from the Apostolic time.

There is a self-correcting factor in scholarship, and the period that has been dominated by secular thinking about Jesus is probably ending. Professor Ernst Kasemann may be seen as 'a sign of the times'. He began as a follower of Bultmann, and was almost completely doubtful about knowing anything of the historical Jesus. But he now writes in *The Problem of the Historical Jesus*:

> We have been told by the Form Critics, that the early Church was not interested in history, that the glorified Christ had practically swallowed up Jesus of Nazareth, and that events in the earthly life of Jesus had but little

---

38 The Ante-Nicene Fathers, i. 153.

interest for Gentile believers in post-Resurrection days. Yet the plain fact is we have four Gospels that relate a great deal about that life on earth. They had their feet squarely in the footsteps of the Man of Nazareth. They were not willing to let a myth take the place of history, or to substitute a heavenly being for the historical Jesus. We no longer think of the Evangelists as pale compilers, but as men giving a true impressionist portrait of Jesus as he was in the years between 6 BC and ad 29.

In Kasemann's view there is enough in the Synoptic Gospels 'to confront us with a figure so awe-inspiringly outstanding and significant that we begin to understand why those who knew Him did not find it impossible to believe about Him that He had triumphed over death and been raised to the right hand of God.'

Likewise after the most detailed study of all the evidence concerning the historical Jesus, Dr Howard Marshall, an outstanding New Testament scholar, affirms:

> So the reader of the Gospels is brought face to face with the biblical Jesus as the Son of the living God. These accounts, seen in the light of the resurrection, call out for the reader's decision and invites them to faith. And the object of their faith is then the Jesus whose existence and ministry have been confirmed and illuminated by their historical research, but whose significance is only fully seen in the light of that experience of the risen Lord which has coloured the interpretation of Jesus offered in the Gospels and the rest of the New Testament and which continues to illuminate the mind of the believer.[39]

[39] I. H. Marshall, *I Believe in the Historical Jesus*.

PART THREE:

Synthesis

The nature of the universe – evidence of Mind and purpose – grounds of Theistic belief – reasonableness of revelation – significance of Old Testament – preparation – expectation – evidence of fulfilment in Christ – historic character – claims of uniqueness – portrait of man in highest definition – truest mirror of God – possibilities Christianity opens up for fullest development of humankind. Jesus 'speaks for himself'. His affirmation in the Court of the Sanhedrin.

CHAPTER SIXTEEN

The Nature of the Universe

> I was delighted with this idea—that Mind was the disposer and cause of all, and I said to myself, If this be so—if Mind is the orderer, it will have all things in order and put every single thing in the place that is best for it.
>
> Plato

> It is not Mind we should want to know. We should want to know the Thinker.
>
> Kaushitaki Upanishad

Before we can take our argument further, we must decide something, not so much about Jesus, as about the nature of the universe, and the character of the Being behind it. Is this universe the result of blind chance, or is it the product of a supreme creative Mind? A positive answer may enable us to continue the consideration of Jesus' significance at a new level.

Numerous and weighty arguments, on which a belief in God may be reasonably based, are readily accessible, and the reader will be aware of their cumulative force.

At this point, however, we are satisfied with the way the modern physicist concurs with the view of the classical Greek philosophers, that the Ultimate Reality behind the flux of visible phenomena is to be understood in terms of mind. For if there is a Mind behind the universe, it is plain that a whole world of theological and philosophical speculation is opened up. What kind of Mind is meant? Some physicists throw out a clue when they speak of God as ‘a consummate mathematician’. But plainly we cannot stop there. If reason is to be satisfied, we must see what more is implied.

The idea of ‘a consummate mathematician’ is itself unintelligible apart from conceptions of what we call personality. Do the physicists believe in a personal God? By definition, a consummate mathematician would have a supreme intelligence and a precise regard for mathematical truth. But ‘truth’ is variously apprehended. It has protcan qualities. Who would argue that God would not bc also interested in scientific truth, artistic truth, moral truth, spiritual truth? Would the God of the physicists be as interested in a peacock’s tail as in a calculus, as jealous of the integrity of a person as of the integrity of a formula?

We are not seeking a scientific opinion to vindicate Christianity, we are, however, pointing out that when science refers to God in terms of Mind, it is coming close to Natural Religion—that God is religiously apprehended through his works.

Scientists, like other people, show the polarisation of thought that afflicts the contemporary world. Some are militantly anti-God, others are Christians, or represent the great theistic religions, are convinced believers in God. Dr E. H. Leach, for instance, of the Cambridge Humanist Society, ‘takes the line,’ as he says, ‘that in these scientific days all religions are out of date’. Professor C. A. Coulson, in *Science and Christian Belief*‘ on the other hand, finds science a spur to faith. ‘I find myself,’ he says, ‘confronted in some utterly personal way with the spiritual quality of the whole universe. I receive the revelation of science and rejoice to call it the work of the Holy Spirit... All life is sacramental; all nature is needed that Christ should be understood; Christ is needed that all nature should be seen as holy.'

The issue of belief in God is of profoundest importance. When Nietzsche (1844–1900) said 'God is dead', he said it with intensity of anguish strikingly absent from those who have complacently revived the phrase in recent years. Nietzsche was an atheist in a profound sense, and faced, until madness came upon him, what it meant to live without God. He did not merely push his unbelief to a point where it ceased to be convenient. He did not say it lightly to be slightly shocking, as though 'the death of God' left everything where it stood. He saw it as meaning the disappearance of everything for which God was responsible. It was the end of all moral judgment, of all sense that science looked for in the universe, of all basis for reason and truth. Meaning dropped out of life leaving only a cold despair.

This is something very different from the casual dismissal of God which is frequently a pose that seems to bolster up and justify an irresponsible society. Attempts to consider it in depth, and logically carry it to its stark philosophical conclusion are strangely shirked. True, in an early essay, *Mysticism and Logic*, Bertrand Russell wrote the deeply moving, and frequently quoted passage:

> That man is the product of causes which had no prevision of the end they were achieving; that his origin, his growth, his hopes and fears, his loves and beliefs, are but the outcome of accidental collocation of atoms; that no fire of heroism, no intensity of thought and feeling can preserve an individual life beyond the grave; that all the labours of the ages, all the devotion, all the inspiration, all the noon-day brightness of human genius, are destined to end in extinction in the vast death of the solar system, and that the whole temple of man's

> achievement must inevitably be buried beneath the debris of a universe in ruins—all these, if not quite beyond dispute, are yet so nearly certain, that no philosophy that rejects them can hope to stand. Only within the scaffolding of such truths, only on the first foundation of unyielding despair, can the soul's habitation henceforth be safely built.

In Russell's case, having rendered this shattering statement, he continued to live within the framework of a very different philosophy, like protesting against the atomic bomb, and in *The Impact of Science on Society* saying 'the root of the matter was a thing so simple that he was almost ashamed to mention it, for fear of the derisive smile with which wise cynics will greet my words. The thing I mean—please forgive me for mentioning it —is love, Christian love or compassion.'

Why, one wonders, did so great a mind not see the irrationality of a universe producing within itself a human being so obviously beyond itself in sensitivity, integrity, and compassion? Or why did he not question the very purpose of continuing beyond the bomb, a universe so productive of feelings of 'unyielding despair'?

Nietzsche and Jean-Paul Sartre made no attempt to take the edge off the despair. They carry atheism to its bleak conclusion, and in so doing they produce an impact from which a healthy mind instinctively recoils. As D. E. Roberts, Professor of Philosophy and Religion, New York, makes plain, 'They offer us the strongest possible argument FOR God that can possibly be conceived.'

We all have to choose. The issue is simply, whether, with Jesus, we are to believe in a universe that makes sense, or, with Nietzsche, in a universe, that makes no sense at all.

We ask ourselves, therefore, if the general consensus of human opinion is true—that there is a God, or whether the universe as it is now revealed makes it an absurdity to believe in a Divine Creator, a Cosmic Mind. What impression comes to us as we consider, as far as we can, the totality of our environment, and the interpretation that seems valid to great scientific minds?

We turn to Sir James Jeans who says, 'We discover that the universe shows evidence of a designing and controlling power that has something in common with our own individual minds.' Or to the words of the physicist, Sir Ambrose Fleming:

> There are unquestionably in the physical universe things that stimulate our appreciation of order, beauty, adaptation, numerical relation, and purpose in our minds —we who are thinking, feeling persons—and hence these qualities which excite these psychic reactions must have been bestowed on the universe by a sentient intelligence at least as personal as ourselves.[40]

Now it is an easy step to believe that a Mind capable of creating the infinities of the universe, and human rationality, would take an interest in human beings. It would be unreasonable to suppose otherwise. No consummate Mind would be likely to withdraw interest from his handiwork. One would anticipate the likelihood of Mind making contact with mind. This, long ago, was the thought of Greek philosophers like Plato and Philo, who envisaged Reason as the intermediary, or bridge, spanning the gulf between God and human beings.

And by what means could the mind of God, using the bridge of Reason, communicate with humanity? In the first instance the Reason of God could display itself in the very structure of the universe. Further, it could be of such a kind that human reason, observing it, could know that the world was not the result of a blind chance, but the product of supreme intelligence, and from that fact, could realise that people were

---

[40] Sir Ambrose Fleming, quoted in *The Miracle of Man* by Dr. Harold Wheeler.

not due to some fortuitous accident, but had their place in the Creator's plan.

In point of fact, is not this the very thing that has happened? People have arrived at ideas of the Creator by scrutinising his work, by observing its orders, its laws, its beauty, its evidences of Mind.

Looking at us from his wide observations, Charles Darwin exclaimed, 'The grand sequence of events cannot be the result of blind chance. The mind revolts against such a conclusion.'

But what is the alternative to 'blind chance'? Is it not meaning and purpose? So Paul thought when he framed these words: 'Ever since the creation of the world His invisible nature, namely, his eternal power and deity, has been clearly apparent in the things that have been made' (Rom. 1: 20).

By way of simplest philosophical illustration, one imagines a mountainside in Wales. It is strewn with boulders and stones of all sizes and shapes, flung there by centuries of cosmic weathering. But by contrast the eye catches a few score of stones that trace a definite pattern. Just a coincidence, we say, that out of such tens of thousands upon the hillside, this tiny number might by chance fall into a pattern. But this pattern in fact spells out the word 'Welcome', and happens to be of stones all about the same size, all spaced regularly in precise letters. The idea of chance recedes. The idea of purpose is inescapable. This word too, we note, is just at the place where it would catch the eye of anyone about to cross into the Principality from England by road and is the word used in the current song being broadcast to Wales' exiles and visitors, 'We'll keep a Welcome in the hillside'. The design is intentional. The mind would revolt from any other conclusion. There is design corresponding with purpose, and as such is meant to be understood.[41]

---

[41] cf. Richard Taylor, *Metaphysics*.

This casual illustration, however, is as nothing, when we think of the myriad evidences of Mind in the order and design everywhere displayed in the physical world. Some controlling Mind, through infinite evidences of intelligent purpose, caused Kepler to cry out, 'O God we read Thy laws after Thee.'

But once we realise that 'Mind is the Orderer' and 'all things have their place', we have to ask if such a Mind would leave humanity entirely dependent on deductions from the physical world, or would it be reasonable that God would contact human beings more directly, placing in the human heart some inner knowledge of himself and of his will?

At least three lines of thought suggest that God has, in fact, done this. We cite the universality of religious experience; the phenomenon of conscience, found at varying levels in all humankind; and, thirdly, the argument for God presented by our highest ideals. We will look briefly at each of these lines of thought in turn.

Religious experience has been universal. One of the oldest and widespread human ideas is that of God. At least since the time of Plato, Seneca, and Cicero, arguments for God have been based on the fact that 'man is incurably religious'. Professor Eddington testifies in *The Nature of the Physical World*, to 'regions of the human spirit untrammelled by the world of physics. In the mystic sense of the creation around us,' he said, 'in the expression of art, in the yearning towards God, the soul grows upward, and finds fulfilment of something implanted in its nature. The sanction of this development is within us, a striving born of our consciousness of an Inner Light proceeding from a Power greater than ourselves.'

As architecture bears the impress of the style and mind of the architect, so human beings have felt that they were not made to be out of harmony, or beyond the possibility of harmony, with the Mind that created them. All the highest and purest forms of philosophy and religion have conceived of God as a personal and spiritual Being, with whom we are related, and to whom we had a sense of responsibility.

Is this evidence subjective, due to illusion or self-deception? It might be considered so, if only a few individuals had such ideas, but when one realises that in all ages, people have associated their highest experiences and thoughts with the idea of God, the evidence is so universal and consistent that it has an *objective* quality.

The phenomenon of conscience points directly to the existence of a Supreme Being, who has placed this monitor in the human heart. A thinker, like Immanuel Kant, thought conscience the strongest argument for belief in God; while C. S. Lewis, in his book called *Right and Wrong*, described our sense of right and wrong as a 'clue to the meaning of the universe'.

Conscience is something that all human beings are aware of. It is the basis of our sense of moral responsibility. It explains why we have a sense of conviction that, regardless of pleasure or profit, we 'ought' to do this or that.

The prayer called the General Confession, expresses the well-nigh universal feeling of those whose natural conscience has not been choked. 'We have left undone those things which we ought to have done, and we have done those things which we ought not to have done, and there is no health in us.'

The more one ponders the implication of that word 'ought', the more one sees the impossibility of explaining it, except in terms of a personal God who has placed this inner voice in the centre of our being.

A third evidence that God has not made the human soul without placing in it some witness of himself, is given by the considerations evoked by the study of our ideals.

The very 'reasonableness' of God would lead us to expect that human beings, his chief creation, would not be made impervious to those ideals and principles which God himself cherished. When we scrutinise our ideals we find that this is exactly the case.

Whenever people have tried to come to terms with their highest perceptions they have tended to become metaphysical.

They have asked, 'What is the Mind behind all things, which has given us an appreciation of beauty, an apprehension of truth, and a sense of justice?'

We cannot, as Professor T. E. Jessop points out in *Science and the Spiritual*, question the validity of ideals without becoming less than human. To deny their validity is to come perilously near denying the validity of thought itself. Yet once we admit their validity, we have to believe in a universe that makes sense of them, that 'takes sides', for instance, with us as we contend for harmony against discord, for truth against lies, for love against hate, that gives us backing in our belief that the foundations of the earth are laid in righteousness, and that in consequence it is 'better' to be pure than licentious, brave than cowardly, good than bad.

From such considerations we see that if we contemplate our ideals, they are able to lead us forward to a clearer apprehension of what the character of God must be.

If we put the argument in another form, this point appears more vividly. Since the lesser does not create the greater, nor surpass it, whatever ideals and values we apprehend, must, *a fortiori*, be more perfectly apprehended by their Creator, who is both their source, and the ultimate ground of their truth.

The alternative is untenable. The stream does not rise higher than its source. What I derive from God, I cannot possibly possess more fully than he. If I am capable of hungering and thirsting after righteousness, much more intensely must God love justice and hate iniquity. If I know love, so much more unfathomed must be his love who bestowed it on me. If I perceive beauty how much greater must be his perception of it?

Plainly this line of thought links up with what we are discussing—that God would be likely to communicate with people. For if earthly parents would leave their children bereft of guidance and help when they asked for it, is it conceivable that the one great Father of all would leave human beings destitute in a universe otherwise so bewilderingly mysterious?

Thus, by the argument from analogy, we connect with the sublime idea that glows in the Old Testament, and that reaches full explicitness on the lips of Jesus—God's Fatherly attitude to humankind.

But we have not said all. Reason and analogy have carried us to a point where God becomes conceivable in terms of Fatherhood. But who could feel deeply convinced about it while it remains on a theoretical level? To have confidence in the Fatherhood of God we need some practical evidence that he has shown towards the human family some Fatherly care. Failing that, God's Fatherhood falls short of the love and guidance that a normal human parent shows to their offspring.

What earthly parents leave their children entirely dependent on their own unaided reason, or upon their own brief experience? Do they not directly, and by teachers, supplement their unsure gropings after knowledge and wisdom? Do they not take pains to see that they are clearly warned against what is wrong and unhelpful?

Do they not steady and encourage them along every right path by a sense of their love and encouragement? Certainly nothing less than this could we expect from him whom we believe to be the one great Father of all.

It is the claim of Christianity that, within the sphere of history, these expectations have been abundantly fulfilled. Christianity faces us with a mass of evidence accumulated over many centuries, that God has in remarkable fashion supplemented human reason and experience. The evidence is recorded in the Old Testament, where the Hebrew people claim that their probings after God had been met by direct revelations; that a long line of prophets had declared God's character and will; that, in the commandments to Moses, God had provided precisely those warnings and admonitions to his children which, in the analogy of human parenthood, we felt should be their due; and, further, that God had steadied and encouraged them throughout a long history by practical evidence of his love and guidance, and that eventually, after a period of progressive enlightenment covering some two thousand years, he had crowned his revelation by sending to humanity one long foreshadowed as the Messiah.

Here is a tremendous chain of testimony and events that precisely satisfies all that we considered essential if God was to be understood on the analogy of human fatherhood.

We are aware, however, that the argument from analogy can be exceedingly deceptive. It can readily carry us beyond what the evidence warrants, or it can prevail upon us to swing the evidence in its direction. If, therefore, numerous lines of thought converge to support the idea of God's Fatherhood we must weigh the evidence by that Reason 'that lighteth every man that cometh into the world'.

Reason can investigate the lines of probability and state, as it were, in advance, certain principles to which any revelation calling itself Divine would be likely to conform. For while the ways of God would almost certainly transcend human reason, they would not be likely to be at variance with it.

Naturally, we could believe in no revelation that did not fulfil certain conditions. It would have to be wholly in keeping with our highest possible idea of God. It would, also, have to be distinguished by considerations that ruled out the possibility of it being mere chance or coincidence. If it were of God, some indications of the fact would have to be reasonably certain.

We say 'reasonably certain' rather than absolutely certain, because an absolutely certain revelation would be a kind of threat to humanity, depriving them of that freedom of choice which, we believe, characterises us, and makes possible individuality. It is the distinctive mark of people that they are free agents, endowed, indeed, as we have seen, with a sense of moral responsibility, but, nevertheless, free to do what they choose.

Now earthly parents, not wishing to crush their child's freedom of development, do not tyrannise them, but temper authority and coercion, by appealing to the child's own reason and experience. Similarly, if God gave humanity an overpowering revelation of himself, they would be bound to obey it, and God would forfeit Fatherhood for dictatorship, and change children into slaves. This affronts our highest idea of God. We would expect him to be courteous to the souls he has made, and that having made people free, he would not wish to see them bound.

From such considerations, we would expect God to reveal himself in a way that would awaken reason and tend to encourage free response and yet not remove the human beings' power to disbelieve it, if they choose.

We shall see that Christianity fulfils this condition. It appeals to nobility in people. It can meet their intellects by its reasonableness, their souls by its spiritual quality, and, when put to the test, it can be verified by personal experience. It does not compel allegiance, however. If people are victims of self-deception or mental pride, or if they are so absorbed with the material that they refuse to explore the spiritual, then nothing that God can do will be invincible enough to convince them.

In the Old Testament we are told that God is not found in uproar and turbulence but in the still small voice that speaks to the human heart. In the New Testament Jesus speaks of God as one who stands at the door of the heart and knocks. He does not overpower human free will. He does not invade or coerce. As is his love, so is his courtesy and restraint. While he would call all people unto him, he compels none.

Now plainly this attitude on the part of God—nobler than any other and full of the highest possibilities for the fullest development of human personality—can readily be abused.

Many a human parent, extending freedom to a child, has seen that child abuse its freedom, misunderstand the ends for which it was given, and move from the standards set in the home, to a life wasteful and prodigal in a far country. Similarly, God by his very gift of free will has made it possible for people to spurn his fatherly guidance and to bring ruin upon themselves and others.

That this has happened time and again is one of the unchallengeable facts of history. The whole tragedy of human history could be written in terms of high insights scorned, great principles forsaken, of people's fatal tendency to make the worse appear the better reason, of their abandonment of the God of truth and love, for the idolatries of the world, the flesh, and the devil.

Seeing the resultant chaos what more could God do? How could God more fully reveal himself? Many a religion has wistfully spoken of the need of an incarnation, of the necessity of God entering the human scene, and meeting personality through personality. Philosophy, too, has envisaged, precisely what Christianity has affirmed has happened, that God should himself find means of entering the human drama. Plato spoke of the reasonableness of the Author of the Universe, on beholding it tempest-tossed and in peril of going down to the place of chaos, taking his seat at the helm of the soul, and coming to the rescue to correct all calamities, as quoted in Athanasius' *On the Incarnation*.

Athanasius gives a further helpful analogy. He speaks of a kind teacher caring for his pupils, and finding some of them unable to profit by indirect instruction, taking it upon himself to come nearer the pupils' level by giving them personal help and encouragement.

It is the belief of Christendom that such an idea did in actual fact commend itself to God, and that in the Incarnation we see God expressing himself in terms of human personality, and that, as St John phrased it, Jesus came forth from the Father into the world' (John 16: 28), or as Paul said, 'When the fullness of time was come God sent forth his Son born of a woman (Gal. 4: 4).

The rationale of Christ's coming, we find in the Messianic passages of the Old Testament, where the prophets set forth their belief that only direct supernatural intervention could save humankind; or we find it on the lips of Jesus, in a parable that would be luminously direct in its implication to anyone familiar with the story of Israel—the Parable of the Vineyard (Mark 12). After long entreaty with his people through prophetic messengers, God chooses to make a final appeal through his Son.

Certainly there is nothing philosophically difficult in believing that God, the creator of humanity, should, out of love for people, send an ambassador to them. Indeed, we have seen that human intuition had already anticipated such an action, and that a mind like Plato's counted it both intellectually acceptable and morally commendable.

Let us, therefore, for the furtherance of our argument, assume the possibility of a divine Incarnation. Let us imagine that the Divine Mind should choose to make himself known through a human personality. Can we now suggest any considerations that might commend themselves to him? Would God, for instance, allow the coming of the Messiah to go unheralded and to arrive unexpectedly? Or would he prepare the stage of history and allow people to have some intimation of the Messiah's coming?

Can we venture to postulate the conditions that might reasonably be fulfilled before the Messiah came? At least five anticipations suggest themselves, three of which are obvious preconditions.

1. We would expect God to prepare people's minds by raising them to a level at which the teaching of the Messiah would be intelligible;
2. We would expect God to give humankind some ideas by which they could, if they were true to the best insights that they had received, recognise the Messiah when they saw him;
3. We would expect God to choose an opportune time for the Messiah's birth and for the fruitful planting of his teaching;
4. We would anticipate, also, a fourth attendant consideration, namely, that the character of the Messiah, when he came, would be such as to commend itself to people as fitting one

who was indeed bearing a message of august and sublime significance;

5. Finally, it would be reasonable to suppose that the coming of a transcendent figure who could say, 'The Father and I are one' would result in a religion viable for all, everywhere, in all ages. Evidence of its reality would be manifest: (a) in the spiritual satisfaction it would give; (b) in the way it enhanced the human sense of life's meaning and purpose; (c) in the new standard of humanity it would supply; (d) in the highest possible idea of God it would reveal.

Could it possibly happen that all five of these logical anticipations were met in Christ, would we not be filled with amazement and awe? We discover that, in fact, every single one of these anticipations became luminously evident in the first century of our era. We will naturally deal with the evidence, point by point.

CHAPTER SEVENTEEN

The Significance of the Old Testament

> The Bible is more than an historical document to be preserved. And it is more than a classic of English literature to be cherished and admired. It is a record of God's dealing with men, of God's revelation of Himself and His will. It records the life and work of Him in whom the Word of God became flesh and dwelt among men.
>
> Preface to the Bible (RSV)

Higher education would be lost on people who had not had long years of preparatory training. 'See' says the educationist, 'before you can impart advanced information on any subject, the road must be cut that leads to it.'

So obvious a fact need not be laboured. No one expects a child engaged on five-finger exercises to tackle Bach, nor a person lacking all literary appreciation to enjoy Chaucer or Milton, or the *Oxford Book of English Verse*.

How did it happen, then, that the teaching of Jesus, so highly demanding on moral and spiritual perception, was not wholly lost on those who heard him?

For an answer one has to turn to the long centuries of training and enlightenment recorded in the Old Testament. It provides precisely that evidence of preparation that we felt we should expect if Jesus were in fact a messenger from the Most High.

But is it not antecedently improbable that God would make a special revelation of himself to any one people? Was it not 'odd of God to choose the Jews'? Does God have racial favourites?

The difficulty dissolves if we realise just what being 'favourites' meant. It meant, as Jeremiah said, 'great things and difficult'. It meant being set apart, shaped, used. It meant being the servants of a purpose beyond their inclinations and national prejudices. They were told, as indeed it happened, that the revelation was not for them only, but that 'through them all the families of the earth should be blessed' (Genesis 12: 3).

As a scientist will isolate a specimen for special culture or experiment, or as a teacher will choose some pupils for intensive training that others might afterwards benefit from their work, so the Bible states that God chose the Hebrews to be the bearers of his truth before all nations. 'I, the Lord, have called thee in righteousness and will hold thy hand and give thee as a covenant to the people, as a light to the Gentiles' (Isaiah 42: 6).

Much in the character of the Hebrews fitted them to be chosen for special training. Sensitive to illumination, and yet slow to live up to it, their very 'toughness' as a people required that emphasis and repetition, that frequency of occurrence, that those of critical mind might look for in a revelation purporting to be divine.

The very grimness of their experiences when they defied God's will, as they frequently did, may have been intended to serve as proof of the truth of God's word, and as a warning for all time, of the consequences that follow its rejection. Certainly all subsequent history has borne witness that it is by the principles enunciated by the Hebrew prophets that nations rise and fall. If any truths have been proved by events, then the truths of the Old Testament have that permanence of application that we should expect of a revelation emanating from God.

The inspirational nature of Hebrew enlightenment is strongly suggested by the way it led them intuitively, and almost despite themselves, to levels of knowledge above that of their contemporaries. Consider the sensitive moral perception behind teaching like this: 'When an alien settles with you in your land you shall not oppress him. He shall be treated as a native-born among you. You shall love him as a man like yourself because you were aliens in Egypt. I am the Lord your God' (Lev. 19: 33). Again, 'If I have ever rejected the plea of my slave or of my slave-girl when they brought their complaint to me, what shall I do if God appears? What shall I answer if he intervenes? Did not he who made me make them?' (Job 31: 13–14).

Does history show any people as God-conscious, as Godfearing as the Hebrews? Think of the prestige and authority accorded to their holy leaders, and the vehemence and power of the voices that proclaimed without fear or favour 'Thus saith the Lord'.

The same reverent awe is apparent in the scrupulous way they preserved their records. Dr Davidson in *The Old Testament* quotes the strict rules by which the copyists were bound: 'No word, letter, or even accent was to be set down without checking from the codex. Should a king address a scribe while he was writing the divine name, the scribe must ignore him.'

Old Testament texts discovered among the Dead Sea Scrolls witness to the care with which such rules were obeyed, for here we have copies of Old Testament writings that are a thousand years older than any previously known, and they correspond with remarkable fidelity to the later manuscripts, establishing how faithful was the transmission of the holy word when checked for variations over a thousand years.

'Modern archaeological and linguistic methods of study have further confirmed our confidence in the Biblical story. Biblical archaeology has illuminated the historical setting of the events and cultural background with which Biblical faith is concerned.'[42]

Tens of thousands of texts like those found at Mari, Nuzi, Ras Shamra, Tell-el-Amarna, take us right back to Old Testament times, and the result is reassuring. But more important than the historical basis underlying the Old Testament is the theological interpretation that is given to the events described. The Old Testament was written and cherished by people convinced that they had things of supreme importance to pass on.

Looked at objectively, it is plain that the illumination that came to the Hebrews was of such a nature, and so scaled to meet them at successive stages of development, that it cannot be explained save by the fact of divine inspiration— mediated indeed, through fallible human agencies, but unmistakably showing signs of God's over-ruling purpose.

And what was the purpose of this illumination, this age long discipline and instruction, if it were not to prepare people's minds for the teaching of Jesus?

If a drama moves along reasonable lines of development, if there is evidence of grasp and mastery in the unfolding of the plot, we hopefully anticipate that we shall be granted an equally reasonable and satisfying conclusion.

The Old Testament invites a similar confidence. It unfolds a sublime drama, but it breaks off rather than reaches an end. We look for some gathering up of the themes, some satisfying conclusion, but without the coming of Christ the Old Testament would merely tantalise us, with problems unanswered, promises unfulfilled, themes loose and without pattern. But with the life and teaching of Jesus, the Old Testament finds its logical fulfilment. The Old Testament illuminates the New, and the New gives point and sublime significance to the Old. There is

---

[42] Dr. G. E. Wright, *Biblical Archaeology*, pp. 19, 25.

an organic relationship between them. They are as related as root and blossom.

Jesus assumed a knowledge of the Old Testament in those who heard him. It had laid a foundation on which he could build. For it was more than a rough foundation. It was, in itself, a piece of massive architecture—needing something, but demanding that 'something' to be of surpassing excellence.

When an architect has designed an arch, and when numerous workers have slowly brought it to completion, there comes the moment when the keystone is required. Without the coming of Jesus, the arch of the Old Testament, spanning so many centuries, would have lacked its keystone. It stands now locked into organic unity, a process-built, progressive revelation.

Naturally it took time. God who in nature works through slow processes, abiding his time for every fruit to come to its perfection, would not act differently, or be less patient, in the nurture and training of complex humanity.

The Old Testament seems scaled to meet humanity's growing apprehension. Every main idea starts from simple beginnings and with many setbacks and delays, grows in scope and height towards the fullness that enabled the contemporaries of Jesus to understand his teaching.[43]

Without the basic morality of the Mosaic code how could the Sermon on the Mount have been understood? The acceptance of the old was the necessary condition for the perception of the new.

It was necessary for Moses to forbid specific acts. It was possible for Jesus to deal at a higher level with the inner thoughts from which such acts proceed. Moses dealt with visible deeds, Jesus could go on to speak of invisible motives. Moses dealt with sin, Jesus with the roots of sin.

---

[43] H. E. Fosdick, *Guide to Understanding the Bible*; G. Herbert, *The Authority of the Old Testament*.

The continuity is obvious. The development inevitable. Obviously if God was to be known in terms of Fatherhood, his revelation could not stop with the disclosure of Law. No fatherly relationship can be based on tablets of stone. As Jeremiah foresaw, a new and more intimate relationship had to be established. The time had come for God to say, 'I will put my law in their inward parts, and write it upon their hearts, and I will be their God, and they shall be my people' (Jer. 31: 33). It was the work of Jesus to fulfil that prophecy in very truth.

As morality advanced, moving from the act to the thought, from the deed to the motive, from the legal relationship to one of voluntary response, so the theology that gave rise to it in the Old Testament moves upward to meet the full revelation of Christ, and shows similar progressive advance.

Every prophet seems to have been entrusted with some special contribution to the knowledge of God's character. Amos stressed his justice, Hosea his loving kindness, Isaiah his holiness, Jeremiah his demands on the community, and Ezekiel his call to the individual.

These broad conceptions of God's character were well known to those who heard Jesus. He addressed a people who had reflected on the prophetic revelation and had accepted it as authoritative.

The time had come then, when the revelation could be completed; and who could do that save the one described by Hegel as 'the unique figure in whom the whole history of religion culminated'?

By the fullness of his teaching, by the sublimity and faultlessness of his life, Jesus gave 'the good life' a new persuasiveness, and a new dimension, and a more intimate relevance for human need. By him, too, the full portrait of God was made real to humanity. Schooled as he was, in the finest Old Testament theology, even St Paul found that he had gained a wholly new conception of God by thinking of him as 'the God and Father of our Lord Jesus Christ'. The first two verses of the Epistle to the Hebrews expressed what centuries of faith have confirmed: 'God, who at sundry times and in divers manners spake in times past by the prophets has in these last days spoken unto us by his Son.'

There is no suggestion of two separate revelations. The one is the perfect flowering of the other. Jesus himself was explicit about the relationship between himself and the Old Testament. He knew that it was the older teaching that made his own possible. 'Other men have laboured,' he said to his disciples, 'and ye have entered into the fruit of their labours.' He was equally confident that the older teaching looked to him for completion. 'I am come,' he said, 'not to destroy but to fulfil.'

It is hard to have this vision of a slowly heightened and progressive revelation, moving upwards from the implicit to the explicit, from the partial to the perfect, without seeing behind it the continuous love and purpose of God, which Christians have seen as the key to the understanding of the life and purpose of Jesus.

CHAPTER EIGHTEEN

The Atmosphere of Expectation

Prophecy never came by human impulse.

2 Peter 1

We are following out the possibility that God might reasonably choose to communicate with humanity. On that assumption, what might we expect? Not a sudden apocalypse in the heavens, nor a dramatic take-over of outer space communication, but something more in keeping with the gradual growth of other forms of knowledge, something that might pass for normal, like the gradual deepening of the insights of good people, so that a man like Moses might come from his meditations on a mountain with a revised version of the laws of Hammurabi in his head, or the awakening of a hope that one day an utterly worthy figure might represent God to humanity.

In our last chapter we saw that the Old Testament was just such a record of a long-term, but growing, enlightenment, and after many centuries it did in fact, seem to prepare the way for a supreme Teacher to come among people.

We now come to the strange, but utterly historical fact, of the expectation of the Messiah. It is a phenomenon which must be judged on evidence, rather than on presuppositions this way or that. The subject calls for open-ended inquiry, avoiding on the one hand the dogmatism of faith, and on the other the equally trying dogmatism of doubt.

As there is artistic inspiration, musical and poetic inspiration, is it unreasonable to speak of prophetic inspiration? Even some scientists have claimed to receive insights beyond their actual knowledge, which later research has enabled them to verify.

Certainly the prophets were by no means merely political and social reformers. They were in their impressive succession people of towering spiritual greatness and moral stature, so that while looking at the contemporary scene they sometimes looked above and beyond it, and speaking to their time, they also spoke truths for all time. It is to them that we owe those flashes of insight, and the illuminating portraiture that impressed upon the Hebrew mind the ideal of the Messiah, and the hope of his coming.

They saw things in new perspectives. While the poetry and mythology of ancient peoples tended to be retrospective, wistfully extolling some golden age in the past, the prophets looked hopefully forward. The Hebrews had had eras of splendour and many notable leaders in their not inglorious past, but these were never idealised by the prophets in the way that they idealised the mysterious figure, whom, they believed, was to shape their future greatness.

The Greeks and Romans, like Eastern philosophy, were without a sense of progressive purpose in the world. Any movement they envisaged was cyclic. Only from the religious insight of Israel came the conception of a divine purpose running through all things and destined, despite human's rebellion, to final effectiveness.

The picture of the Messiah was fragmentary and composite. It was the work of many hands over a long time. There is wide difference of spiritual tone; earthly hopes and spiritual mission move at different levels. Yet there are large general agreements.

The prophets agree in sharply denouncing the present, yet they are filled with irrepressible hope for the future. They lament the feebleness of their nation, yet predict for it a world-wide mission. They despair of human agencies, yet are confident that a Messiah was coming who would usher in a new era.

The Messiah was to sum up all ideas in himself. He was to be a veritable King of Righteousness, and through him God's will was to be revealed. Peace and a beneficent change in all human relationships were to be the result of his rule, and all nations were to be gathered into his kingdom. A new Covenant was to be established and there was to be an outpouring of the Divine Spirit.

Scholars differ widely in their interpretation of Messianic passages. Some rightly point out that a number of passages formerly counted Messianic are in fact topical references to persons or a person known at the time. Others say, like Dr Westcott, 'God through His Spirit so speaks that words not directly addressed to Christ, find their fulfilment in Him.' Others, again, agree with Dr A. G. Herbert who argues in *The Authority of the Old Testament* that while passages must not be pressed to detail, yet 'Old Testament prophecies run to Christ as tidal rivers to the sea, only to feel his reflex influence upon them'.

On any reckoning we have to account for the fact that the Messianic hope came to take an increasing place in the Hebrew mind. This cannot be left hanging in the air without reasonable explanation.

If there is no such thing as prophetic inspiration, how did it happen that the idea of a Messiah ever arose? If it was the outcome of 'wishful thinking', how did it happen that some significant Messianic passages allude to things that were far from wished? Some of the ideals voiced in them cut across Israel's material and national aspirations.

Popular hope for example centred round the idea of a Messiah as one who would revive the national glory of Israel, restore worldly power and prosperity, and break off the yoke of oppression. But there were prophets who had a very different message.

The Messiah was to be sought by the Gentiles (Isaiah 11: 10), the Jews were to share their covenant status with the Gentiles and give light to them (Isaiah 42: 6), his followers were to be called by a new name (Isaiah 62: 2), and instead of founding a merely national religion, it was to be 'great among the heathen from the rising up of the sun unto the going down of the same among the Gentiles' (Mai. 1: 11).

Only one acquainted with Jewish history can appreciate how grudgingly the Jews of that time could have entertained the thought of sparing any comfort to the Gentiles. No wonder Isaiah exclaimed 'who hath believed our report?' How bewildered they must have been at the portrait of one 'despised and rejected of men, brought as a lamb to the slaughter, bearing griefs and carrying sorrows', a Saviour redeeming humanity at the cost of his own life (Isaiah 53). The author of the Suffering Servant Songs was not afraid to think of suffering as it had been found to be in the Exile, a road to new and larger thoughts of God, a way of showing that evil at its worst can be made to fail before goodness at its best.

Plato, the Greek philosopher, held the view that if a perfect person appeared on this planet, death would be their portion. But the author of the Suffering Servant passages reached the higher truth that such a death might be a refining and saving thing, even perhaps, that the nature of God could be revealed in it.

No wonder, perhaps, despite the voices of the prophets, the more material, the more national idea, held sway, and that the people entrusted with the portrait of the Messiah, refused to recognise him when they saw him.

Yet, is not this just what we should expect, if prophecy were indeed a revelation from God? We would be prepared to find it bigger than the measure of the human mind, purer than ideas mixed with national desires and worldly hopes. We would expect it to contain a challenge to higher and wider thinking.

But the unaccountable sweep of prophetic vision, offering a spiritual mission to the whole world, is not so astonishing as the way the picture of the Messiah tended to encroach even on the Hebrews' cherished thought of God as one, absolute and transcendent. Such fighters against polytheism as the prophets, vehemently contending for the holiness and oneness of God, undoubtedly on occasion, startle us by pointing to a figure who has the Name of God upon Him. The writer of the book of Daniel, for instance, describes a vision of 'The Ancient of Days' enthroned in fiery flame and with hundreds of thousands standing before Him, and one 'like the Son of Man' receiving from him the promise of a Kingdom wherein all peoples, nations and languages should serve him, a Kingdom that should increase and not pass away (Dan. 7: 13, 14). With a Hebraic assurance of reality Isaiah proclaims, 'Unto us a son is born, a child is given, and the government shall be upon his shoulder: and his name shall be called, Wonderful, Counsellor, Mighty God, Everlasting Father, Prince of Peace' (Isaiah 9: 6, 7). What is the significance? To the Hebrew the Name of God was so unutterably holy that none but the High Priest could utter it, and even he but once a year.

It was such thoughts as these that in one form or another entered the Hebrew consciousness, just as they have undoubtedly contributed to the Church's devotion to Christ. They are likely to continue to hold their place in Christian thought, and to be variously interpreted.

As we attempt to sum up five facts seem clear. First, the reality and spread of the great hope in the quantity of Messianic and Apocryphal literature, and the gleams of it in the Qumran Scrolls. 'It shows,' as Professor N. K. Gottwald says in *A Light to the Nations*, 'that the Jews were more keenly aware at the time of Christ of some impending great act of God than they had been at any time in their history.'

Secondly, even if prophecy is taken at its lowest valuation, as merely a 'showing forth' of the ideal man, the perfect servant of God, it is bound to remain significant that only one figure in history, Jesus of Nazareth, has brought that idea to vital reality.

Thirdly, 'filled with the spirit Jesus seemed to have known that he had been called to translate prophecy into history'. To the question, did Jesus accept the Name of the Messiah, or Christ? Dr A. M. Ramsey replied in *God, Christ and the World*: 'Certainly Jesus did and said things appropriate to one who was the Messiah, and his enemies set out to destroy him, because his behaviour added up to a claim to Messiahship and more... The Synoptists record him as avowing Messiahship in his reply to the High Priest in the Sanhedrin when he was at the point of condemnation to death.'

Fourthly, there is much to suggest that Jesus had no idea of Messiahship that was his alone, and it included new elements that even his disciples realised but dimly, if at all. He *was* the Messiah. It explains his agony in Gethsemane; his courageous admission before the High Priest when on trial, when he knew his admission would be taken as blasphemy, and send him to his death; and it explains his first resurrection message to the disciples on the Emmaus road, 'when beginning with Moses and all the prophets, he interpreted to them in all the scriptures the things concerning himself (Luke 24: 27).

Fifthly, proof-texts were used with powerful effect by the first preachers of the faith. To many scholarly minds today they were excessively used, and sometimes misapplied. 'To Christ,' said Peter, 'give all the prophets witness' (Acts 10: 43); and the appeal was convincing. By Messianic explanation, Philip converted the Ethiopian (Acts 8: 10); Stephen spoke with invincible spirit at the immediate cost of his life (Acts 6: 10), and Paul was able to throw the Jewish colony into complete confusion by the way he demonstrated that Jesus was the Christ (Acts 9: 22).

Finally, it is a generally admitted fact that the Messianic doctrine provided a terminology and background of ideas, without which the significance of Jesus could hardly have been so immediately interlocked with the Old Testament, and so readily interpreted in the primitive Church.

CHAPTER NINETEEN

Flood-tide

When the fullness of time was come God sent forth his son.

Epistle to the Galatians

One of the remarkably fortunate things in history was the extraordinary timeliness of Jesus' coming. Had he come either earlier or later he would have missed the one moment in history that was most likely to favour the reception, the understanding, and the spread of the Gospel.

Let us summarise the evidence.

We have already seen how by the time of Christ's birth the Jews had been progressively raised, through centuries of discipline and enlightenment, to a level at which the teaching of Jesus about God and human duty was broadly intelligible. We have noted also the amount of thought that focused on the arrival of the Messiah.

Granted, that the light of what we must call 'revelation' had filtered through human channels, and had suffered a good deal in transmission, yet it was sufficient to provide a remarkable background, that Jesus and the Apostolic Church used with tremendous effect.

Even outside Judaism a good deal was known of this background. The very Dispersion of the Jews had been a singularly fortunate happening. Wherever they had gone, they had carried with them their characteristic beliefs, and, outside the narrower sects, there was missionary zeal. 'The Pharisees,' said Jesus, 'compassed land and sea to make one proselyte.' Nor was it only spiritual motives that made people take an interest in Judaism. Relief from military service and the sabbath day rest from work rewarded the proselyte.[44]

Thus over most of the ancient world, various factors had aided the spread of Old Testament ideas, including the Messianic hope.

Either by influence from Judaism, or by simultaneous thinking along similar lines, we find the Roman poet, Virgil, anticipating that one would soon be born who would usher in a golden age, while Suetonius, the historian, bears witness that a certain and settled belief prevailed in the East that about this time Judaea would bring forth a personality who would win universal homage.

The atmosphere of the time just before Christ's coming was charged with Messianic excitement. In Palestine there was a remarkable personality, John the Baptist, who had already launched a final campaign, pleading that the clock of destiny was actually about to strike, that 'the Kingdom of heaven was at hand'.

The reception given to John the Baptist's words, the multitudes that flocked to hear him, the numbers of all classes that were stirred to repentance, all indicate how strong was the conviction of the nearness of the Messiah's advent.

Further, these facts, convincing as they are in themselves, combine with others to show that Christ's entrance into history was timed and ordered in a fashion that invites illustration, not from the annals of religious mysticism so much as from the

---

[44] Juvenal, *Satires*, vi

sphere of mechanical and scientific precision. One thinks of some great mechanism swinging into pre-deter- mined engagement, wheel with wheel, cog with cog, mesh with mesh. One is reminded of something planned and ordered by the good pleasure of God himself.

At no other time in the history of the world was the stage so perfectly set for a divine revelation as it was at the time of Christ's birth. Not only were the Hebrews themselves ripe for the Messiah's coming, but the Graeco-Roman world was also literally at its wit's end for a credible faith. The old polytheisms had had their day. Their confused mythologies alienated the better minds and baffled the simpler. If ever the death of old beliefs opened the doorway to the new, this was the time.

But what religion could seize an opportunity that was hedged round by so many conditions? Consider the varied needs and yearnings of that troubled world. There was a demand for a religion that at one level could meet the exacting demands of philosophy, and at another could free people from the gross superstition and emotionalism of the mystery cults, and at still another level could meet the desire for an improved moral code, evidenced by the Stoics and the followers of Mithra. Any religion hoping to be all-embracing had thus to satisfy a three-fold demand—the demand of philosophy, the demand of the emotional side of human nature, the demand of rising ethical standards.

The religion of Jesus met every such need. Its doctrine of God was acceptable to philosophy, and by its earliest writers was readily united with it. It even fulfilled the longing for an intermediary between God and humanity that had entered human thinking.

There was the concept of an almost personified Wisdom, standing alongside God as a 'master-worker' effecting God's great purposes, and there was Philo's handling of the tremendous doctrine of the Logos—the very expression of the divine Reason personified, and even incarnate, and these two wonderful terms were ready for describing the innermost meaning of the Christ.

One can only marvel that it should have happened that, before Jesus came, both Jewish and Greek ideas had glimpsed the possibility of God breaking silence through an intermediary, and that they should have spoken of the intermediary as his 'well-beloved', his 'first-born', his 'image', as one 'coeternal with him before the worlds were made'. In the fusion of Greek and Jewish thought in cities like Alexandria there 'tended to be an identification of the Logos of the Greeks with the Messiah of the Jews. Everything, therefore, was ready for the appearance of the Son of God,' as we find Temple saying in *Mens Creatix*.

At no time before or since have such ideas occupied human thought, and the theory of chance, or coincidence, hardly explains the extraordinary way such ideas gave a background, and even the very language by which Christ's coming could be understood and interpreted. The fitness of current thinking, for an interpretation of the Incarnation, is evidenced by the ready way the author of the Fourth Gospel could speak of Jesus in terms of the Logos (John 1: 1—14) to his Greek readers.

Christianity, however, did more than agree with philosophical trends. It stood on historical facts that were open to examination. The early Church depended on those whose authority rested on their having been eyewitnesses of Christ's life, death, and resurrection. For them it was but incidental that many of the Christian doctrines had become philosophically respectable. One cannot imagine the respectability of the idea of immortality, for instance, weighing greatly with the five hundred eyewitnesses of Christ's resurrection that Paul refers to, or with the Apostles, or with Stephen, the first martyr. But as Christianity moved into the wider world and sought to make its faith articulate, it was immensely fortunate that vivid personal experience, and a chain of historical events, could be expressed in a medium of thought that others, without that experience, could understand and find credible. Without that medium it is not likely that the wider world would ever have been won.

Nor was Christianity merely intellectually and historically respectable. It glowed with life and reality. It exalted human emotions where the mystery cults had debased them. In the purity of Mary, and in the Christian consecration of home life, a new and much needed change of direction was given to the sex element in life and religion. In the Christian sacraments, the mystic and emotional elements, sought after in the weird practices of the mystery cults, were sublimated, and combined with an ethical emphasis completely absent at the pagan shrines. In the breaking of bread, and in the promise of Christ's spiritual fellowship, there was available precisely that sense of mystic union with the divine which people had sought in vain in the pagan rites. In the teaching of the Cross there was that promise and forgiveness and renewal, that hope of 'salvation' and 'grace' which the ancient world craved.

So Christianity offered people all that they were dimly seeking – and at an entirely new level. The rapid rise and spread of the new faith was itself a testimony to the way in which Christianity fulfilled that 'God-shaped blank' in the heart of the ancient world.

Facts, such as these, deserving, of course, much fuller treatment for an appreciation of their full force and cogency, are coupled with numerous 'practical' considerations that also indicate how timely, in an historical sense, was Christ's arrival on this planet.

Christianity was a world-religion. It sought universality. Yet how could it reach the world? For its expansion it needed a world more or less unified and at peace. It needed roads and systems of communication. It needed a world in which there was at least a semblance of law and order.

Remarkably enough, all these conditions were fulfilled in the first century of our era. In the swift growth of Christianity they played their part.

But these conditions had been ripening over a long time. When Alexander the Great was alleged to have sat down and wept because there were no more worlds to conquer, he little dreamt that his conquests had paved the way for the far-reaching unity that Rome was to bring to the Empire by the time of Jesus.

As though in readiness for the transmission of Christianity, we find in every important district Roman roads providing main arteries of traffic and communication. Sea traffic in the Mediterranean was well organised and protected. There were probably more and better facilities for travel in the eastern Mediterranean and the adjoining lands at this period than at any subsequent time until the nineteenth century. A glimpse of Paul's journeys shows how he made use of them. He seems to have kept deliberately to the main roads connecting the main centres of Graeco-Roman civilisation.

The language problem was solved also. Greek provided the universal language that Christianity needed. Even districts which retained the use of local dialects were largely bi-lingual. In Jerusalem, Antioch, Colossae, Ephesus, Philippi, Corinth, and Rome alike, the New Testament could be read and comprehended, and for over three hundred years this remained the case.

Roman jurisprudence, too, running to the farthest province, curbed lawlessness and violence, and provided a universal standard of law, to which a man like Paul could appeal, and which, when occasion arose, could even get him, as a Roman citizen, an audience with Caesar.

In short, surveying the general scene, one gets an impression of seeming unity in the ancient world, with the only elements lacking in that unity being the very ones that Christianity seemed precisely fitted to provide.

For the unity imposed by Rome was external and not organic. Within the strong shell of external authority there existed an impossible moral and spiritual diversity. Apart from their common membership in the Empire, there was no idea, moral, social, or religious that was shared by the rustic of Lycaonia, the intellectual of decadent Athens, or the idolator of

Ephesus. The Empire enclosed its varied elements without amalgamating them.

In the ancient world no human union was durable without a religious bond. The Emperors tried to provide such a bond by promoting the worship of the State and its visible head, but a living religion is one thing and a political contrivance another.

To this world Christianity came with its Gospel of one God, a God towards whom many had been reaching; a Gospel that soon rose above all national qualifications; that could be a force of practical improvement here below, and that looked for its consummation to a world beyond; a Gospel that united the moral and the mystical, the individual and the social sides of life; an historical religion that alone could supply the principles of unity of which the world was in need; and a faith, which, as a matter of historical fact, gave the Empire a new framework of organic unity and which stood not utterly overwhelmed when the Empire went down.

These facts taken in their cumulative force speak for themselves, and, like arrows, point to the truth of Paul's reiterated statements, 'that when the fullness of the time was come, God sent forth his son' (Gal. 14: 4), or again, that it was God's mysterious purpose 'in the fullness of time to gather together all things in one in Christ' (Eph. 1: 10).

When Jesus announced 'the time is fulfilled', his words were fraught with a sense of destiny.

CHAPTER TWENTY

The Clear Mirror

> A Light we can bear to look at … comes to us from a Light we cannot bear to look at.
>
> Evelyn Underhill

We come now to the pivotal question on which our main argument swings. Does the character of Jesus commend itself to us as being in keeping with one who claimed to be uniquely related to God? Is what we know of the character of Jesus suggestive of such a relationship?

We may well begin to answer this momentous question by examining our own reactions to the picture that has been unrolled before us. Has it not been, in itself, highly suggestive?

Recall the position we took up at the commencement of our inquiry. 'We are modern people,' we said. 'We are not prepared to take on trust any traditional view of Jesus. We cannot accept large affirmations that we have not checked.' We made an empirical inquiry. We examined what in fact he had done.

But what emerged was more stirring and full of implication than we had realised, or expected it to be. We saw his place in world-history. We measured his impact on the life of humanity as a whole. We saw the width and worth of the work his teaching had done in the moral conscience. We noted the excellence of his contribution to all that was highest in human culture. With a quickening of our own mind and spirit, we saw the imperishable glory of what he had added to the otherwise mediocre, and frequently tragic, story of the human race. Was it merely a young carpenter who had done all this, or was there the suggestion that higher forces were behind him?

Opposing forces from position after position had obstructed, or caused doubt to fall upon the faith. But as a unique phenomenon, Christianity had a foothold in every land, and to many in every age Jesus had proved a catalyst of the pure fire of God in innumerable souls.

But in conducting this inquiry, we were trying to be objective. We were not being swayed by emotional appeals. No emphasis was being laid on his alleged divinity. Our attention was being held by facts. We were hearing the plain testimony of the human conscience, the clear witness of the human soul. Yet, was all this accountable on the rational assumption that Jesus was just a man, merely a human figure? Or did we perhaps catch ourselves saying, 'Of course this is Jesus, he is different'? In short, did we almost unwittingly to ourselves invest Jesus with a strange 'plus-element'?

Yet if the suggestion of his 'difference', an awareness of a strange 'plus-element' attending him, came to us, did it not come from the facts themselves, and not from any dogmatic supposition arbitrarily introduced?

Further, if we sensed such a 'difference' in Jesus, were we not doing just what the first disciples did? They, too, were conscious of a 'plus-element', the sense of supernatural endowment of which we ourselves have felt aware. But, mark the extraordinary point! While they reached their view by seeing him, we have reached ours by realising what he had done. They had facts to guide them. We have had facts to guide us. But the facts are wholly different ones.

Is not this then in the highest degree curious, that from an accumulation of facts, we begin to think of Jesus as 'different', while his disciples, with wholly dissimilar facts before them thought that he was 'different' too? Why should approaches, from such completely different starting points, converge?

Thus the sense of what, for lack of other terms, we must call the 'Sonship', the 'divinity' of Jesus, comes to humanity from the scrutiny of his life, and the hallowed graciousness of his influence, whereas it came to the disciples from their personal contact with him.

But how can we grapple, in terms amenable to reason, with the problem raised by this recognition of the supernatural in Jesus?

Recall how we have been attempting to do so in recent chapters. We have been exploring the possibility, envisaged alike by religious and philosophical thinkers, that God himself might choose to make himself known. We have, therefore, been considering what is involved in the thought of an incarnation, of a revelation of God in human terms. And we have found actually that a number of facts and attendant considerations wonderfully suggest that the coming of Jesus was such an incarnation, and not to be explained otherwise.

We have noted, for instance, that such an incarnation could only be reasonably effective if certain preconditions were first satisfied. We have concentrated on three such preconditions in our three last chapters.

We must ask indulgence for repetition, because as Athanasius pointed out, when one is dealing with the Christ it is better to err on the side of repetition, rather than run the risk of something important being left out.

Recall then the three matters we predicted would have to be fulfilled before the Messiah could come.

First, we saw that, preparatory to a Messiah's coming, humankind would have to be raised to a level of moral and spiritual perception that would enable them to grasp and transmit something of the Messiah's teaching. Secondly, we noted that they would have to be acquainted with a matrix of ideas that would enable them to understand and interpret the

Messiah's personality and work. Thirdly, we postulated the likelihood that God would make his revelation at a time favourable to its reception and dissemination.

Supposing that such preconditions were fulfilled, then the coming of the Messiah would not be an abrupt intrusion, but in accord with the gradual and evolutionary control of events that we have come to associate with the normal working of Providence.

Consider, then, the astonishment with which we found that once, and once only, in human history these three conditions were satisfied, and demonstrably satisfied— and that at the time of Christ's coming. In our last three chapters we gave the evidence. Now we but tabulate it:

1. In the Old Testament we found precisely the sort of moral and spiritual preparation that fitted the coming of Christ.
2. In the Wisdom and Messianic literature, and in the philosophical conception of the Greek Logos, was the very matrix of thought that enabled Christ's contemporaries to interpret his person and work.
3. In the first century of our era were present all those propitious circumstances that favoured the rise and growth of Christianity.

Would it not have seemed tantalising and ironical if, when all these three preconditions were fully satisfied, no Messiah had come? On the other hand, how inevitably suggestive of a Higher Hand, if, when the stage was set, when expectation ran high, when every circumstance favoured the appearance of the Messiah, one actually came who both claimed the title and was, in actual fact identified as the Messiah by his contemporaries!

Could the fourth point now be established, that Jesus made his claim to have 'come forth from the Father', in terms worthy of the Father, would we not have to say that the circle of evidence was complete and that there was no reasonable doubt possible about the reality of the incarnation? Next to being compulsive, would it not be as far as God could go without actually coercing people's minds?

But how can we establish that the revelation brought to this earth by Jesus was 'worthy of the Father'? Which is easier to believe—that the coming of Christ was an accident, or a revelation; that it was a fortuity, or the fulfilment 'of the eternal purpose that God purposed in Christ Jesus'?

Assuredly, Hegel is right. 'The real attestation of the divinity of Christ, is the witness of one's own spirit, for only spirit can recognise spirit.' But, as we have noted elsewhere, spiritual discernment varies greatly between people, and is, by its very nature, impossible to establish by argument as such. What 'argument' establishes, for instance, the claim of a work of art, or literature, or music, to be a classic? Do we not have to enter the sphere of 'appreciation'? Are we not dependent on what is called a 'value-judgment'?

Let us therefore enter that sphere now, taking for the establishment of a value-judgment on Jesus both the considerations we have already dealt with earlier in this chapter, and a number of affirmations by responsible thinkers that may serve to stimulate and confirm 'the witness of our own spirits'.

We shall assume as the background of our thought the stockpile of evidence accumulated throughout our study, but now into the foreground of our thinking we shall bring particular evidence to show that, in moral perfection and absoluteness of his surrender to the Divine Will, Jesus was uniquely fitted to bring into the world of time God's truth from the eternal world. We shall show, too, that in the experience of people, Jesus has actually had the value of God. He has made them realise God, love God, and enter into a relationship with God with wholly new vividness and reality.

We have already mentioned in Chapter 9 the sinlessness of Jesus, so that neither his friends nor even his foes could convict him of moral blemish. But is not such moral perfection in itself suggestive? Would we not count it a prerequisite in anyone claiming to be a special messenger from God? Could we imagine that for a perfect work God would use an imperfect instrument? Is it not moral excellence that most becomes those who seek to be channels of God's grace? But even in Jesus' case can we sustain the doctrine of moral perfection? Do we like the tone, for instance, of the story of the Syro-phoenician woman? (Mark 7: 24–30). Has it been unduly abbreviated? Or the fierce denunciation of the Pharisees? (Matt. 23). Did the Evangelist make additions? In any case was he not dependent on a memory? Is the story of the cursing of the barren fig-tree (Mark 11: 14) an example of a parable being rendered as a wonder-story?

How far, in short, can we go with J. A. Baker in *The Foolishness of God* in questioning the consensus of New Testament opinion on Jesus' sinlessness? Do we see a rising reticence in the modern mind about affirming anything that may impair Jesus' utter 'oneness with ourselves' in all things? He can only help us as he is like us, they say.

But nowhere does the New Testament present Jesus' moral excellence as meaning his immunity to temptation, but always his complete ability to resist it. 'We have not a high priest that cannot be touched with the feeling of our infirmities', says the Epistle to the Hebrews (4: 15) 'for he was in all points tempted like as we are, yet without sin.'

See, then, how the Apostolic writings deeply emphasise this remarkable feature of Christ's character. 'Who did no sin,' says the Epistle of Peter. 'He who knew no sin,' is the kindred expression of Paul. 'In him is no sin,' says John's first Epistle. 'Without sin,' is the similar description of the Epistle to the Hebrews.

In the Gospels, the evidence direct and indirect is convincing. Pilate, after examining Jesus, declared, 'I find no fault in this just man.' His wife, haunted, even in her dreams, lest her husband should have the blood of Jesus upon his hands, speaks of him as ‘this just person’. Judas, too, who had known Jesus, as Peter had known him, for three intimate years; Judas the very man who would have been glad to justify his treachery by any flaw he could have pointed to Jesus’ character, was forced to declare that the blood which he had betrayed was ‘innocent’.

But what of Jesus himself? He presents his sinlessness not as inability to fall, but as an ability to resist the suggestion of evil and to hurl it away. At no time does he see himself to have failed. We note in his life no awareness of moral fault. He never prays for forgiveness, but he directs others to do so; he expresses no need of reconciliation; he has no sense of transgression, no sense of conflict between himself and God.

This fact becomes the more wonderful when we realise that in the case of all other spiritual leaders, a deepening sense of sin is the unvarying accompaniment of their moral growth. They are conscious of a duel between flesh and spirit, between their own imperfection and God’s holiness, that intensifies at every stage of their moral growth, but in Jesus there is nothing of this. The serenity of his vision of God is never clouded. He lives, and everything shows that he lives, in perfect harmony with the divine will. But how shall we account for this save that he realised the completeness of his at-one-ment with the Father?

The earliest heresy, the Docetic, is suggestive. It was not that a man like Jesus could not be God. It was that one so divine as Jesus, so perfect and without fault, could not be man. He was an appearance rather than a reality.

The heresy was thrown out of the Church. The full humanity of Jesus is rooted in the Gospels. He was ‘tempted in all points like we are, yet without sin’.

It was no life so hidden in God as to be withdrawn from humanity. He knew that goodness was the reconciliation of extremes. He praised the successful, yet mixed with the failures. He shared the purest, highest thoughts with sinners, and rightly guessed unexpected ‘types’ could be comprehending. Noblest among others he mixed without harm among the polluted. He identified himself with all knowing God had made them, and he himself would die for them. One with God he was without partiality like God 'making his sun rise on the evil and the good'.

What was his life to look like as the centuries went by? What higher test can there be than to take a life lived out in the first century of our era, and set it alongside the saints and mystics of a later time: men and women who had the advantage of knowing him and starting from the level he had reached? Of the answer there is no doubt. With one voice they have acclaimed his eminence, like an eagle mounting to heights they could never attain, and for even such excellence as they have achieved they claim to owe everything to his grace.

Of course, it may be said that the world's saints and mystics may have their own particular partialities, and terms of reference. What would the intellectuals of humankind think, the savants? On an international scale they too have spoken.

'There is only one figure in all the world of absolute beauty —Christ,' averred the Russian, Dostoevsky. 'I bow before him as the divine manifestation of the highest principles of morality,' proclaimed Goethe, the German poet and thinker. 'God's eternal wisdom which has manifested itself in all things has done so most in the human mind, and supremely in Christ Jesus,' declared the Jewish philosopher Spinoza. 'Jesus,' testified the sceptical Frenchman Renan, 'is the highest of those who show to man whence he is and whither he ought to tend. In him was condensed all that was good and elevated in our nature.' 'The life of Christ,' declares the British mathematician and scholar A. N. Whitehead, 'has the decisiveness of a supreme ideal, and that is why the history of the world divides at that point of time.'

Such testimonies then from representative and liberal minds, who have some claim to be typical of humanity at his intellectual best, speak of Jesus in startling terms. They say he has presented the world with something 'decisive', 'absolute', ‘eternal’. Nor are these overstatements, for it will be recognised that in still higher and more emphatic terms could be expressed the unequivocal convictions about Jesus that uphold the universal Church.

If we inquire, now, how Jesus has given this sublime impression we discover at least six truths, all of which suggest how pure was the light that shone through him. Let us tabulate them briefly:

1. Jesus has given the world its loftiest ethical ideals. ‘Attempt to reach righteousness by any way except that of Jesus,’ cried Matthew Arnold, ‘and you will find your mistake.’
2. Jesus has made people believe in the possibility of moral victory and renewal. ‘Again and again I have been tempted to give up the struggle,’ declared George Tyrrell, ‘but always the figure of that strange man upon the Cross, has sent me back to fight again.’
3. Jesus has given the world its most moving and effective instance of love and sacrifice. ‘The Cross of Jesus,’ says Dr Fosdick, ‘is the most subduing, impressive, and significant, fact in the spiritual history of man.’
4. Jesus has immeasurably heightened men and women’s estimate of their own worth and possibilities. ‘Jesus alone in history,’ said Emerson, ‘estimated the true greatness of man.’
5. Jesus has, by his historical resurrection, and by the spiritual values which he has made real, lifted unnumbered multitudes out of the fear of death, and has made inviting and meaningful the prospect of a life beyond the grave.
6. Finally, and most important of all, Jesus has given the world its most significant and compelling idea of God. The word ‘God’ is only a picture frame; all its value depends on the quality of the portrait that the frame encloses. It was the distinction of Jesus that he lived such a life that the best picture we have of God is to say He is like Jesus.

You can look down on a lake in Switzerland and see a great deal more than the lake. You can see mirrored in its clear waters the dark green forests leading up to snow-capped mountains, and the procession of the clouds, and by night the shining stars. You can, in the same way, look at the man Jesus, and see more than a man, for mirrored in his goodness, and the total mystery of his being, you may be taken above manhood until you wonder if what is reflected in him is God.

CHAPTER TWENTY ONE

Finality

The glory of Christ is for those who can discern it.

Alfred North Whitehead

We set out to make a fair-minded and objective study of Jesus, but we find ourselves with a number of facts on our hands that do not submit to explanation, and refuse to be honestly explained away. They have to be accounted for. The Church says, 'O God, Thy hand is here.' Can they be accounted for otherwise?

We found a number of facts in the earlier section of this book that related to the impact and influence of Jesus. We examined and tested these facts. We found them very suggestive, certainly undeniable, and plainly, humanly speaking, unaccountable.

In the next section we saw Christianity advancing through storms that might well have been expected to overwhelm it. Repeatedly one thought the faith would founder. But it sailed on, even though with torn sails, decks awash, and mutiny, so to speak, among the crew.

In our last sequence of studies we have had to face the unaccountable. Apart from saying again, 'O God, Thy hand was here,' how can we explain the evidence of the Old Testament that seemed to be preparing the way for Christ? Or how can we explain the build-up of the sense of expectancy that preceded the Messiah's coming? Further, was it merely coincidence that he came at the most opportune time in all history for the planting, rootage, and growth of Christianity?

Can it be imagined that the world will ever look upon such a sequence of facts again? Does it not set Jesus in lonely eminence?

When Jesus actually came, he was a man of flesh and blood like the rest of us. But he lived a human life in a God-like way His life, death, and resurrection was utterly congruent with the New Testament faith that 'God was in him', and that, as far as his humanity could express it, God was manifest in him.

'I will found my Church,' he said, and the most daring of all dreams was carried into effect, and instead of being confined to a faithful few has spread over all the world, and when thus exposed to unequalled strain, has remained remarkably resilient, capable of renewing, and re-shaping itself, and yet obviously utterly dependent on its original Founder at every stage of its ongoing life.

Today if people looks for a viable faith can they do better than choose Christianity? Consider some of the essentials we might look for in an ideal religion.

We would expect it to be free of narrow particularity binding it to time and place. Christianity has this freedom.

A religious leader like Mohammed is plainly the product of a particular age and culture. No one could say this of Jesus. Nothing that he taught depended on special conditions of culture, date, race, or government. His outlook owed little to the circumstances in which he grew up. 'It is more startling,' writes Professor C. F. D. Moule in *Is Christ Unique*?, 'that the outlook of Jesus does not seem to have derived from his upbringing and environment; and what his disciples found in him was contrary to their expectations.'

No one in the Empire of Tiberius Caesar thought as he did and even when he meets with the religious groups of his own race and church, his thoughts are not their thoughts, nor his ways their ways. He dwarfs them.

They were concerned with particularities of ritual, legalism, race. He is concerned with the timeless and the universal. His God loves the whole world. Jesus' family is all humankind. His ethical principles apply to any age or place. He holds time and eternity itself in a total vision.

It was a Jewish scholar, Dr Klausner, who said that Jesus brought a conception of God and of morals applicable to all humankind, and because these clashed with Jewish national peculiarities they rejected him.

In a literal sense Jesus created his own environment. He called it the Kingdom of God. It was a timeless concept, so that people in all generations, and in all lands, and even in the realm beyond time, could belong to it. It was the Kingdom of his Father. Jesus lived in it, and it lived in him. Therefore, to be 'in him' as the New Testament put it, was to be 'in the Kingdom'. It was a Kingdom that was to be 'an everlasting Kingdom'.

Such a thought challenges an age committed to modernity in all things. Some consider it humiliating for people to exist under the spiritual Lordship of any single person, especially one who walked the earth so long ago. May not the time be coming for him to be superseded and a new Kingdom arise? Granted Jesus was a torch bearer. But torches go out, or pass to other hands!

But there is confusion of thought here. The revelation of God in Christ cannot be repeated. Christ once manifest remains manifest. If the Gospel was God's word to humanity, it remains God's word to humanity. True once, the passage of time does not influence its truth.

When Rodin wanted to represent a Thinker he sculptured a man, apart, alone. He gave him no clothes to denote any period.

He gave him no historical setting. He knew thought would go on as long as human beings go on. Still more emphatically Christians believe that 'Jesus Christ is the same, yesterday, today, and forever', and that to believe in him is to be incorporated into his life and into his Kingdom.

It was the liberal critic, Renan, who said in Vie de, 'Whatever the expected phenomena of the future, Jesus will not be surprised. His worship will constantly renew its youth. His sufferings will soften the best hearts, and all the ages will proclaim that among the sons of men there is none born greater than Jesus.'

The evolutionary mystic Pierre Teilhard de Chardin, author of *Hymn of the Universe* goes to the ultimate limit, making Jesus the culminating figure of evolution itself. 'Lord Jesus,' he wrote, 'you are the centre towards which all things are moving.' Bishop David Jenkins, puts it, 'The person who is designated Jesus is at the very centre of our understanding of God, man, and the universe.'

A ribbon of film that is once exposed to the sun must keep ever afterwards its decisive encounter with the light, so the rule of God made evident to the world in Jesus' life, death, and resurrection, must ever remain, with the terms of it, like mathematical laws, outside chronological change.

A further feature of an ideal religion would surely be its ability to provide spiritual satisfaction so that it would enhance the idea of life's worth and meaning and deepen a sense of God's reality.

Has it not been one of the sublime achievements of Jesus that he has awakened and deepened the spiritual sense of countless multitudes? Millions have had their lives changed by contemplating the cross and meditating on the one who hung and suffered there. The thought that 'He loved me and gave himself for me' has dramatically invested their lives with a new dignity, worth, and value.

Still more life-enriching has been the fact of the resurrection. It is impossible to explain the power of

Christianity without it. Not only did it establish people's faith in Christ, but it added a new dimension to human thinking. It hallowed life. It added a new incentive to lives of sacrifice and service. It has meant for millions 'being steadfast, immovable, always abounding in the work of the Lord, knowing that their labour was not in vain in Him'. It has meant a decisive change, not in God's love for humanity, but in people's understanding of the divine love, and the eternal purpose, purposed in Christ Jesus.

These matters are not amenable to 'proof. But those who have attested them, undoubtedly believed them true, and there has been an immense weight of 'inner evidence' from those who have perceived them true, and experienced their truth through the power of the Holy Spirit.

Moreover, if a country once brought to greatness by Christianity, loses that faith, it may somehow be seen to lose the secret of its greatness. Given the choice then between two philosophies—one that affirmed life's meaning and worth, developed conscience and character, spread love and happiness, and another philosophy that tended to empty life of meaning, increased cynicism, spread greed, and increased stress of every kind, would it not be philosophically sound to choose the former? Even scientifically sound, too, in so far as a positive result is preferable to a negative?

So we come to two important demands we might make on any religion claiming to be ideal. We would look for it to provide both the highest idea of humanity, and the highest idea of God. It is the central affirmation of Christianity that both may be seen in Christ.

While this is a matter that is usually accepted or rejected, in proportion to faith or the lack of it, it is not something that cannot be brought nearer our understanding by reason. To vindicate its underlying meaning, or at least to get closer to it, let us recall two propositions from a modern thinker, and then consider each of the propositions separately.

‘If, in Jesus Christ, God lived on earth a human life,’ said Dr Temple in *Christus Veritas*, ‘then it must be true that in Jesus Christ we see two things. First, one adequate presentation of God, as far as the human mind is concerned, for it shows us God in terms of our own experience. Secondly, one adequate presentation of man—when glorified by the in-dwelling of God.’

Is it possible that Jesus satisfies both these conditions? Do we, in fact, find that Jesus gives humankind its most adequate presentation of God?

While earlier in our study, in Chapter 9, we found that ‘God had nowhere left Himself without witness,’ did we not also find that this witness seemed to have been stronger and better attested in the Old Testament than in any other Scripture, and that the Hebrews had been brought to a knowledge of God progressively, so that they had a fuller and more satisfying idea of him than any other people? In Chapter 19 we also saw the height to which this revelation attained.

But the conclusion that was forced upon us then was that Jesus crowned and completed the Old Testament idea of God; that he himself was the unique figure in whom the whole history of Hebrew religion culminated, and that, since his coming, Christians have never been able to think of God in higher terms than to say ‘God was in Jesus’.

The importance of the confession ‘Jesus is Lord,’ says Dr A. M. Ramsey, in *God, Christ and the World*, ‘is not only that Jesus is divine, but that God is Christlike, and in him was no un-Christlikeness at all.’

In Rome, a mirror, conveniently placed, reflects perfectly a masterpiece of Michelangelo’s that is painted on the ceiling. Visitors no longer have to peer awkwardly to behold the painting above them. The mirror brings it within the natural focus of their eyes.

It is the testimony of Christian experiences that illustrates the truth about Jesus. He is the mirror of God. Can we in fact grasp the thought of God, or envisage him save as we see him reflected in Christ? We may affirm with Paul that 'God who commanded the light to shine out of darkness, has shined in our hearts, to give the light of the glory of God in the fact of Christ Jesus' (2 Cor. 4: 6).

We move on to the second proposition, therefore, 'That in Jesus we have one adequate presentation of humanity—when man is glorified by the indwelling of God.'

Again, there is a powerful consenus of opinion that Jesus is the supreme revelation who presents us with ideals of character that cannot be bettered. Here is what Tertullian meant by saying 'the soul of man is by nature "Christian"'. It is what all people at their best might wish to achieve. This is strongly confirmed in experience, for as we approximate to Jesus we have inward persuasions that we are becoming the sort of people God himself wishes us to be. In short Jesus presents us with humanity in finest definition.

Nor has this view been confined to those of orthodox belief. There is a widespread human conscience that in the Christian character lies the answer to most human problems, as in the absence of it we find their cause. 'Not even an unbeliever,' said John Stuart Mill, 'could find a better translation of the rule of virtue from the abstract to the concrete, than so to live that Christ would approve his life.'

Acceptance of these facts, then, logically establishes the finality of Christianity. If we have been given an adequate knowledge of God what more do we need? What would be the use of asking for a fuller knowledge of God than we could receive? Similarly, if we find in Jesus the highest conceivable definition of humanity, what more again could we look for?

When a religion offers us the purest idea of God that we can receive, and the highest pattern of virtue that we can envisage, its finality seems established. And how could this have been made available save by an Incarnation?

CHAPTER TWENTY TWO

Jesus Speaks for Himself

> Better to rend our clothes with a great cry of 'Blasphemy' as Caiaphas did in the Judgment Hall, or to lay hands on him as his kinsmen did, and try and get him away quietly, than to stupidly tone it down.
>
> G. K. Chesterton

No words have been studied so deeply, or have affected people so powerfully, as the words of Jesus. To come to them now, after industriously tracing their influence and exploring other's views of them, is like coming up from a subway to the freshness of the open sky.

There is a power in these words by which one's whole attitude to living and dying may be changed. To study the records of the Bible Society, or simply to arrange, as the Gideons do, to leave the Gospels about in hotel bedrooms, or in the wards of hospitals, is to learn that they have their own eloquence and their own way of changing human lives.

To concentrate on the words of Jesus in a life-time's preaching, or to work on them over many years as translators do, is to feel their spirit and life. 'The whole material is extraordinarily alive,' says J. B. Phillips, 'it has the ring of truth.' 'My work changed me,' says Dr E. V. Rieu, 'I came to the conclusion that these documents bear the seal of the Son of Man and of God. They are the Magna Carta of the human spirit.'

Yet Jesus was a man. The New Testament never attempts to treat his humanity as unreal. How could we be expected to 'follow in his steps' if he had not experienced the challenge of life to the full?

We see him in the world of his day. Individuals, groups, and crowds are drawn to life. Here is the topography of first-century Palestine. Here the political, social, and religious milieu of his time is authentically portrayed. To suppose that such verisimilitude was ever concocted is incredible.

It is the very realism of Jesus' humanity that has caused a variety of writers to look at him with fresh eyes and to seek to interpret him differently. Uninhibited by Christian beliefs, they have featured him as a purely ethical teacher, as a mistaken apocalyptist, as a model for successful businessmen, as the mouthpiece of the Church of the second century, as a myth, as a champion of social reform, and so on.

Such reconstructions have their own interest. But their variety indicates the impossibility of accounting for Jesus on naturalistic lines. They turn back the quest for the meaning of Jesus to the evidences of the Gospels themselves.

It is easy to assume that since Jesus was a man, he was someone like ourselves. 'Jesus reached his high excellence as a man,' said Stopford Brooke, 'and by a man's power alone, and it is a clear disclosure that our nature is capable of reaching such a height.' A direct approach to the Gospels themselves makes us less confident. Jesus is far ahead of human nature as we know it.

The way people react to him in itself sets him apart. Perhaps long familiarity with the Gospels has taken the edge off our surprise at the way he is approached, spoken to, regarded. Is it just literary skill that gives Jesus always the central place, and causes people to react to him as though he were different, special, holy? Or is the most reasonable, and natural, conclusion that Jesus was just such a person as would create this impression, and make this impact? Has anyone else lifted such a variety of people to such experiences, feelings, and aliveness to God?

Astonishing things are expected of him. Astonishing things are said of him, still more astonishing things are said by him.

When he is but an infant being presented like any other baby in the Temple, the aged Simeon takes him in his arms and says, 'This child is to be a sign that men reject. Many in Israel shall stand or fall because of him, and thus the secret thoughts of many hearts will be laid bare.' Strange words that a child should grow up not only to read the secrets of human hearts, but to cause them to read their own. Yet he did grow up to cause people such deep heart-searchings as they never expected to experience. So we find Peter drew back from him so astonished that he said, 'Depart from me, for I am a sinful man, O Lord'; and Zacchaeus was called down from his perch in the sycamore tree so shaken in conscience as to give half his goods to feed the poor, and to restore money taken by false accusation four times over.

At the age of twelve, when others thought him 'lost', he had been entirely at home in the Temple, 'both hearing the scholars and asking them questions so that they marvelled at his understanding and answers'.

'What made you search?' he asked his mother. 'Did you not know that I was bound to be in my Father's house?' Even so, he went back with them to Nazareth and was obedient to them.

What was the mystery of the hidden years that followed of which we know nothing, save that the Father claimed them. When at about thirty years of age Jesus came to be baptised by John the Baptist, he heard the call of approval that sealed his destiny: 'Thou art my Beloved Son. With thee I am well pleased.'

The account of the Temptations must have come direct from the lips of Jesus. If he had not told us we might not have suspected that he knew persuasions so alluring that he personified their force in the graphic phrase 'tempted of the Devil'. What was to be the nature of his Messiahship? To satisfy with God-given powers humanity's material wants? To claim heaven's might for the protection and advancement of heaven's cause? Or to take the path of the conqueror as young Alexander had done, and win the kingdoms of the world and the glory of them by military might? He chose instead to inaugurate God's Kingdom by a complete surrender to God's will, and trust that a slow diffusion of his spirit would cause others to seek it as the supreme good.

What makes the Temptations remarkable is the level of possibility they imply. Was there anything Christ could not have achieved if he had made it his heart's desire? Who then, save Jesus, would have seen the Kingdom of God as the one thing worth living and dying for, and, knowing his own powers, have chosen the path of sacrifice rather than ambition and unflinchingly kept to it to the end?

In the familiar synagogue of Nazareth he opened the scroll of the prophet Isaiah at a passage that described the Messiah's mission of saviourhood: 'The spirit of the Lord is upon me because he has anointed me; he has sent me to announce good news to the poor, to proclaim liberation for prisoners, and recovery of sight to the blind; to let the broken victims go free.' Then, with all eyes fixed upon him, he says, 'Today in your very hearing this text has come true' (Luke 4: 21).

There was a general stir of admiration, we read, and they wondered at his gracious words. His teaching was acceptable enough. But could they accept 'the scandal of particularity' and his lowly origin, 'Is not this Joseph's son?' they asked.

In essence that dilemma is with us yet. Many accept the compelling wisdom of Jesus' moral teaching, but impatiently reject his transcendent status. But was Jesus unerringly right in his moral teaching, and hopelessly mistaken about his divine call? We must be guided by our views of the teaching, and still more by our views of the Teacher.

'His word was with power.' He does not depend on the Scripture's absolute authority as the Rabbis did. When he chooses, he questions it, amends it. He does not refer back to his original call as the prophets did, to say with delegated authority, 'Thus saith the Lord'. He speaks in his own name, 'I say unto you'. This emphatic personal authority is a significant feature of Jesus' ministry both as healer and as teacher. He approaches the bedside of Jairus' little daughter, and takes her by the hand and says with infinite tenderness, 'Little girl, I say to you, arise.' He takes his position on the Mount to declare with greater authority than Moses the new laws of the Kingdom, and the 'I say unto you' has the force of finality.

Those who speak of the 'simple' ethics of the Sermon on the Mount have hardly taken the measure of that teaching, of the momentous claims implicit in it.

The commandments of Moses were to the Hebrew nation the final summary of the moral Law. Upon them their faith centred, and they were sure that only in keeping them could their nation find blessing. Yet Jesus stood before his countrymen and declared that it had, in a measure, served its purpose, and must take its place under a higher law of which he himself was the legislator, so that he could establish one part of it, and supplement, or abrogate, another, giving no authority, save that of his own word.

Take but a few instances: 'You have heard that it was said to the men of old, "You shall not kill: and whoever kills shall be liable to judgment," but I say to you that everyone who is angry with his brother shall be liable to judgment.' 'You have heard that it was said, "You shall not commit adultery," but I say to you that everyone who looks at a woman lustfully has already committed adultery with her in his heart.' 'You have heard that it was said, "You shall love your neighbour and hate your enemy," but I say to you, Love your enemies and pray for those who persecute you, so that you may be sons of your Father who is in heaven, for he makes his sun rise on the evil and on the good, and sends rain on the just and on the unjust' (Matt. 5).

During the Maccabean wars thousands of pious Jewish soldiers allowed themselves to be cut to pieces on the Sabbath day rather than break the Law by fighting. But Jesus declared 'The Sabbath was made for man, and not man for the Sabbath.' Nor in his legislating did Jesus consider he was destroying the Law but rather expressing its highest intention. Far past Laws of the outward, visible act, went his probing of the secret thoughts and motives of the mind and heart.

Who is this, we ask, who claims such authority, and compares those who obey him to the wise who build on rock, and those who reject him to the fools who build on sand?

The startling thing is that when we submit the judgments of Jesus to the tribunal of our own hearts and consciences, we know he is ineffably right. But who is this who so unhesitatingly and unerringly can appeal from himself to us, and whose reference is to no God of the past, but to the ever-present Father who gives authority to the Son? 'He must have regarded himself,' says Ernst Kasemann, 'as the very instrument of that living spirit of God.'

Let us consider further aspects of this teaching.

It seems clear that the mournful pictures of Jesus in mediaeval art do not capture Jesus' victorious spirit. The Beatitudes, or, as we may describe them, the beautiful attitudes, do that more accurately. Time and again the words 'grace', 'wisdom', and 'authority' are used to describe his teaching, and one of the reasons must be that the teaching puts into words the very attitudes that graced the character of the Teacher. He knew the joy of the humble, the happiness of the merciful, the reward of the pure in heart, the bittersweet of saviourhood. He was ready to 'go the second mile'. He was always the volunteer of whom the stern centurion, Life, could never ask too much.

It was the joy of his life to win people for God. There was never so radiant a leader. The faces of the disciples light up at his approach. The description of John is like a snapshot that could have been taken on many occasions, 'Then were the disciples glad when they saw the Lord.' He delights in his work as a shepherd who calls his friends and neighbours to rejoice with him over a sheep that is rescued, or as a father who throws open his arms to welcome home an erring son.

It was the distinction of Jesus to discern the inmost secret of life itself. That secret was love. Not love as a passion, not love as an emotion, but love as the creative force in the universe radiating from the very nature of God. He was himself the embodiment in history of the love of the one Father of all. None loved like this one. With every characteristic of an heroic leader, he was yet gifted with a love that embraced the whole human family.

It was love that accounted alike for the tenderness and the severity of his teaching, for as he taught with loving patience the truths of the Kingdom, so he spoke with utmost sternness to those who disregarded that Kingdom, despised his little ones, and deserted the weak and broken.

It is a mark of rank in human nature when such teaching and attitudes awaken a response, and sometimes considerable numbers were drawn by the magnetism of Jesus to come back for more. We read of those who were prepared, on at least one occasion, to go as long as three days without food to share the privilege of Jesus' teaching. In the Gospel phrase 'to what can we compare it?'

Some music is transitory, the passing expression of a trend. Other music lasts, and repetition only increases the taste for it. Some thoughts are ephemeral. They have their headline and cease to matter. Other thoughts touch that which is immortal in the human spirit. Such were certainly the thoughts of Jesus. Of any teaching of his William Watson's words are true,

This savours not of death
It has the relish of immortality.

Is it possible to be taken beyond the teaching to the Teacher? 'Studying the earliest biographies and interpreters of Jesus,' says Evelyn Underhill, 'we find it was neither his moral transcendence, nor his special teaching which struck men most. It was rather the growing certainty that something was here expressed, in and through humanity which was yet other than humanity.'

There is the suggestion of power and of limitless resources implicit in every reference to him. He dwarfs strong personalities into insignificance. 'He goes before his disciples and they are amazed, and as they follow they are afraid.' Even those who opposed him bitterly had to acknowledge his mighty works, and unable to say—without looking absurd for opposing him—that his power was from above, they said 'he was in league with the mightiest powers of darkness, the Prince of Devils' (Mark 3: 22).

If, as Harnack pointed out, 'a great personality is to be understood, not only by his words and deeds, but by the impression he creates on those who come under his influence', we may well ask what must have been the force and elevation of personality that are reflected in the fact that some loved Jesus so deeply they were ready to die for him, and others hated him so bitterly that they killed him?

Such was his holiness and power that his disciples saw him as the perfect channel for the divine love, a Revealer who was one with the Reality Revealed. He irradiated love and it found natural expression in works of love. The Kingdom of God was manifest in Jesus both in word and in power.

'Jesus passed along the Sea of Galilee,' writes Matthew, 'and Jesus went up into the hills and sat down there. And great crowds came to him, bringing with them the lame, the maimed, the blind, the dumb, and many others, and they laid them down at his feet, and he healed them, so that the throng wondered … and glorified God. There were evenings, long after the sun had gone down, when it seemed the whole city was gathered at the door, and he healed many'.

Such unsparing demands drained Jesus of power, but if power flowed from him it equally flowed to him. 'Rising a great while before dawn,' says Mark, 'he went to a lonely place and there prayed.' No one has ever prayed with such intensity. It revitalised him. On one occasion his observing disciples commented that his very face was changed. On another the disciples saw Jesus suffused in a nimbus of awe inspiring light. On another occasion one of his disciples heard him say, 'Father, I thank Thee that Thou hearest me at all times'. His disciples longed to pray in the same way, 'Lord,' they said to him, 'teach us to pray.' So clearly they prayed as humanity to God, while he prayed as Son.

In the light of such experiences we understand Matthew Arnold's question:

Was Christ a man,
Then let us see
If we can be
Such men as he?

Mark (2: 1–12) records the healing of a paralysed man, but it was not the physical cure that astounded the onlookers but the deeper psychosomatic healing, 'My son your sins are forgiven.'

Here was a claim that, as his opponents immediately saw, was tantamount to a divine claim. 'Who can forgive sins,' they asked, 'except God only?' But this was no chance utterance, we need to link it with Jesus' still more astounding claim to be the veritable Judge of the quick and the dead (Matt. 21: 42–45; Luke 12: 8–9; Luke 20: 7–18; Matt. 24: 31). Claims of such awe-inspiring magnitude exceed all Messianic ideas, and place Jesus at the right hand of God himself.

Who is this, we have to ask, who in the most accredited documentary records sets aside the accepted authorities of his Church; who claims for his words a final authority; who asserts that on our love and obedience to him depends their final destiny; who looks into the future and sees all the nations of the world gathered before his judgment seat and who presents himself as humanity's Judge and Saviour?

These are no statements that we can take or leave as we please. They are his terms. He concentrates humanity's gaze upon himself. He expects obedience. For his sake, if necessary, they are to sever the sacred ties of home and kinship. He asks, as though it were the most natural thing in the world, that they must live for him alone. They must be like a merchant who having found one shimmering, priceless pearl, gives all that he has to possess it.

Is it possible to read these Gospel evidences without seeing that we face in Jesus a Person in whom the relationship of human to God, and of God to human, appears to be distinct from anything to be found even in saints and prophets?

We seem presented with a figure that is both human and more than human. If we imagine ourselves at the Crucifixion knowing nothing but the dread drama before us, we see a man whose life-blood is ebbing away in agony. A mission that promised so much has ended in this. He had hoped to reorientate humankind to the divine will. He had sublimely led the way. But all he had come to do and be, and even the Kingdom of God on earth was a shattered dream. Rejected, forsaken, spat upon, crowned with thorns, was there any sorrow like his sorrow? Yet this is the moment he chose to pray: 'Father, forgive them for they know not what they do.' Does this quality of forgiving, pleading, love, belong to the rest of us? Does the frame of humanity accommodate Jesus, or is this the spirit of God?

We cannot portray Jesus as other than he is. Portraiture has to be true to scale. Michelangelo visited the studio of Raphael when the younger painter was absent. On the easel was a picture of Christ that Raphael was painting. Michelangelo made his comment. He took a brush and wrote '*Amplius*—Larger'.

Is this what the New Testament compels us to do? One school of scholars (represented by Wellhausen and Weiss and their varied successors) insists on Jesus' humanity. He was an ethical teacher. The transcendental is cut out. Another (represented by Schweitzer and his followers) fastens on the very elements the others discard. They concentrate on the supernatural, apocalyptic elements of his divine nature.

Plainly both groups cannot be right. They cancel each other out, or perhaps we should say they supplement each other, and together secure what the Gospels present, namely the mystery of the divine and the human both meeting in Christ.

Go back to the disciples at Caesarea Philippi. Calvary was hidden in the future. There was no knowledge of God's verdict on his Suffering Servant supplied by the resurrection. In that Greek city Jesus asked his disciples, 'Who do you say that I am?' Peter gave the answer of the apostolic group, 'Thou art the Christ, the Son of the Living God,' and Jesus answered him, 'Blessed art thou Simon Baqona, for flesh and blood has not revealed this to you but my Father who is in heaven' (Matt. 16: 17).

Humanly speaking what facts had the disciples to go on? The supreme fact that into the here and now had come a man who lived totally for God, whose belief in God determined all he said and did, and who daily made the power of God and the wisdom of God a reality to their own souls.

Without some such relationship of Sonship they could not account for the Person before them. Did not his very prayers use that particular family word '*Abba*—Father' with undertones of affection not employed by any other lips?[45]

After Caesarea Philippi,[46] Jesus increasingly speaks of God as Father, but always the word is used with a vivid and sacred sense of reality and revelation, either in prayer, or directly to his disciples. It means too much to be lightly used.

---

[45] See C. F. D. Moule, *The Phenomenon of the New Testament*, pp. 48, 67.

[46] See T. W. Manson, *The Teaching of Jesus*.

Such awareness of direct filial relationship finds expression in one of the most accredited passages in the whole of the New Testament. 'All things,' says Jesus, 'have been delivered unto me of my Father, and no one knoweth the Son save the Father; neither doth any know the Father save the Son and he to whomsoever the Son willeth to reveal him' (Matt. 11: 27; Luke 10: 22). Here the word translated 'knoweth' bears an intense meaning such as 'knows fully' or 'understands wholly'. But what of the august solemnity of such a claim?

This passage gives us the most important and characteristic thought of Jesus concerning his own relationship to God. It suggests a range of consciousness limitless in its extension, a mutuality of love and knowledge, a sense of affinity and oneness that none other could share.

Such an utterance could only have fallen from the lips of one who had passed through the highest and most wonderful spiritual experiences; who had seen veil after veil between God and himself going down, until he stood in the immediate presence of the Most High, knowing that it was God's will that was done by him, God's word that was spoken by him. Realising, in short, that the kinship was so close, the identity so real, that in human language only the word 'Sonship' could describe it.

In the Fourth Gospel we get this, the deepest and most sacred faith of Jesus, receiving the ampler exposition that he most naturally gave to his most spiritual followers. It is the unveiling of the most vivid truth in the inner consciousness of Jesus, and with compelling emphasis the relationship is stressed. 'He that hath known me hath known my Father also; I came out from the Father into the world, again I leave the world and go unto the Father.' Certain passages make explicit the astounding claim to have pre-existed with the Father from all time. 'Verily I say unto you, before Abraham was I am.' 'Father, glorify me with the glory that I had with Thee before the world began.'

Truly the more the uniqueness of Jesus' personality is perceived, the more it baffles analysis.

So our quest into the mystery of mysteries draws to its conclusion. But what is that conclusion to be? In our first chapter we asked, 'What can modern people believe about Jesus?' In all subsequent chapters we have been accumulating the evidence on which an answer can be based. Now certain conclusions seem inescapable.

Jesus is the one transcendent figure who has given humankind its highest interpretation of life's significance, here and hereafter. The best we know of humanity and the best we know of God are alike revealed in him.

A life like his, followed by an influence so hallowed and eternal, must be either an incredible fortuity or a divinely intended revelation. Was he an intruder or a messenger? Did Jesus 'just happen'? Was he the product of a blind, chance happening in a world that never purposed him, and that cared nothing for him? Or were the disciples on the trail of a tremendous truth when they accepted the Old Testament revelation of God, as the Creator of the world and the Lord of history, and then went on to acclaim Jesus as his supreme revealer?

If they were right then, their verdict is right still, although we ourselves may seek to state the meaning of Jesus in different categories of thought—provided we could find them.

Meanwhile, the thought-forms of the New Testament have timeless significance, as frameworks of thought, from which the truth they enclose is separable. Phraseology has sometimes to be decoded before we can arrive at its abiding meaning.

Recall then some of the categories of thought that the New Testament writers use to express their convictions about Jesus. He is the long promised Messiah, the supernatural figure in whom the whole story of revealed religion culminates, say the Synoptic Gospels. He is the Logos, the divine Reason of Greek thought, says the Fourth Gospel, 'full of grace and truth'. He is the incarnate Wisdom says the Epistle to the Hebrews, 'reflecting the glory of God and bearing the very stamp of his nature'. The Epistles of Paul speak of him 'who is the image of the invisible God' (Col. 1: 15), who was 'equal with God, but emptied himself to become as men are, and being as all men are, he was humbler yet, even to accepting death on the Cross. But God raised him on high and gave him the name that is above every name so that all beings in the heavens, the earth, and in the underworld, should bend the knee at the name of Jesus, and every tongue should acclaim Jesus Christ as Lord to the glory of God the Father' (Phil. 2: 7–11).

Here the changing categories of thought do not mean changes of underlying conviction. They are attempts to make plain a truth too big for one mode of expression, and all point to one historic figure through whom, as through a prism, there shone the authentic radiance of the Eternal to spread and become the light of the world.

But how true are these statements to what Jesus would himself have said, and did, in fact, say? We ask, as the disciples once did: 'If you are the Christ, tell us plainly'. We are people of secular cities and not at home with the terms of mysticism and theology found in sanctuaries and studies, but rather with the terms of the workshop floor, the laboratory, the courtroom, the atmosphere of fact and precise statement.

Even at such a level the Gospels meet us. We find Jesus after a brief, but completely unique ministry, standing in a courtroom at Jerusalem on trial for his life. He is arraigned on a charge of alleged blasphemy, of claiming to be the Messiah, of being so knowledgeable of God's mind and will that he could claim a filial relationship and speak of himself as God's 'Son'.

In the centre of the court stands the highest representative of the Jewish Church, Caiaphas, the High Priest. To Jesus he applies the solemn Oath of the Testimony: 'I adjure you by the living God.' 'Now if,' says the Mishna, the Jewish Law, 'one shall adjure you by one of the Divine titles, behold, you are bound to answer.'

Consider, therefore, what the three Synoptic Gospels record: 'And the High Priest said unto him, "I adjure you by the Living God, that thou tell us plainly if thou art the Christ the Son of God?"

'And Jesus affirmed, "Thou has spoken it. Hereafter ye shall see the Son of Man sitting at the right hand of power, and coming in the clouds of heaven." Then the High Priest rent his clothes, saying, "Ye have heard the blasphemy! What need have we for any further witnesses?" ' (Matt. 26: 63–65).

By his own testimony under oath that he was the Messiah, Jesus was passed from the High Priest to Pilate, and thence to crucifixion.

Nineteen troubled centuries, lit by the gleams of the Gospels, have passed since that claim was made and that verdict delivered. We now know that Caiaphas had his own reasons for engineering a verdict that would result in a capital sentence. Despite his words, therefore, we have called 'further witnesses'. As time goes on they still come forward and evidence accumulates. Even as this is written, over one-third of the inhabitants of the globe believe that Caiaphas was wrong and that Jesus was right. What are we to think? Should the verdict of Caiaphas stand, or should it be wiped out?

No one can answer for another. Taking the evidence as a whole: What is your Verdict?

PART FOUR:

Twenty-first Century Developments

The challenge of the 'new atheism' – the acceptance of evolution by mainstream Christianity – creation stories in the Bible and in the thought of Origen of Alexandria, Augustine and Aquinas – the harmony between religious and scientific thinking and the global revival of philosophy of religion.

The third quest of the historical Jesus – the revival of scholarly confidence -Jesus as 'by disciples and eyewitnesses – the Jewish context of Jesus' life and work – his ongoing influence.

Jesus as a Jewish Rabbi and thinker – Jesus as a Prophet in Islam – the Quran's acceptance of his miraculous status – his impact within the Sufi movement. Acceptance and resistance to Jesus in Hindu traditions and Buddhist approaches to Jesus as both a limited and a universal figure.

CHAPTER TWENTY THREE

The Reasonableness of Belief in a Creator God in the Twenty-first Century

Paul Badham

The new atheism

The twenty-first century has begun badly for Christianity in Britain. There has been a surge of enthusiasm for books highly critical of religious belief The most influential of these have been Richard Dawkins' *The God Delusion* and Christopher Hitchens' *God is Not Great,* both of which topped the best-seller lists for months. Both take for granted that belief in God is incompatible with modern science and that from the perspective of modern philosophy, 'there almost certainly isn't a God.' Dawkins' challenge carries great weight, not only through his former position as Professor for the Public Understanding of Science at Oxford University, but as one whose own pioneering scientific work was profoundly and rightly influential. He is also exceptionally good at presenting his case on television and in the media, and he used the one hundred- and-fiftieth anniversary of the publication of Darwin's great work *The Origin of Species* to revive the old canard that religion is opposed to science. His book and those of other so-called 'new atheists' have been subject to detailed criticism by

Alister McGrath, Keith Ward, and many other writers.[47] I do not propose to duplicate their responses here. Instead I shall seek to reply to the central proposition of the new atheism, which is its claim that modern science and philosophy have made the existence of God highly improbable.

Christian fundamentalists and Genesis 1

One reason why the claims of the new atheists seem plausible is that there are today Christians, particularly in the USA, who treat the creation narrative of Genesis i as if it were intended to give us factual information about the mode of divine creation. On the basis of this belief they reject all the findings of evolutionary biology. Richard Dawkins rightly criticises such obscurantism. But regretfully he treats such opinions as if they were widespread among Christians and central to Christian believing. He seems unaware of the fact that it is false to the Christian tradition to treat Genesis i as if it had been intended to give a scientific account of how things began. Over a hundred years ago Bishop Charles Gore documented that belief in the special creation of each species was not an idea drawn from Genesis i. Rather it was a scientific theory of the seventeenth century derived from observations about the limits within which interbreeding is possible. It was first taught by John Ray (1628–1705), affirmed as a kind of dogma by Carl Linnaeus in 1751, and made a basis for popular Christian apologetic by William Paley in 1802.[48]

Though subsequently fundamentalist Christians have proclaimed the fixity of the species as 'Biblical', it was a belief read into, rather than out of, the Bible. Christians had read

---

47 Alister and Joanna McGrath, *The Dawkins Delusion* (London: SPCK, 2007); Tina Beattie, *The New Atheists* (London: DLT, 2007); Keith Ward, *Why There is Almost Certainly a God*.

48 Charles Gore, *Belief in God* (London: John Murray, 1921), pp. 6-7.

Genesis for seventeen hundred years without drawing such a conclusion from it.

The speedy acceptance of evolution by nineteenth-century Christians

The development of geology as a serious science in the nineteenth century and the subsequent formulation of evolutionary theory in biology matter because they showed the falsity of what some nineteenth-century Christians had come to believe both about science and religion. Darwin himself was clear that what his theory critiqued was not belief in a Creator God as such but solely the kind of interventionist God Paley had argued for. The initial opposition to evolutionary theory famously articulated by Bishop Samuel Wilberforce in his debate with Thomas Huxley in i860 was not derived from theological reasoning but came from the world view that Wilberforce shared with many of his scientific contemporaries. Darwin himself thought that there was no necessary conflict between the theory of evolution and belief in a Creator God. Consequently in the second and all subsequent editions of *The Origin of Species* he amended its concluding sentence to make this clear:

> There is grandeur in this view of life, with its several powers, having been originally breathed by the Creator into a few forms or into one; and that, whilst this planet has gone cycling on according to the fixed law of gravity, from so simple a beginning endless forms most beautiful and most wonderful have been, and are being, evolved.

What is more remarkable than Wilberforce's initial opposition is the speed with which the theory of evolution came to be accepted even among 'diehard clergymen'.[49] Certainly by 1884, Darwin's burial in Westminster Abbey was enthusiastically supported by all the religious press as well as by the national dailies, who additionally took the view that Darwin had been 'shabbily treated' by a political establishment which had withheld the knighthood or peerage his achievements so richly deserved.[50] It was therefore particularly significant that the religious establishment gave Mr Darwin the public endorsement of an Abbey funeral and a memorial committee which included the Archbishops of Canterbury and York and the Bishop of London. By the end of the nineteenth century almost all thoughtful Christians had come to take evolution for granted. In the wider Church the watershed came in 1889 with *Lux Mundi*, edited by Charles Gore, a book which presented Christianity wholly within an evolutionary framework.

The 'monkey trial' of 1925 and the birth of young earth creationism in the 1960s

For most of the twentieth century, creation through evolution was taken for granted as the position of educated Christians in Britain and throughout Europe. It was also the position of mainstream churches and academic institutions across most of the USA, though during the 1920s the teaching of evolution in publicly funded schools was banned in Tennessee, Mississippi, and Arkansas. In 1925 John Scopes, a young biology teacher in Dayton, Tennessee, was fined $100 for teaching evolution. The trial was widely reported because

---

[49] Fern Elsdon-Baker, *The Selfish Genius: How Richard Dawkins Rewrote Darwin's Legacy*, cited from a review by Janet Smith in Times Higher Education Supplement, 17-24 December 2009, p. 55.

[50] Cf. the account in Adrian Desmond and James Moore, *Danvin* (London: Penguin, 1991), p. 671.

William Jennings Bryan, former Secretary of State and three times Democratic challenger for the presidency of the USA, gave evidence for the prosecution. The defence counsel, Clarence Darrow, showed that Bryan had little real knowledge either of the theory of evolution or of the Bible. Bryan tried to reconcile his belief in Genesis with what he knew to be the great age of the earth by suggesting that each of the Biblical 'days' was really a great geological age. Darrow was thereby able to show that Bryan's supposed defence of the accuracy of Genesis was incoherent.[51] The publicity surrounding the trial seriously weakened popular support for anti-evolutionism, which lapsed into relative quiescence for the next thirty years.[52]

According to R. J. Berry, 'the calm was shattered in 1961 when *The Genesis Flood* appeared, a book written by John Whitcombe, a Bible teacher, and Henry Morris, a hydraulics engineer.'[53] They rejected 'all the established findings of geology, palaeontology and archaeology' on the grounds of the flood's supposed impact and argued for what has come to be known as 'young earth creationism', affirming the essential truth of belief in a recent creation and of a universal flood. The impact of their work, and of the subsequent claim by biochemist Michael Behe that some biological mechanisms are incapable of evolution by natural selection and therefore require individual 'intelligent design', has been quite

---

51 <http://en.wikipedia.org/wiki/William_Jennings_Bryan>.

52 R. J. Berry, 'Darwins Legacy", in John Quenby and John MacDonald Smith, *Intelligent Faith* (Winchester: O Books, 2009) p.no.

53 J. C. Whitcombe and H. M. Morris, *The Genesis Flood* (Philadelphia: Presbyterian and Reformed Publishing Company, 1961).

incredible.[54] Though rejected by mainstream churches and the academic world alike, 'young earth creationism' and 'individual intelligent design' have impacted on millions through the influence of televangelism, the internet, and American publishing houses located in the Deep South. This recent and bizarre development poses a major threat to the credibility of Christian believing in the twenty-first century

The variety of creation stories in the Bible

Belief in a single divine creator is one of the key contributions of Biblical theology to human understanding. This belief is celebrated in a wide variety of imaginative pictures, the best known of which is the account of the creation of everything by divine fiat over a six-day period culminating in the creation of a Sabbath rest on the seventh day. But it would never have occurred to the priestly author of this beautiful story that he was either writing or editing a divinely revealed account of how the creation actually came about. We know this because in chapter 2 he included an entirely different creation narrative. In this second account, creation is not spread over six days but is all compressed into a single sequence of events. First God made man from the dust of the ground before there were any plants or shrubs (Gen. 2: 5). Then God created a garden for the man, followed by animals to provide him with company. Only when it became apparent that no animal was a suitable partner for the man did God anaesthetise Adam, take out one of his ribs, and build it up into a woman (Gen. 2: 21–22).

Psalm 104 tells a different creation story in which God spreads out the heavens over the earth like a tent and then fixes the earth on a firm foundation. At this point the waters are high above the mountains, so God gets rid of the waters by ordering them to pour down into the valleys (Ps. 104: 8). Another picture

---

54 R. J. Berry, 'Darwin's Legacy', pp. 110-112.

is presented in Job 38–41, where God is pictured as laying the foundations of the earth, stretching a measuring line over it like an architect, and ensuring that the world is adequately supported on pillars. God also proclaims the rules that govern the heavens, bringing the signs of the zodiac out in their appropriate seasons (Job 38: 5, 32). Second Isaiah pictures God working like a potter 'fashioning the earth and everything that grows on it' and shaping human beings out of clay (Isa. 42: 5; 45: 9, 18; 64: 8).

The poetic character of Biblical creation stories becomes even more apparent when we come across traces of old Babylonian mythology in some of the creation accounts. The books of Job, Psalms, and Isaiah all draw on the ancient myth that creation began with the defeat of a great dragon from whose body the earth was formed. So, as well as the imagery of the potter and the architect, we hear how God 'hacked the Rahab in pieces and ran the dragon through' (Isa. 51: 9, NEB; cf. Job 26: 12, Ps. 89: 10).

No Christian today would dream of seeking to rehabilitate myths of the great dragon, yet that myth is embedded in at least three Biblical creation accounts. More sophisticated accounts using the imagery of a potter and a pot, or of an architect with a measuring rod, or even accounts of God simply creating by calling everything into being, are all alike human attempts to make sense of the cosmos and of our place in it. At its best the Christian tradition from the earliest days has recognised this.

The earliest Christian commentary on Genesis

The earliest theological reflections we have on Genesis 1 come from Origen in the third century. He pointed out that it is impossible to take the account as literally true because its ordering of creation simply doesn't make sense:

> What intelligent person would fancy for instance, that a first, second, and third day, evening and morning, took place without sun, moon and stars; and the first, as we call it, without even a heaven? Who would be so childish as to suppose that God after the manner of a human gardener planted a garden in Eden towards the east, and made therein a tree, visible and sensible, so one could get the power of living [for ever] by the bodily eating of its fruit with the teeth; or again could partake of good and evil by feeding on what came from that other tree. I fancy that no one will question that these statements are figurative, declaring mysterious truths by the means of a seeming history, not one that took place in bodily form.[55]

St Augustine's understanding of the literal meaning of Genesis

St Augustine, though claiming to defend the literal meaning of Genesis in his work of that title, acknowledged that one could not and should not seek to defend such details as the creation of light before the creation of the sun. More generally he insisted that we should form our judgments on questions in the natural sciences by reasoning and observation rather than seeking to derive such information from the Scriptures:

> It frequently happens that there is a question about the earth, or the sky or other elements of this world, the movement, revolutions, or even the size and distance of the stars, the regular eclipses of the sun and the moon, the course of the years in seasons; the nature of animals, vegetables, and minerals, and other things of the same

[55] Origen, *On First Principles* 4.16, cited from H. M. Gwatkin, *Selections From Early Christian Writers* (London: Macmillan, 1920), pp. 137-8.

kind, respecting which one who is not a Christian has knowledge derived from most certain reasoning and observation. And it is highly deplorable and mischievous and a thing to be specially guarded against that he should hear a Christian speaking of such matters in accordance with Christian writings and uttering such nonsense that, knowing him to be as wide of the mark as the, to use the common expression, East is from West, the unbeliever can scarcely restrain himself from laughing.[56]

St Augustine's own understanding of God's creation was that it was a gradual event. In his magisterial summary of early Christian thought, Bishop Charles Gore pointed out that St Augustine himself followed the view of St Gregory of Nyssa, that God in the beginning created only germs or causes of the forms of life which were afterwards to be developed in gradual course. Gore notes wryly that accommodation between religion and science would have been much easier in the fourth century than it was in the nineteenth.[57]

Aquinas' understanding of scientific and religious modes of explanation

The Christian thinker who expressed most clearly the classic arguments for the existence of God was St Thomas Aquinas. However it is vital to study his arguments in full, because his famous 'five ways' of demonstrating divine existence are preceded by a brilliant summary of the case for atheism. His first argument is that since the concept of God implies 'limitless goodness', evil should not exist at all. 'But evil is encountered

---

[56] Augustine, *The Literal Meaning of Genesis* 1.19, cited from J. G. Langmead Casserly, *The Retreat from Christianity* (London: Longmans, 1953), pp. 21-22.

[57] Charles Gore, *Belief in God*, p.10.

in the world, therefore God does not exist.' His second argument is that everything we observe within the world can be fully accounted for by natural causes, 'therefore there is no need to suppose that God exists'.[58] Nothing that Aquinas subsequently wrote takes away the reality of these two observations. Christians always have to live with the 'problem of evil' and with the fact that belief in God is not a replacement for the search for natural explanations for what we encounter within the world.

As one proceeds to the study of Aquinas' arguments from causation and design, it is important to notice that they presuppose that there are always natural explanations to be found for the interconnectedness of all life. Everything we observe in the world is causally related to, and moved by, other realities which become the 'natural cause' or 'efficient cause' of what develops. God, for Aquinas, is not within this natural cycle of 'efficient causation'. Aquinas' five ways are a sustained argument that the discovery of the 'natural' cause of why things happen is insufficient. We need also to think in terms of 'first cause' and 'final cause'. Since God for Aquinas is outside time, his understanding of 'first cause' does not imply temporal priority but simply his belief that the whole created order in the past, present, and future is all equally dependent on God. Likewise his argument from design supplements, but does not compete with, his ongoing conviction that there can be a naturalistic explanation for everything that happens within the world which in its own terms is complete.

For Aquinas, belief in God is not some kind of rival explanation to what the sciences disclose to us about how the universe operates. For Aquinas, belief in a Creator God goes alongside and complements what science can discover about the natural order. As a matter of history, belief in a universe created by a single divine mind, within which there is a

---

[58] St. Thomas Aquinas, *Sutntna Theologica* 1a, 2, 3.

'natural' explanation for everything waiting to be discovered, is why science as we know it began in Western Europe rather than elsewhere. Within Britain, the founders of the Royal Society acknowledged that they wanted to think God's thoughts after him and discover how God's universe worked. In principle therefore there should never be a clash between religion and science, since belief in God is not in competition with natural explanations for the way things are.

The paradox of the present situation

When we reflect on Origen's belief that no intelligent person would ever take the Genesis stories literally, or St Augustine's belief that building scientific hypotheses out of Biblical texts was a thing to be 'specially guarded against', or Aquinas' assumption that there is a natural explanation for everything, then the development of fundamentalist attitudes in the early nineteenth century and their revival in the twenty-first is utterly bewildering. It is false to the Christian tradition itself, let alone to the evidence from historical and Biblical criticism and from the data of the natural sciences. The tragedy is that this resurgence of belief in a fundamentalist creationism is happening at a time when a number of philosophers and scientists believe that a stronger case can be made for Christian theism than for many centuries.

The harmony between religious and scientific thinking

There is a widespread consensus among scientists that the universe has not always existed. It came into being from nothing some thirteen billion years ago. This does not of course prove that God created the universe out of nothing. But the two beliefs are very readily compatible with each other. The scientific belief that the universe came into being out of nothing and the Christian belief that God created the universe out of nothing fit very easily together. They are parallel beliefs and it is entirely rational for a person to hold them both.

Similarly there is a scientific consensus that the universe appears to be 'finely tuned' for the emergence of life and mind, since if the conditions just after the big bang had been even fractionally different the universe could not have evolved in the way it has evolved. For example, in his *A Brief History of Time* Stephen Hawking has shown that the heat of the universe one second after the big bang had to be exactly as it was, because a decrease in heat of as little as one part in a million would have caused the universe to collapse.[59] Similar fine tuning is necessary for about fifty constants of nature, a fact that readily lends itself to the idea that there may be a cosmic mind behind all this. But once again, scientific belief in the fine tuning of the universe does not require belief in God: Hawking is not a believer. What one can legitimately say, however, is that scientific belief in the fine tuning of the universe and Christian belief in God as the mind behind the universe go very happily together.

This was a phenomenon noted by philosopher Antony Flew, who preceded Richard Dawkins as 'the most notorious atheist in the world'.[60] At an early stage of his 'Pilgrimage from Atheism to Theism',[61] Flew came to think that 'if a cradle Roman Catholic' believes that 'the universe has a beginning and will have an end' then acceptance of the big bang 'surely does provide empirical confirmation of the first part of that belief'. Likewise, if a person believes in a purposeful creation

---

59 Stephen Hawking, *A Brief History of Time* (London: Bantam, 1998), p. 127; John Leslie, *Universes* (London: Routledge, 1989), pp. 3, 28, 29, 37.

60 Antony Flew, *There is a God: How the World's Most Notorious Atheist Changed His Mind* (New York: Harper One, 2009).

61 Antony Flew, 'My Pilgrimage from Athiesm to Theism', <http:biola.edu/antonyflew/flew-interview.pdf>; see also *Philosophia Christi*, Winter 2005.

then 'it is entirely reasonable to welcome the fine-tuning argument as providing confirmation of that belief.'[62] Later Flew went further than this and in January 2004 announced that he had come to believe in God. He 'simply had to go where the evidence leads', and it now seemed to him that the case for God 'is now much stronger than it ever was before'.[63]

The revival of interest in the philosophy of religion

The idea that the case for God is now much stronger than it ever was before can be seen in the way philosophy of religion was transformed in the later years of the twentieth century. As an undergraduate at Oxford in the early 1960s I was very conscious that it was regarded as a fringe subject. In theology it was an optional extra rather than part of the normal syllabus. In philosophy the positivistic school led by A. J. Ayer took the view that religious claims were not so much false as meaningless. When Ian Ramsey left the Nolloth Chair of the Philosophy of Christianity in 1966 to become Bishop of Durham, there was a strong movement not to appoint a successor on the grounds that the subject was not really needed. Fortunately, a decision was made to appoint Basil Mitchell to the Chair and under him and his successors, Richard Swinburne and Brian Leftow, the subject blossomed as never before.

In a foreword to a book on the philosophy of religion, Professor William Abraham comments that, when he arrived in Oxford as a graduate student in 1973, he little knew that he was 'at the beginning of a golden period in the philosophy of religion' in which believers could 'take a lead and create the intellectual space in which Christian belief could be taken seriously once again. The outcome was seen in the wealth of

---

62 Antony Flew, in Stan Wallace, *Does God Exist?: The Craig-Flew Debate* (Aldershot: Ashgate, 2003), p.190.

63 Antony Flew, 'My Pilgrimage from Atheism to Theism'.

material that has been published, has been startling in its originality and depth.'[64] The book for which this foreword was written is *The Agnostic Inquirer* by Sandra Menssen and Thomas Sullivan, two formerly agnostic professors of philosophy who have gradually reasoned their way to a rational faith. They wrote their book to help fellow agnostic inquirers follow them to their new convictions. They show in a work of outstanding logical force that a cumulative rational case for God's existence can be carefully developed in which natural theology and revelation combine to mutually support each other as components of a reasonable faith in a Creator God who has willed to become known to humankind.

William Abraham's assessment of the emergence of a newly confident Christian philosophy is confirmed by the Canadian atheist philosopher Kai Nielsen. Writing in 1971, Nielsen had said that philosophers who took the claims of religion seriously were very much in the minority and their arguments have been forcefully contested'. But nearly twenty years later Nielsen's estimate of philosophical attitudes was quite different: 'Philosophy of religion in Anglo-American context has taken a curious turn in the past decade … what has come to the forefront... is a group of Christian philosophers of a philosophically analytic persuasion, but hostile to even the residues of logical empiricism or Wittgensteinianism, who return to the old topics and the old theses of traditional Christian philosophy and natural theology.'[65] We need to notice that Nielsen describes this development as 'curious', indicating that he himself remains unconvinced. None the less it is intriguing that Richard Purtill similarly claims: 'All the

---

[64] Sandra Menssen and Thomas Sullivan, *The Agnostic Inquirer* (Grand Rapids: Erdmans, 2007), p. xi.

[65] Kai Neilsen, *Contemporary Critiques of Religion* (London: Macmillan, 1971), p. 19; foreword to K. Parsons, *God and the Burden of Proof* (Buffalo: Prometheus, 1989), p.7.

traditional arguments have able and respected defenders, and if there is not a consensus in favour of philosophical arguments for God's existence, it is no longer true that there is a consensus against.'[66]

Why philosophy of religion has revived

It is important not to overstate the case. Arguments about God remain strongly contested. The difference is that in the twenty-first century the arguments are taken seriously on both sides. Factors which have changed the situation include the collapse of logical positivism and of atheistic Marxism, together with a distrust of Freudian analysis. Within philosophy an important development has been the recognition that 'the justification of religious belief' depends on a recognition that knowledge cannot be simply confined to what we discover through the natural sciences, but that disciplines like history, law, literary studies, politics, sociology, aesthetics, and philosophy, as well as theology, while unable to provide logical certainty, can yet still provide sensible arguments for the support of one theory rather than another.[67] In all such cases certainty is not available, but argumentation may convince some that one view is more probable than its alternative.

In this climate philosophy of religion has dramatically revived. In his introduction to the twentieth-century section of a five-volume *History of Western Philosophy of Religion*, Professor Charles Taliaferro writes:

> One general observation seems secure: philosophical reflection on religion has formed a major vibrant part of

---

[66] Richard Purtill, 'The Current State of Arguments for the Existence of God', *Review and Expositer* 82 (1985), pp. 521-33.

[67] Basil Mitchell, *The Justification of Religious Belief* (Oxford: Oxford University Press, 1982).

> some of the best philosophy in the past century. We now have a virtual library of a hundred years of first-rate, diverse philosophy of religion. At the close of the century there are more societies, institutions, journals, conferences and publishing houses dedicated to philosophy of religion than any other area of philosophy.[68]

Although Taliaferro was largely speaking of philosophy in the English-speaking world, similar comments could be made of the situation in continental Europe. Friedrich Nietzsche and many other leading intellectuals including Feuerbach, Marx, Freud, and Sartre had confidently predicted the imminent 'Death of God in the hearts of men'.[69] This has not happened. According to Paul Johnson, author both of a *History of Christianity and of Modern Times,* 'The most extraordinary thing about the twentieth century has been the failure of God to die … At the end of the twentieth century the idea of... God is as lively and real as ever.'[70] The profoundly influential philosopher Jurgen Habermas argues that secular citizens need to accept the insight that 'they are living in a society that is epistemically adjusted to the continued existence of religious communities'.[71] Likewise Gianni Vattimo believes we are

---

[68] Graham Oppy and Nick Trakakis (eds), *The History of Western Philosophy of Religion* (Durham: Acumen, 2009), vol. 5 p. 1.

[69] Cf. Friedrich Nietzsche, *The Gay Science*, Aphorism 125, cited from Walter Kaufmann, *The Portable Nietzsche* (New York: Viking, 1954), pp. 95-6.

[70] Paul Johnson, 'Peaceful Co-existence', *Prospect* 7 (April 1996), pp. 34-8.

[71] Jurgen Habermas, 'Religion in the Public Sphere', *European Journal of Philosophy* 14.1 (2006), pp. 1-15 (p. 15).

'entering a new age where religion is taken seriously by philosophy'.[72]

Philosophy of religion in Russia and China

What is true of Europe is even more true of the revival of philosophy of religion in both Russia and China. I have had first-hand experience of both. In 1991 I was invited to speak on 'Faith and Reason' to the Philosophy section of the Russian Academy of Sciences and later gave the same lecture in the Department of Philosophy at the People's University in Beijing. My department at Lampeter subsequently obtained a grant from the European Commission to help in the transformation of a former 'Institute for Scientific Atheism' in Leningrad into an 'Institute for Religious Studies' in what is now called St Petersburg. It is significant that this kind of development has taken place throughout the former Soviet Union and that priority was sought for it.

Subsequently Professor XinzhongYao and I secured a four-year grant from the John Templeton Foundation to compare religious experience in Britain and China. Working with colleagues from seven Chinese universities we found that after sixty years of atheistic indoctrination, the number of firm atheists corresponded almost exactly with the number in Britain (in both cases around 26 per cent). The biggest surprise in our China survey was that 56.7 per cent reported that they had been influenced or controlled by a power that they could not understand or explain clearly and that they identified this power with a religious entity or force. We also found that 31.3 per cent of those Chinese who had described themselves as 'firm

---

[72] Thomas Guarino, *Vattimo and Theology* (London: T. & T. Clark, 2009), p. 14.

atheists' believed that 'religion contains profound truth'.[73] We discovered that between 2001 and 2005, each of the five main religions in China had increased its membership by an average of 5.9 per cent each year.[74] We were also told by several Chinese philosophers that from being a banned subject thirty years ago, philosophy of religion is now the most popular area of philosophical inquiry in China.

How modern knowledge may help belief in a Creator God

We saw earlier that a key factor in Antony Flew's move from atheism to theism was his belief that this made better sense of the data now available within the natural sciences. The reason behind this is that as we explore the 'fine tuning' of the universe, it seems as if some kind of 'anthropic principle' is at work guiding the evolution of the cosmos in ways necessary for the emergence of life and mind. The odds of all the constants of nature being exactly as they are is utterly astronomical, and it is this fact that has caused some to think that alongside naturalistic explanations it could be helpful to think of personal explanation as well. Even Richard Dawkins acknowledges this:

> There are possible good reasons for believing in some sort of grand supernatural intelligence. They are never anything to do with the biblical God, which is just an ancient bronze age belief having no semblance of reality. But there are modern physicists who believe that the universe— if you actually look at the laws of the

---

[73] Xinzhong Yao and Paul Badham, *Religious Experience in Contemporary China* (Cardiff: University of Wales Press, 2007).

[74] Yuli Liu, 'A Buddhist explanation of religious experience', paper presented to a conference of the British Association for the Study of Religion in Edinburgh, 2007.

> universe, they are to some physicists too good to be true. This suggests a very interesting case for a possible very, very deep reason why we might believe in some sort of grand fundamental intelligence underlying the universe.[75]

Dawkins goes on to stress that this 'grand supernatural intelligence' has nothing whatever to do with the kind of God that people go into a church to worship. That may sometimes be the sad reality of some contemporary church worship, but it ought not to be the case. The New Testament belief in a Creator God is belief in the 'Word' or *Logos* which was 'with God' and 'was God'. The Greek concept of the Logos is precisely belief in some sort of grand fundamental intelligence underlying the universe; an eternal mind in whom 'we live and move and have our being'; a divine 'light that enlightens every man' and 'was coming into the world' (John 1:1; Acts 17: 28; John 1:9, RSV). It ought to be axiomatic that this is indeed the Christian vision of the Creator, and the object of Christian worship. It is a remarkable phenomenon that many scientists see an 'anthropic principle' at work in the way the universe has evolved. It is also surprising that the universe should be comprehensible to our minds in the way it is. But because this seems to be the case, we can postulate that some fundamental intelligence analogous to our own minds underlies the way things are. This is precisely what the classic Logos doctrine actually affirmed about a mind behind the universe.

But if there is a supernatural intelligence analogous to our own minds, then it is reasonable to suppose that that intelligence should wish to make itself known to us. In Stoic

---

[75] BBC talk given 16 March 2003, retrieved 28 August 2004 from <www.bbc.co.uk/northernireland/religion/sundaysequence/archive-interviews.shtml>, cited in Sandra Menssen and Thomas Sullivan, *The Agnostic Inquirer*, p. 117.

philosophical thought, the idea of the Logos includes the notion that there is a spark of the divine in each of us. My father argues in Chapter 20 (pp. 180–1) how opportune it was both that the concept of the Logos existed in the first century as a widely understood idea and that there was an understanding that the Mind (or Logos) of God could find expression in human life. Hence the prologue to St John's Gospel was able to draw on a philosophical understanding which made it possible to affirm both the divinity and humanity of Jesus. The verdict of Christian orthodoxy on Jesus is that he really did incarnate the divine Logos in his life and teaching, so that in Jesus was seen the character of the mind behind the cosmos expressed in the language of his human life.

CHAPTER TWENTY FOUR

Jesus in the World's Religions

Gregory A. Barker

In the Pulitzer Prize-nominated novel, *The Accidental Tourist,* we meet a middle-aged travel writer who hates to travel. Interestingly he capitalises on his dislike by writing travel guides for reluctant travellers who long to feel at home in strange places. These guides help businessmen and women locate a McDonald's in France, a Taco Bell in Mexico and canned spaghetti in Italy. These books, with their elaborate systems designed to help people feel that they've never left home, reflect the main character's struggle as he realises that he is becoming 'a dried up kernel of a man that nothing real penetrates'.

One of the most fascinating journeys for a traveller in the field of theology or religious studies is to investigate how the central figure of one religious tradition is viewed by another tradition. This journey can lead to startling discoveries which challenge theological, political, and social assumptions, causing the traveller to re-evaluate cherished notions and reach an enhanced sense of belief and identity. In the history of the Christian Church, however, exploration into how Jesus has been viewed by the world's religions has often resembled journeys described by the 'Accidental Tourist', where one looks only for the familiar, seldom the new and challenging. Too many explorations on the subject of Jesus in the world's religions have merely helped travellers feel that they have never left home.

Christian theology has generated several systems through which truths proclaimed by the world's religions may be viewed.[76] As important as these approaches are, we must recognise that they are systematic positions that channel data into existing categories of thought. In other words, one works from a general position when accounting for particular points of view. This has the advantage of giving the theologian or religious believer a firm identity in the face of claims that may be at odds with his or her commitments.

One might legitimately ask if this approach needs to be complemented by a temporary suspension of a general framework, a working from the particulars to the general. After all, we are often changed through personal encounters rather than abstract principles; if the abstract has an ironclad grip on the data, we may miss a chance to discover new insights that might enhance or change our point of view. When it comes to views of Jesus from the world's religions, a theological system can make it possible to miss challenging and intriguing viewpoints that could lead to rich new insights. There can be real discomfort in temporarily setting a system aside, but then there is also the reward of travelling on new roads and returning 'home' with added depth and understanding.

This chapter, then, is an invitation for Christians to examine some verdicts on Jesus from those with no commitments to the classic creeds of the Christian Church.

A thoroughly Jewish Jesus?

Perhaps the most distorted portraits ever produced are mediaeval works of a gentle and fragile-looking Jesus surrounded by grotesque and twisted faces representing

---

[76] Alan Race has helpfully outlined three such systems in *Christians and Religious Pluralism: Patterns in the Christian Theology of Religions*, 2nd edn. (London: SCM, 1993). See also Alan Race and Paul Hedges (eds), *Christian Approaches to Other Faiths* (London: SCM, 2008).

European Christian perceptions of Jews.[77] These works deny the truth that Jesus himself was a Jew among Jews; they also reflect Christian hatred of Jews and Christian denigration of Jewish traditions, demonstrating Rosemary Radford Ruether's thesis that anti-Semitism is indeed the 'left hand' of Christology.[78] Much scholarly and ecclesiastical work has challenged the prejudices conveyed by these portrayals, demonstrating Jesus to be firmly rooted in his Jewish setting. Indeed, to divorce Jesus from this setting is to miss keys to the meaning of his message and constitutes a denial of the Christian insistence upon his full humanity.

What do Jews think of Jesus? This question has to be handled with care, as for centuries it was used not as an invitation to genuine discussion but as a cloak to deny the validity of Jewish traditions and as a mask for a converting and persecuting agenda. In light of centuries of persecution in 'Christian' countries, Jews have had their own questions for Christians: when will you stop killing us, declaring that we are 'God killers' (deicide), burning our sacred texts, denying our humanitarian rights, and declaring our faith to be nothing more than dead legalism? Many Jews found Christian devotion to Jesus to be the reason why these questions needed to be asked, so one should not be surprised that Christian questions to Jews about Jesus have often been met by silence. Added to this is the fact that Judaism developed its rich and nuanced traditions without reference to someone who is, for Jews, a relatively minor figure from the late Second Temple period.

---

[77] For instance *Christ Carrying the Cross* by Hieronymous Bosch (01490). See Mitchell B. Merback (ed.), *Beyond the Yellow Badge: Anti- Judaism and Antisemitism in Medieval and Early Modern Visual Culture* (Leiden and Boston: Brill, 2008).

[78] Rosemary Radford Ruether, *Faith and Fratricide: The Theological Roots of Anti-Semitism* (New York: Wipf and Stock, 1996 [1975]).

Yet this silence is not the only story; there are significant reactions to Jesus in Jewish traditions that can inform and deepen Christian approaches.

Initially, Jesus was perceived as a threat to Judaism. As the early Christian movement denied key Jewish approaches to Messiahship and divinity, and appeared to transgress monotheism, Jews charged Jesus with having denied the faith in the manner described in Deuteronomy 13—teaching heresy about his identity. As Christianity emerged as a power within Graeco-Roman culture, Jewish resistance to less than benign policies was sometimes channelled into pictures of Jesus as a supernatural arch-deceiver who spurned authority, was sexually promiscuous and performed magic for self-aggrandisement. These approaches can be seen as reactions from a religion under threat.[79]

Some Jewish leaders and scholars in the mediaeval era asked a question that would lead to an entirely different set of perceptions about Jesus: what if it was the Church and not Jesus that was responsible for transgressing key Jewish tenets about the Messiah, divinity, and law? In other words, what if Jesus had been a Jewish Rabbi who was turned into a god after his death? Asking this question led to insights which anticipated Enlightenment-inspired views of Jesus by several centuries:

---

[79] Recent work by Peter Schafer yields important insights concerning perceptions of Jesus by the Jewish community behind the redaction of the Babylonian Talmud. See *Jesus in the Talmud* (Princeton and Oxford: Princeton University Press, 2007). For Jewish views on Christian violence see the perceptive reflection of Rabbi Nachmanides (Rabbi Mosche ben Nachman [by acronym, Ramban], 1194-01270) Hyam Maccoby (ed. and trans.), *Judaism on Trial: Jeunsh- Christian Dispuations in the Middle Ages* (Oxford and Portland, Oregon: The Littman Library of Jewish Civilization, 1982), pp. 121-2.

> The more clearly we examine into the purport of the New Testament, the more clearly we perceive its general intent is not to deify Jesus; and that the doctrines which assign to him the title of God, have arisen from want of due investigation and are not upheld by the force of sound argument.
>
> (Isaac of Troki, 1533–1594)[80]

This approach to Jesus was soon to be developed in significant directions by the Jewish Reform movement. Reform thinkers claimed that prophetic traditions formed a bridge between Enlightenment philosophy and a distinctive Jewish identity. In other words, one could realise the heights of Jewish identity not through strict adherence to the law but through an enlightened ethic, informed by the prophetic tradition as well as by philosophical and historical approaches then current in Europe. Many innovations lay ahead for Reform Jews: modernisation in worship and synagogue architecture as well as extensive re-interpretation of theological concepts. Reform Jews, however, faced criticism from Orthodox Jews for the abandonment of a strict adherence to the law and Christians wondered why reform-minded Jews did not go further and simply convert to Christianity.

In answering their Christian critics, Reform Jews noted that Jesus wasn't so much a 'Christian' as he was a charismatic Rabbi shaped by prophetic traditions and principles. In fact, if one studied Jesus in his context, one would conclude that he

---

80 Isaac ben Abraham Troki, *Faith Strengthened*, trans. Moses Mocatta [from the Hebrew] (London: n.p., 1851). For a more recent source see Isaac of Troki, *Faith Strengethend*, trans. Moses Mocatta (New York: Ktav Publishing House, 1970), pp. 87-93, 264. See World Karaite Movement <http://faithstrengthened.org/index.html> (accessed 26 February 2010).

had more affinity with the Pharisees than with subsequent generations of his self-professed followers. Abraham Geiger (1810–1874) noted that anti- Jewish sentiments had blinded New Testament explorations from seeing Jesus' relationship with Judaism:

> He was a Jew, a Pharisean Jew with Galilean colouring —a man who joined in the hopes of his time and who believed that those hopes were fulfilled in him. He did not utter a new thought, nor did he break down the barriers of nationality. When a foreign woman came to him with a request to heal her, he said, 'It is not meet to take the children's bread and cast it to the dogs.' He did not abolish any part of Judaism; he was a Pharisee who walked in the way of Hillel, did not set the most decided value upon every single external form, yet proclaimed 'that not the least tittle should be taken from the Law;' 'The Pharisees sit in Moses' seat, and whatsoever they bid you observe, that observe and do.' It is true that, if the accounts are faithful, he allowed himself to be carried away to trifling depreciatory expressions concerning one subject or another, when he was opposed; but he never faltered in his original convictions.[81]

Certainly there was polemic built into early Reform arguments about Jesus: Jesus uttered nothing new; his teaching was simply a reworking of aspects of Jewish traditions. It should be noted, however, that many of Geiger's insights remain at the heart of Jewish and Christian scholarly approaches to New Testament studies today

In fact, one of the most lively areas of New Testament study is now occurring among Jewish and Christian biblical scholars

---

[81] Abraham Geiger, *Judaism and Its History in Two Parts*, trans. Charles Newburgh (New York: Bloch, 1911), pp. 130-1.

who have renewed the quest for the historical Jesus by examining his place in the shifting sands of first-century Judaism.[82] The best way to understand Jesus, these scholars maintain, is not to contrast him with his surroundings as had been done in earlier historical explorations. Rather, it is to understand how Jesus lived in both affinity and tension with various Jewish tendencies and groups of his time. Sources such as Josephus, the Dead Sea Scrolls, and a plethora of Rabbinic writings, as well as the New Testament, are used to understand Jesus the Jew. Geza Vermes, for example, has received much attention for his view that the ministry of Jesus resembles that of other charismatic miracle-working Hasids from Galilee in the same period.[83] Furthermore, Vermes argues, many of the New Testament titles for Jesus (such as 'Lord' and 'Prophet') would have been applied to other Jewish figures of Jesus' day and not understood as a departure from Judaism.

Recent Jewish assessments of Jesus have followed both the more resistant approaches outlined earlier and the Reform pictures. However, there is an outstanding Jewish scholar who has done much to build a positive relationship between Jews and Christians when it comes to interpreting the meaning of Jesus: David Flusser (1917–2000). Flusser's work on Jesus is notable not only because it has been praised by key Christian scholars and leaders, nor because his work on Jesus has been

---

[82] This is sometimes referred to as the 'third quest' (after the initial Enlightenment-inspired explorations ending with Schweitzer, the 'no quest' period of form criticism, and the renewed quest of the 1950s-shaped by concerns raised by Ernst Kasemann). Prominent 'third quest' scholars include Marcus Borg, John Dominic Crossan, Paula Frericksen, Gerd Thiessen, E.P. Sanders, Geza Vermes, and N. T. Wright.

[83] See works by Gaza Vermes including his seminal study, *Jesus the Jew: A Historian's Reading of the Gospels*, 3rd edn (London: SCM, 2001 [1973]).

the recipient of two of the highest literary awards in Israel, but because Flusser is the author of the article on Jesus in the *Encyclopaedia Judaica*, a resource used across Jewish traditions.[84]

Before one can appreciate the originality of Jesus, Flusser insisted, one must first appreciate the ways in which he was not original. Echoing earlier Jewish works, Flusser demonstrated how the miracles, the embracing of poverty, the teaching of love of God and neighbour, and the 'but I say unto you' sayings of Matthew 5 had their foundations and parallels in the Jewish teaching and spirituality of Jesus' day.[85] Furthermore, a detailed study of Gospel passages confirmed for Flusser that nowhere did Jesus transgress any of the Mosaic laws. When Jesus appears in the Gospels to be at variance with the practice of the Pharisees, this represents an intra-mural debate about non-binding applications of the Law rather than a transgression of Jewish legal codes. Thus it was only a fringe group of Pharisees who viewed Jesus as breaking laws; the wider Jewish community accepted variations in the application of traditions. It is also misleading to say, as Christians have insisted, that Jesus held the moral to be higher than the ritual—since Jesus sought faithfulness to the Mosaic code. Jesus' uniqueness,

---

[84] David Flusser, 'Jesus', in Cecil Roth and Geoffrey Wigoder (eds) *Encyclopaedia Judaica*, vol. 10 (Jerusalem: Peter Publishing House, Ltd, 1971), pp. 10-18. This article has been reprinted without change in the 2007 edition Fred Skolnik (ed.), *Encyclopaedia Judaica*, vol.n (New York and London: Thomsen Gale, 2007), pp. 246- 51.

[85] David Flusser, *Jesus*, trans. Robert Walls (New York: Herder and Herder, 1969), 2nd. edn (Jerusalem: Magnes Press, 1997). See especially his chapter 'The Law" pp. 44-64. Those interested in reading more of Flusser are directed to the newly revised edition of this work: David Flusser with R. Steven Notley, *The Sage of Galilee: Rediscovering Jesus' Genius* (Grand Rapids and Cambridge: William B. Eerdmans, 2007).

rather, is to be found in specific revolutionary points of his life and teaching, including the radical commitment to love one's enemy.

In other words, the teaching of Jesus may be viewed as difficult for Jews in the same way as it is difficult for Christians: it is never easy to love one's enemies. By embracing this challenge, Jews and Christians can truly find common ground.

Jesus: a prophet of Islam?

Islam is the only religion other than Christianity that requires its adherents to hold Jesus in reverence. As a result, there is a rich history of reflections, poetry, and accounts of Jesus across Muslim traditions. At the very centre of Islamic interpretations of Jesus is the Quranic testimony of Jesus as a prophet—quite a contrast from the world of Judaism where the prophet-hood of Jesus remains at the edge of interpretive possibilities. But has this reverence for Jesus in Islam been a source of peace between Muslims and Christians? The answer to this question lies in understanding the Islamic view of a prophet.

According to Islam, during troubled times when humans have forsaken the path of God, a prophet appears. The circumstances each prophet addresses are unique to that prophet's era; however all prophets issue a judgment on idolatry and ungodly behaviour as well as a challenge to submit to the one true God. When Muslims call Jesus a 'prophet of Islam' they are referring to the centrality of this prophetic mission. In fact,'Islam', related to the Hebrew 'shalom', has an intriguing double meaning: 'submission' and 'peace'; the teaching of the Quran is that humans will find peace as they submit the entirety of their lives to God.

As a result of this prophetic model, the unique teachings of Jesus are not a central concern in the Quran. The Quran, however, does extol Jesus as unique in the sense that God granted a special confirmation of his prophetic work through his miraculous birth (similar to Adam's) and numerous miracles performed during his life. In fact, Jesus is known by several beautiful titles including 'spirit of God' and 'word of God'; however, these titles are not signs of divinity but of the divine hand of a sovereign God working through his life. This explains why the Quran clearly rejects the Christian conviction of Jesus partaking in God's nature:

> People of the Book, do not go to excess in your religion, and do not say anything about God except the truth: the Messiah, Jesus, son of Mary, was nothing more than a messenger of God, His word, directed to Mary, a spirit from Him. So believe in God and His messengers and do not speak of a 'Trinity'—stop [this], that is better for you—God is only one God, He is far above having a son, everything in the heavens and earth belongs to Him and He is the best one to trust. The Messiah would never disdain to be a servant of God, nor would the angels who are close to Him.[86]

As Muslims and Christians interacted through the centuries, the Quranic viewpoint became a source for sharp polemic and even violence between these religions. Yet is this an inevitable outcome of the Quranic understanding of Jesus?

In the unprecedented consensus statement among Muslims, *A Common Word*, the Muslim community identifies a teaching of Jesus in the New Testament which it believes to be consistent with a prophetic challenge and which holds the possibility of inter-religious peace: the dual commandment to

---

[86] Q 4: 171-72a. Quotations from the Quran are from M. A. S. Abdul Haleem (trans.), *The Qur'an* (Oxford: Oxford University Press, 2004). From *The Qur'an* trans. by Abdul Haleem (2004). By permission of Oxford University Press.

love God and neighbour.[87] This document, which has received much attention in interfaith circles, elicited a positive response by Christian leaders and church bodies. Whether or not this approach can transcend tensions between Muslim and Christian interpretations of Jesus remains to be seen; yet it is noteworthy that such a strong and positive declaration was made.

For Christians, it is tempting to compare the Quran to the Bible as both are the central sacred texts in these traditions. Yet it may actually be more accurate to compare the Quran to the Incarnation of Jesus as, for Muslims, the Quran is a revelatory event, the incarnation of God's way into the world.[88] It is the Hadith, the sayings of the Prophet Mohammed, which may be more equivalent to the Bible, for the Hadith points Muslims to the Quran as the Bible points Christians to the Incarnation. Hadith literature is an unparalleled source of guidance for Muslims as they seek to practise a life that honours God's ways.

It is in the Hadith that we meet images of Jesus as an end-time figure. These images arise from a suggestive passage in the Quran. In speaking of the persecution of Jesus, the Quran declares:

> [They] said, 'We have killed the Messiah, Jesus, son of Mary, the Messenger of God.' (They did not kill him, nor did they crucify him, though it was made to appear like that to them; those that disagreed about him are full of doubt, with no knowledge to follow, only supposition:

[87] *A Common Word between Us and You* (Jordan: The Royal Aal al-Bayt Institute for Islamic Thought, Jordan, ce 2007, ah 1428.) See <www.acommonword.org> or <www.acommonword.com>

[88] Wilfred Cantwell Smith was responsible for this and many other groundbreaking inter-religious insights. See his Islam in *Modern History* (New York: New American Library, 1957), p. 26.

they certainly did not kill him—God raised him up to Himself God is almighty and wise.)[89]

The plain sense of this passage is that Jesus did not die on the cross and was taken up to heaven. This difference in crucifixion narratives between Muslims and Christians is perhaps as significant as the disagreement over Jesus' divinity. It is unthinkable, for Muslims, that prophets should meet an ignominious end. Jesus is, accordingly, viewed as awaiting the end of time when he will return to fight the antichrist and proclaim again the truth of Islam prior to the community of believers being united with Mohammed. Hadith literature paints many striking pictures of the return of Jesus at the end of time.

No reference to Jesus in Muslim traditions would be complete without mention of the rich images of Jesus in Sufism. Rather than being seen as a 'school' or 'denomination' within Islam, Sufism is best viewed as a tendency across all Muslim traditions to realise more fully union with God in this life. Sufism has taken on a variety of forms through the centuries, though the earliest Sufis were ascetics concerned that Muslim wealth and prosperity in the expanding empire would lead to a corruption of the simple and pious lifestyle of the prophet Mohammed and his companions.

These early Sufis believed that Jesus spoke for their cause, especially in his conflict with the Pharisees and in the radical lifestyle he advocated in the Sermon on the Mount. Sufi traditions, accordingly, preserved many sayings of Jesus which relate Jesus to ascetic themes. In addition to sayings that are

[89] Q 4:157-58. From *The Qur'an* trans. Abdul Haleem (2004). By permission of Oxford University Press. The use of parentheses here does not indicate that this sentence is a departure from the literal text of the Quran but is simply a convention to indicate an explanatory statement following a main thought.

more or less direct quotations from the Gospels, there are many which highlight Jesus as an ascetic figure and seek, by implication, to chasten Muslims for diluting the powerful message of the Quran by too close an association with the rich and powerful.

> Jesus said, 'There are four [qualities] which are not found in one person without causing wonder: silence, which is the beginning of worship; humility before God; an ascetic attitude toward the world; and poverty.'[90]
> John, son of Zachariah, met Jesus and said, 'Tell me what it is that draws one near to God's favour and distances one from God's wrath.'
> Jesus said, 'Avoid feeling anger.' John asked, 'What arouses anger and what makes it recur?' Jesus replied, 'Pride, fanaticism, haughtiness, and magnificence.' John said, 'Let me ask you another.' 'Ask what you will,' replied Jesus. 'Adultery— what creates it and what makes it recur?' 'A glance,' said Jesus, 'which implants in the heart something that makes it veer excessively toward amusement and self-indulgence, thus increasing heedlessness and sin. Do not stare at what does not belong to you, for what you have not seen will not make you wiser and what you do not hear will not trouble you.'[91]

As Sufism grew and developed, so too did the image of Jesus as a prophet of the heart or conscience who called people to a radical break from egoistic living. Moving reflections of

---

[90] Tarif Khalidi, *The Muslim Jesus: Sayings and Stories in Islamic Literature* (Cambridge, MA and London: Harvard University Press, 2001), 'Abdallah ibn al-Mubarak (d. 181/797).

[91] Tarif Khalidi, *The Muslim Jesus*, saying no. 18, 'Abdallah ibn al-Mubarak (d. 181/797).

Jesus, containing rich imagery, can be found also in the works of Al-Ghazali (1058–1111), Ibn al-Arabi (1165–1240), and Jalaluddin Rumi (1207–1273).[92]

Because of the Muslim commitment to the Quran and to the prophetic model, Jesus will never eclipse Mohammed in importance for Muslims, yet Islamic traditions will continue to inspire Muslims with Jesus as a miracle worker, end-time figure and prophet of the heart.

Threads in the Hindu tapestry of Jesus

"Westerners have long been fascinated with India, its exotic tastes, vivid colours, and striking images of gods and goddesses. India, for many, has become a destination for religious quests; its traditions appear to offer radical alternatives to monotheistic approaches. For those with a Christian heritage, these spiritual journeys to India have sometimes resulted in dramatic re-interpretations of Christian doctrine, the establishment of Christian ashrams, intriguing fusions of Eastern philosophies with Christian thought, and, of course, new interpretations of Jesus. But can one easily say what 'Hinduism' really is?

Scholars of the past century have become suspicious of simplistic definitions of the world's religions, especially of Hindu traditions. After all, Hinduism has no single historical founder, no central authoritative structure, no central religious text (though many appeal to the Vedas in this regard), nor a single approach to key questions of how best to manifest religious truth and achieve ultimate liberation. It is better to view the many approaches on the Indian subcontinent as a rich tapestry of traditions offering various ways to discover the

---

[92] For an anthology of relevant writings by these and other Muslim authors, see Gregory A. Barker and Stephen E. Gregg, *Jesus Beyond Christianity: The Classic Texts* (Oxford: Oxford University Press, 2010), pp. 83-149.

Sanatana Dharma, or 'the eternal truth/ law' which lays claim to all dimensions of human life.

Just as there is no single approach which can be called 'Hindu', there is no single Hindu interpretation of Jesus. There are, however, several threads in the tapestry of Hindu interpretations that emerge as prominent. Some of these may be unexpected or surprising to Christians. There certainly is admiration for Jesus in Hindu traditions; and there is a wealth of Christian literature that speaks approvingly of such admiration. However examining the many threads of these interpretations reveals that this admiration is frequently accompanied by both a robust critique of Christian doctrine and a well-developed world view that sees itself in tension with Western interpretations.

When did Hindus first hear about Jesus? It is possible that some Hindus heard of Jesus in the first centuries of the Common Era, as we know of trade routes that existed between the Roman Empire and some areas of the Indian subcontinent.[93] In addition to this, there are unsubstantiated accounts of the Apostle Thomas travelling to India as well as evidence (substantiated) of Syrian-speaking Christian churches perhaps composed of traders and their families.

However if there were any Hindu reactions to Jesus in this early period, they no longer exist. One has to wait for the arrival of the European traders and colonisers of the sixteenth century onwards and, especially, to the interactions between Hindus and Christians in the context of British rule before one has access to a diversity of Hindu viewpoints on Jesus.

The most popular thread in the tapestry of Hindu approaches to Jesus is the Bhakti thread. Bhakti is the Sanskrit term that

---

[93] Stephen Neill's exhaustive study, *A History of Christianity in India: The Beginning to AD 1707* (Cambridge: Cambridge University Press, 1984), provides a reliable guide to the historical interactions between Christianity and Hinduism.

can be interpreted as 'devotion' and signifies the path of active worship of the divinities of one's spiritual heritage as the way to a right relation with the world. Perhaps one of the most tangible signs of the popularity of Jesus as an object of devotion is his appearance in 'bazaar art', where he is featured alongside Gandhi, Krishna, and other avatars which lead devotees to a closer relationship to Brahman, the divine ground of all being. Many Hindus accept Jesus as an avatar (lit. 'a descent' of Brahman), a spiritual being who comes during a time of trouble to assist in the restoration of divine order in the world.

Perhaps the great Hindu mystic Ramakrishna Paramahamsa (1836–1886) best exemplifies this approach. Though Ramakrishna was devoted to the goddess Kali, he had mystical experiences of other divine figures, including Jesus whom he described as 'Master Yogi' and 'Love Incarnate', a being who is in eternal communion with God.[94]

Hindus following the path of devotion, however, are often perplexed by the Christian insistence upon the exclusivity of Christ's divinity. Deeply ingrained in Hindu traditions is the belief in multiple manifestations of divinity, though one may legitimately choose to focus upon specific divine figures emphasised in one's tradition. In addition to this reservation, there are some aspects of Jesus' life that appear to fall short of glorious aspects from the narratives of popular avatars: Jesus' humble birth, his lowly status, and his ignominious end on the cross. This may be the reason why Jesus is not destined to play a more central role in Hindu devotion.

A very different approach to Jesus is found in the Advaitic (lit. 'non-dual') thread; this is the approach which stresses the inter-relatedness of all reality. Those on this path do not reject

---

[94] Nikhilananda (ed. and trans.), *The Gospel of Sri Ramakrisna: Translated into English with an Introduction by Swanti Nikhilananda* (New York: Ramakrishna-Vivekananda Center, 1984 [1942]), p.34.

worship, but believe that the highest spiritual expression is the realisation of one's soul as identical to Brahman. This is not a glorified egoism: as one realises that one's fears, jealousies, greed, and various indulgences of the physical senses are not essential characteristics, one begins to discover unity with the divine. There is, for advaitins, a hierarchy of spiritual evolution: from animism and polytheism and other forms in which one is aware of being separate from divine reality through to the realisation of the essential unity of the soul with the divine.

Swami Vivekananda (1863–1902), a disciple of Ramakrishna, identified this hierarchy of spiritual approaches in Jesus' life:

> You will find that these three stages are taught by the great Teacher in thc New Testament. Note the Common Prayer He taught: 'Our Father which art in Heaven, hallowed be Thy name,' and so on; a simple prayer; mark you, a child's prayer; it is indeed the 'Common Prayer', because it is intended for the uneducated masses. To a higher circle, to those who had advanced a little more, He gave a more elevated teaching: 'I am in my Father, and ye in me, and I in you.' Do you remember that? And then, when the Jews asked Him who He was, He declared that He and His Father were one; and the Jews thought that that was blasphemy. What did He mean by that? The same thing has been told also by our prophets: 'You are gods and all ye are Children of the Most High.' Mark the same three stages; you will find that it is easier for you to begin with the first and end with the last.[95]

---

[95] Swami Vivekananda, *Christ the Messenger* (Calcutta: Udbonhan Office, 1984 [1900], pp.19-10.

Accordingly when giving an account of the crucifixion, Hindu philosophers view it not as an exclusivist moment of reconciliation between humanity and the divine realm, but as a metaphor both for the egoistic behaviours which inevitably assault a spiritual quest and for the attitude of forgiveness which must meet such opposition in order finally to overcome it.

One must not overlook the thread of resistance to Jesus that weaves itself through many Hindu traditions. Given that social and religious oppression accompanied the colonial enterprise, and that Jesus was the religious figure of the colonisers, many thinkers and leaders in India have felt that the best strategy for independence would be either to criticise or completely to ignore the question of the meaning of Jesus. This approach actually intensified with the growing support for the specific version of Hindu nationalism represented by the BJP, the RSS, and other groups. Many within this thread consider Jesus to be nothing more than a Western 'export', one who threatens the quest for meaning and identity which can best be found on Indian soil.

The final thread we will consider is a Hindu tradition which can be seen as presenting a challenge to popular Western interpretations: the Sannyasin Jesus. Many Hindus consider it ideal to pass through several distinct stages prior to realising full liberation. One begins as a student of Vedic traditions and moves on to the responsibilities of the householder stage. At the conclusion of these duties, one then begins deliberately to relinquish one's hold on the world. At the end of one's life, there is a complete dedication to the life of the spirit; this is accompanied by disciplines of poverty, celibacy, meditation, devotion, etc. This final stage is called the Sannyasin Asharama, literally, 'renouncer stage'. Although few Hindus today strictly follow this pattern, when Jesus as portrayed in the Gospels is under discussion, he appears, for them, as a Sannyasin whose life resembles more the Eastern holy quest than it does the Western preoccupations with wealth, comfort, and scientific progress.

Vivekananda's earliest response to Jesus is, interestingly, found in the Bengali translation of *The Imitation of Christ*, where he makes the case that Jesus' complete surrender to God is evidenced in his renunciate lifestyle. Mohandas Karamchand Gandhi (1869–1948), renowned for his policy of non-violent active resistance, urged Christians to manifest the life embraced by Jesus rather than seeking Hindu converts through an egoistic show of intellectual prowess. An aspect of Gandhi's rich and nuanced interpretation of the Gospels stressed that to ignore the poverty of Jesus is to negate his spirituality. The renouncing of material possessions as the path to peace is always, according to Gandhi, an aspect of the larger spiritual vision embraced by all great religious leaders: Mohammed, Buddha, Nanak, Kabir, Chaitanya, Shankara, etc:

> ... the *New Testament* produced a different impression [from the Old Testament], especially the *Sermon on the Mount* which went straight to my heart. I compared it with the *Gita*. The verses—'But I say unto you, that ye resist not evil: but whosoever shall smite thee on thy right cheek, turn to him the other also;' and, 'If any man take away thy coat, let him have thy cloak too'—delighted me beyond measure and put me in mind of Shamal Bhatt's 'For a bowl of water, give a goodly meal', etc. My young mind tried to unify the teaching of the *Gita, The Light of Asia* and the *Sermon on the Mount*. That renunciation was the highest form of religion appealed to me greatly.[96]

[96] M. K. Gandhi, *The Message of Jesus Christ*, ed. Anand T. Hingorani (Bombay: Bharatiya Vidya Bhavan, 1963), p.4.

Indian Christians, reflecting on these approaches, have challenged the wider Christian Church both to embrace a Christology which stresses the voluntary poverty of Jesus and to embrace philosophical traditions of the Indian subcontinent as a valid vehicle for Christology, just as the Church has been open to Graeco-Roman traditions in the formulation of historic creeds.

Buddhists and the awareness of Jesus

Buddhism enjoys widespread interest in the West. Its popular spiritual teachers, well- developed approaches to meditation, and nuanced philosophical concepts have helped Buddhism to become the religion of choice for those disenchanted by Christianity but who wish to find a 'religious' rather than a 'secular' path through life. Meditation classes, the appearances of popular Buddhist teachers, and Buddhist retreat centres are now features across Western countries. Christians from Thomas Merton (1915–1968) to Roger Corless (1938–2007) have discovered important fusions between Christian prayer and Buddhist meditation. But what do Buddhists make of Jesus?

The answer to this question may be more difficult to discover than at first appears. In Western countries where Buddhism has been chosen as an alternative to Christianity there has been much discussion of Jesus and Christianity—usually highly critical of Christian doctrine and approving of Jesus as a proto-Buddhist. But what do Buddhists outside of these culture wars make of Jesus?

Lands which have long been centres of Buddhist practice have not had much opportunity to interact with Christianity until more recent times. When the barriers of politics and geography were overcome, additional barriers were found, including one of attitude which has hindered Buddhist reflection on the central figure of Christianity. Because Buddhism grew out of a Hindu religious context, it is Hindu traditions rather than Christianity that have been viewed as the primary area for interfaith reflection. Under the umbrella of Hindu devotionalism, there are non-dual views which, in their distance from a personalistic theism, may provide the basis for philosophical overtures with Buddhism. However Christianity, at first glance, may appear to Buddhists as a degraded form of Hindu devotional tendencies and therefore not worthy of concern. Add to this the fact that Buddhists have had to relate their traditions to Confucian, Shinto, and other Asian traditions and one has an explanation for the dearth of reflection by Buddhists on Christianity's central figure.[97]

When Buddhists have considered Jesus, there are some common themes that emerge across many different Buddhist traditions. First, there is an allergy to Jesus' belief in the personal God of the Hebrew Scriptures. This deity, complete with a full range of emotions, appears to be far from the ideal of non-attachment prized by Buddhists. Buddhist traditions do embrace a wide range of supernatural beings, but these beings are frequently bound to unhelpful cycles which prevent liberation; the Hebrew God appears to be one of these. In the struggle for identity in the face of Christian missionaries who could only see darkness in Buddhism, Buddhist leaders frequently seized upon conceptual differences between the religions to establish Buddhist conceptual superiority, the chief one being personalistic conceptions of God, versus non-personal approaches to reality. Other differences have included creation versus co-dependent origination, sin versus karma and heaven versus nirvana. Jesus is often viewed as tainted by association with a Christian cosmology.

---

[97] For an overview of Jesus in Buddhist traditions see Jose Ignacio Cabezon, Buddhist Views of Jesus' in Gregory A. Barker (ed.), *Jesus in the World's Faiths: Leading Thinkers From Five Religions Reflect on His Meaning* (New York: Orbis, 2008), pp. 15-24.

Few Buddhists would object, however, to the radical approach of Jesus embodied in the Sermon on the Mount. Here, Jesus is viewed as having transcended the narrow confines of his own traditions and having articulated a universalistic ethic which, if followed, could help the entire world to be freed from unhealthy attachments. Furthermore, the teachings of the Sermon appear to grasp the key principles of the interconnection between all things as well as the need for compassion to prevail. The Dalai Lama, reflecting on Christianity, has said,

> These Gospel passages also remind me of reflections in another Mahayana text called *A Guide to the Bodhisattva's Way of Life*, in which Shantideva states that it is very important to develop the right attitude toward your enemy. If you can cultivate the right attitude, your enemies are your best spiritual teachers because their presence provides you with the opportunity to enhance and develop tolerance, patience, and understanding.
>
> By developing greater tolerance and patience, it will be easier for you to develop your capacity for compassion and, through that, altruism. So even for the practice of your own spiritual path, the presence of an enemy is crucial. The analogy drawn in the Gospel as to how 'the sun makes no discrimination where it shines' is very significant. The sun shines for all and makes no discrimination. This is a wonderful metaphor for compassion. It gives you the sense of its impartiality and all-embracing nature.[98]

---

[98] Robert Keily (ed.), *The Good Heart: His Holiness the Dalai Lama Explores the Heart of Christianity and Humanity* (London: Rider, 2002), pp.47ff.

There is one additional area of Jesus' life that is met with admiration when considered by Buddhists: the crucifixion. What is important for Buddhists is not concepts of atonement or sacrifice that have been a part of the fabric of Christian theological development through the centuries. Rather it is the attitude of Jesus on the cross that speaks to Buddhists of an enlightened figure who was not attached to revenge, fear, hatred, or envy. For Buddhists the words of the Gospel of Luke point to this truth: 'Father, forgive them; for they do not know what they are doing' (Luke 23: 34, NRSV). A Buddhist might paraphrase this verse using the term 'aware': 'Father, they are not aware of what they are doing'. To display such a compassionate awareness while at the same time experiencing physical pain is a sign of having reached a highly evolved spiritual state.

In addition to these general themes, there are certain 'inclinations' of interpretations of Jesus which are characteristic of Theravada and Mahayana paths.

Theravada Buddhism (lit. 'the way of the elders') has over 100 million adherents, most of whom live in southeast Asia. This school claims to have preserved the original teachings and practices of the historical Buddha as followed by the first sangha ('community'). Here, the accent is on the need to redeem oneself in the context of a commitment to the three jewels (the Buddha's example, the path of the Dharma, and the discipline of the sangha). Theravada Buddhists are proud of the rich legacy of teaching of their founder over a forty-five-year period. Jesus, in contrast, taught for only three years (at most) and his teachings appear to be sporadically delivered, unorganised, and incomplete. There is a sense that there are nuggets to be found, though one has to sift through much that is culturally and spiritually limited. Perhaps the most influential exponent of Theravada traditions to the West was Anagarika Dharmapala (1864–1933); one can see in his writings both admiration and reservation toward Jesus:

> I compare the teachings of Jesus with the teachings of the Buddha, his parables with the Buddhist parables, his ethical and psychological teachings with the ethics and psychology of Buddhism. Thereby I have been greatly benefited in the intuitional acceptance of Truth. Sometimes I identify myself with Christian teachings so much so that I desire to make an effort to reform Christianity just as Paul did, who had not seen Jesus physically, but had the boldness to challenge and crush Cephas, the personal disciple of Jesus. I … would suggest to ignore the stories of the O. T. as divine scriptures. As folklore stories of a nomadic people we should treat the Old Testament. The pure teachings of the gentle Nazarene we have to sift from the later theological accretions, and then we can make Jesus a central figure in the universal church of truth. Science is progressive, while theology belongs to a decadent age. Buddhism is progressive because it did not touch on theological dogmatics, neither was it agnostic. It taught a discipline and enunciated generalized cosmic truths.[99]

Mahayana traditions have emphasised three themes which have led to much dialogue between Buddhists and Christians: a cosmology of the Buddha as a transcendent being with three 'bodies' (the Trikaya), radical perspectives on the nature of emptiness of all concepts, and an emphasis on the Bodhisattva path for all Buddhists. Accordingly, comparisons between the Trinity and Trikaya as well as Christian mysticism and Buddhist emptiness have become hallmarks in Buddhist–Christian conversations. It is the Bodhisattva theme, however,

---

[99] From Anagarika Dharmapala, 'An Appreciation of Christianity', *Mali a Bhodi Journal*, vol. 35 (December 1927), lecture delivered in the Temple at the City in London, 3 October, 1927.

which has been at the forefront of Mahayana assessments of Jesus.

A Bodhisattva (lit. 'wisdom being') is one who has reached enlightenment but, instead of departing from the cycle of rebirth and entering nirvana, has committed to the path of the welfare of all sentient beings. As Buddhism spread to lands with other religious figures, these often came to be viewed as Bodhisattvas existing in various regions of the universe to whom one could appeal for help on the path to enlightenment. In this understanding, Jesus can be viewed as a Bodhisattva for Christians, one who has taken a vow to give his life so that all may come to enlightenment. The theism which accompanies traditional Christianity can be viewed by Buddhists as the raft in the famous parable attributed to the Buddha: when one has crossed rivers on one's journey to liberation, the raft of theological doctrine (in this case, theism) may then be left aside and the journey continued.

One final approach within Mahayana traditions stands out for its ability to view many of Jesus' teachings in a positive manner. Zen Buddhism should be understood as an intuitive path to the realisation of oneself as a spiritual unity rather than as a systematic philosophy. One does not reach enlightenment by reason but by insights that cannot be confined to a single spiritual tradition or thought process—though training and discipline are certainly necessary. For some Zen figures, Jesus' teaching can be seen as consistently confounding traditional ways of seeing things and thus helping one to let go of rigid ways of viewing reality.[100]

Though Jesus is far from a central figure in Buddhist traditions, Buddhism is providing fresh religious approaches for many who are attempting to re-interpret the meaning of Jesus.

---

[100] For a popular treatment of this approach, see Kenneth Leong, *The Zen Teachings of Jesus*, 2nd revised edn (New York: Crossroad, 2001).

A verdict on Jesus in the world's religions

It is fascinating to see the ways in which Jesus has become a subject of reflection across the spectrum of religious traditions. Predictably, there is resistance to Jesus when he has been closely identified with oppressive colonial efforts. In fact, the criticism of Jesus and his teachings, at times, can be both comprehensive and sharp. Even here these criticisms can be instructive for Christians; it is undeniable that power and status can privilege certain Christian interpretations which may not be consonant with the intentions of this God-centred first-century figure. On the other hand, there are a great number of positive responses to Jesus' teachings, especially to the Sermon on the Mount. Jesus is recognised by many from diverse traditions as having grasped the depth of our alienation from Ultimate Reality and from one another as well as having identified that nothing other than a radical change is needed in order to find a way ahead. Yet, even here we must be careful not to ignore dissonant voices. There are many religious traditions which value the positive role that tradition-specific regulations, laws, and rituals can play in sustaining a community amid oppression and the challenge of larger, more aggressive or popular approaches. These voices wonder if Jesus' radical message, though inspiring for certain individuals, may, in fact, harm culture and community.

Many of the views emerging from this introductory examination of Jesus in the world's religions are not convenient to traditional Christian interpretations. The variety of thought is, in fact, staggering and prevents one from making even the most general statements about the position of Jesus across the world. But isn't facing a lack of convenience a part of any enthralling journey into the unknown? The traveller may not know exactly how to value what she or he has encountered until long after a return home and a time of reflection. As one takes this time to reflect, one is no longer an 'Accidental Tourist', but an informed traveller.

The Greatest Thing in the World

Henry Drummond

New York   Chicago
Fleming H. Revell Company
LONDON AND EDINBURGH

Printed in the United States of America

INTRODUCTORY

I was staying with a party of friends in a country house during my visit to England in 1884. On Sunday evening as we sat around the fire, they asked me to read and expound some portion of Scripture. Being tired after the services of the day, I told them to ask Henry Drummond, who was one of the party. After some urging he drew a small Testament from his hip pocket, opened it at the 13th chapter of I Corinthians, and began to speak on the subject of Love.

It seemed to me that I had never heard anything so beautiful, and I determined not to rest until I brought Henry Drummond to Northfield to deliver that address. Since then I have requested the principals of my schools to have it read before the students every year. The one great need in our Christian life is love, more love to God and to each other. Would that we could all move into that Love chapter, and live there.

D.L. Moody

Love: The Greatest Thing in the World

Every one has asked himself the great question of antiquity as of the modern world: What is the summum bonum—the supreme good? You have life before you. Once only you can live it. What is the noblest object of desire, the supreme gift to covet?

We have been accustomed to be told that the greatest thing in the religious world is Faith. That great word has been the key-note for centuries of the popular religion; and we have easily learned to look upon it as the greatest thing in the world. Well, we are wrong. If we have been told that, we may miss the mark. In the 13th chapter of I Corinthians, Paul takes us to

Christianity at its source

and there we see, "The greatest of these is love."

It is not an oversight. Paul was speaking of faith just a moment before. He says, "If I have all faith, so that I can remove mountains, and have not love, I am nothing." So far from forgetting, he deliberately contrasts them, "Now abideth Faith, Hope, Love," and without a moment's hesitation the decision falls, "The greatest of these is Love."

And it is not prejudice. A man is apt to recommend to others his own strong point. Love was not Paul's strong point. The observing student can detect a beautiful tenderness growing and ripening all through his character as Paul gets old; but the hand that wrote, "The greatest of these is love," when we meet it first, is stained with blood.

Nor is this letter to the Corinthians peculiar in singling out love as the summum bonum. The masterpieces of Christianity are agreed about it. Peter says, "Above all things have fervent love among yourselves." Above all things. And John goes farther, "God is love."

You remember the profound remark which Paul makes elsewhere, "Love is the fulfilling of the law." Did you ever think what he meant by that? In those days men were working the passage to Heaven by keeping the Ten Commandments, and the hundred and ten other commandments which they had manufactured out of them. Christ came and said, "I will show you a more simple way. If you do one thing, you will do these hundred and ten things, without ever thinking about them. If you love, you will unconsciously fulfill the whole law."

You can readily see for yourselves how that must be so. Take any of the commandments. "Thou shalt have no other gods before Me." If a man love God, you will not require to tell him that. Love is the fulfilling of that law. "Take not His name in vain." Would he ever dream of taking His name in vain if he loved him? "Remember the Sabbath day to keep it holy." Would he not be too glad to have one day in seven to dedicate more exclusively to the object of his affection? Love would fulfill all these laws regarding God.

And so, if he loved man, you would never think of telling him to honour his father and mother. He could not do anything else. It would be preposterous to tell him not to kill. You could only insult him if you suggested that he should not steal—how could he steal from those he loved? It would be superfluous to beg him not to bear false witness against his neighbour. If he loved him it would be the last thing he would do. And you would never dream of urging him not to covet what his neighbours had. He would rather they possessed it than himself. In this way "Love is the fulfilling of the law." It is the rule for fulfilling all rules, the new commandment for keeping all the old commandments, Christ's one

Secret of the Christian Life

Now Paul has learned that; and in this noble eulogy he has given us the most wonderful and original account extant of the summum bonum. We may divide it into three parts. In the beginning of the short chapter we have Love contrasted; in the heart of it, we have Love analyzed; toward the end, we have Love defended as the supreme gift.

I. The Contrast

Paul begins by contrasting Love with other things that men in those days thought much of. I shall not attempt to go over these things in detail. Their inferiority is already obvious.

He contrasts it with eloquence. And what a noble gift it is, the power of playing upon the souls and wills of men, and rousing them to lofty purposes and holy deeds! Paul says, "If I speak with the tongues of men and of angels, and have not love, I am become sounding brass, or a tinkling cymbal." We all know why. We have all felt the brazenness of words without emotion, the hollowness, the unaccountable unpersuasiveness, of eloquence behind which lies no Love.

He contrasts it with prophecy. He contrasts it with mysteries. He contrasts it with faith. He contrasts it with charity. Why is Love greater than faith? Because the end is greater than the means. And why is it greater than charity? Because the whole is greater than the part.

Love is greater than faith, because the end is greater than the means. What is the use of having faith? It is to connect the soul with God. And what is the object of connecting man with God? That he may become like God. But God is Love. Hence Faith, the means, is in order to Love, the end. Love, therefore, obviously is greater than faith. "If I have all faith, so as to remove mountains, but have not love, I am nothing."

It is greater than charity, again, because the whole is greater than a part. Charity is only a little bit of Love, one of the innumerable avenues of Love, and there may even be, and there is, a great deal of charity without Love. It is a very easy thing to toss a copper to a beggar on the street; it is generally an easier thing than not to do it. Yet Love is just as often in the withholding. We purchase relief from the sympathetic feelings roused by the spectacle of misery, at the copper's cost. It is too cheap—too cheap for us, and often too dear for the beggar. If we really loved him we would either do more for him, or less. Hence, "If I bestow all my goods to feed the poor, but have not love it profiteth me nothing."

Then Paul contrasts it with sacrifice and martyrdom: "If I give my body to be burned, but have not love, it profiteth me nothing." Missionaries can take nothing greater to the heathen world than the impress and reflection of the Love of God upon their own character. That is the universal language. It will take them years to speak in Chinese, or in the dialects of India. From the day they land, that language of Love, understood by all, will be pouring forth its unconscious eloquence.

It is the man who is the missionary, it is not his words. His character is his message. In the heart of Africa, among the great Lakes, I have come across black men and women who remembered the only white man they ever saw before—David Livingstone; and as you cross his footsteps in that dark continent,

Men's faces light up

as they speak of the kind doctor who passed there years ago. They could not understand him; but they felt the love that beat in his heart. They knew that it was love, although he spoke no word.

Take into your sphere of labor, where you also mean to lay down your life, that simple charm, and your lifework must succeed. You can take nothing greater, you need take nothing less. You may take every accomplishment; you may be braced for every sacrifice; but if you give your body to be burned, and have not Love, it will profit you and the cause of Christ nothing.

II. The Analysis

After contrasting Love with these things, Paul, in three verses, very short, gives us an amazing analysis of what this supreme thing is.

I ask you to look at it. It is a compound thing, he tells us. It is like light. As you have seen a man of science take a beam of light and pass it through a crystal prism, as you have seen it come out on the other side of the prism broken up into its component colours—red, and blue, and yellow, and violet, and orange, and all the colours of the rainbow—so Paul passes this thing, Love, through the magnificent prism of his inspired intellect, and it comes out on the other side broken up into its elements.

In these few words we have what one might call

The Spectrum of Love

the analysis of Love. Will you observe what its elements are? Will you notice that they have common names; that they are virtues which we hear about every day; that they are things which can be practised by every man in every place in life; and how, by a multitude of small things and ordinary virtues, the supreme thing, the summum bonum, is made up?

The Spectrum of Love has nine ingredients:

Patience	"Love sufferers long."
Kindness	"And is kind."
Generosity	"Love envieth not."
Humility	"Love vaunteth not itself, is not puffed up."

Courtesy	"Doth not behave itself unseemly."
Unselfishness	"Seeketh not its own."
Good temper	"Is not provoked."
Guilelessness	"Taketh not account of evil."
Sincerity	"Rejoiceth not in unrighteousness, but rejoiceth with the truth."

Patience; kindness; generosity; humility; courtesy; unselfishness; good temper; guilelessness; sincerity—these make up the supreme gift, the stature of the perfect man.

You will observe that all are in relation to men, in relation to life, in relation to the known to-day and the near to-morrow, and not to the unknown eternity. We hear much of love to God; Christ spoke much of love to man. We make a great deal of peace with heaven; Christ made much of peace on earth. Religion is not a strange or added thing, but the inspiration of the secular life, the breathing of an eternal spirit through this temporal world. The supreme thing, in short, is not a thing at all, but the giving of a further finish to the multitudinous words and acts which make up the sum of every common day.

Patience. This is the normal attitude of love; Love passive, Love waiting to begin; not in a hurry; calm; ready to do its work when the summons comes, but meantime wearing the ornament of a meek and quiet spirit. Love suffers long; beareth all things; believeth all things; hopeth all things. For Love understands, and therefore waits.

Kindness. Love active. Have you ever noticed how much of Christ's life was spent in doing kind things—in merely doing kind things? Run over it with that in view, and you will find that He spent a great proportion of His time simply in making people happy, in

Doing Good Turns

to people. There is only one thing greater than happiness in the world, and that is holiness; and it is not in our keeping; but what God has put in our power is the happiness of those about us, and that is largely to be secured by our being kind to them.

"The greatest thing," says some one, "a man can do for his Heavenly Father is to be kind to some of His other children." I wonder why it is that we are not all kinder than we are? How much the world needs it! How easily it is done! How instantaneously it acts! How infallibly it is remembered! How superabundantly it pays itself back—for there is no debtor in the world so honourable, so superbly honourable, as Love. "Love never faileth." Love is success, Love is happiness, Love is life. "Love," I say with Browning, "is energy of life."

"For life, with all it yields of joy or woe

And hope and fear,

Is just our chance o' the prize of learning love,—

How love might be, hath been indeed, and is."

Where Love is, God is. He that dwelleth in Love dwelleth in God. God is Love. Therefore love. Without distinction, without calculation, without procrastination, love. Lavish it upon the poor, where it is very easy; especially upon the rich, who often need it most; most of all upon our equals, where it is very difficult, and for whom perhaps we each do least of all. There is a difference between trying to please and giving pleasure. Give pleasure. Lose no chance of giving pleasure; for that is the ceaseless and anonymous triumph of a truly loving spirit. "I shall pass through this world but once. Any good thing, therefore, that I can do, or any kindness that I can show to any human being, let me do it now. Let me not defer it or neglect it, for I shall not pass this way again."

Generosity. "Love envieth not." This is love in competition with others. Whenever you attempt a good work you will find other men doing the same kind of work, and probably doing it better. Envy them not. Envy is a feeling of ill-will to those who are in the same line as ourselves, a spirit of covetousness and detraction. How little Christian work even is a protection against un-Christian feeling! That most despicable of all the unworthy moods which cloud a Christian's soul assuredly waits for us on the threshold of every work, unless we are fortified with this grace of magnanimity. Only one thing truly need the Christian envy—the large, rich, generous soul which "envieth not."

And then, after having learned all that, you have to learn this further thing, Humility—to put a seal upon your lips and forget what you have done. After you have been kind, after Love has stolen forth into the world and done its beautiful work, go back into the shade again and say nothing about it. Love hides even from itself. Love waives even self-satisfaction. "Love vaunteth not itself, is not puffed up." Humility—love hiding.

The fifth ingredient is a somewhat strange one to find in this summum bonum: Courtesy. This is Love in society, Love in relation to etiquette. "Love does not behave itself unseemly."

Politeness has been defined as love in trifles. Courtesy is said to be love in little things. And the one secret of politeness is to love.

Love cannot behave itself unseemly. You can put the most untutored persons into the highest society, and if they have a reservoir of Love in their heart they will not behave themselves unseemly. They simply cannot do it. Carlisle said of Robert Burns that there was no truer gentleman in Europe than the ploughman-poet. It was because he loved everything—the mouse, and the daisy, and all the things, great and small, that

God had made. So with this simple passport he could mingle with any society, and enter courts and palaces from his little cottage on the banks of the Ayr.

You know the meaning of the word "gentleman." It means a gentle man—a man who does things gently, with love. That is the whole art and mystery of it. The gentle man cannot in the nature of things do an ungentle, an ungentlemanly thing. The ungentle soul, the inconsiderate, unsympathetic nature, cannot do anything else. "Love doth not behave itself unseemly."

Unselfishness. "Love seeketh not her own." Observe: Seeketh not even that which is her own. In Britain the Englishman is devoted, and rightly, to his rights. But there come times when a man may exercise even

The Higher Right

of giving up his rights.

Yet Paul does not summon us to give up our rights. Love strikes much deeper. It would have us not seek them at all, ignore them, eliminate the personal element altogether from our calculations.

It is not hard to give up our rights. They are often eternal. The difficult thing is to give up ourselves. The more difficult thing still is not to seek things for ourselves at all. After we have sought them, bought them, won them, deserved them, we have taken the cream off them for ourselves already. Little cross then to give them up. But not to seek them, to look every man not on his own things, but on the things of others—that is the difficulty. "Seekest thou great things for thyself?" said the prophet; "seek them not." Why? Because there is no greatness in things. Things cannot be great. The only greatness is unselfish love. Even self-denial in itself is nothing, is almost a mistake. Only a great purpose or a mightier love can justify the waste.

It is more difficult, I have said, not to seek our own at all than, having sought it, to give it up. I must take that back. It is only true of a partly selfish heart. Nothing is a hardship to Love, and nothing is hard. I believe that Christ's "yoke" is easy. Christ's yoke is just His way of taking life. And I believe it is an easier way than any other. I believe it is a happier way than any other. The most obvious lesson in Christ's teaching is that there is no happiness in having and getting anything, but only in giving. I repeat, there is no happiness in having or in getting, but only in giving. Half the world is on the wrong scent in pursuit of happiness. They think it consists in having and getting, and in being served by others. It consists in giving, and in serving others. "He that would be great among you," said Christ, "let him serve." He that would be happy, let him remember that there is but one way—"it is more blessed, it is more happy, to give than to receive."

The next ingredient is a very remarkable one: Good temper. "Love is not provoked."

Nothing could be more striking than to find this here. We are inclined to look upon bad temper as a very harmless weakness. We speak of it as a mere infirmity of nature, a family failing, a matter of temperament, not a thing to take into very serious account in estimating a man's character. And yet here, right in the heart of this analysis of love, it finds a place; and the Bible again and again returns to condemn it as one of the most destructive elements in human nature.

The peculiarity of ill temper is that it is the vice of the virtuous. It is often the one blot on an otherwise noble character. You know men who are all but perfect, and women who would be entirely perfect, but for an easily ruffled, quick-tempered, or "touchy" disposition. This compatibility of ill temper with high moral character is one of the strangest and saddest problems of ethics. The truth is, there are two great classes of sins—sins of the Body and sins of the Disposition. The Prodigal Son may be taken as a type of the first, the Elder Brother of the second. Now, society has no doubt whatever as to which of these is the worse. Its brand falls, without a challenge, upon the Prodigal. But are we right? We have no balance to weigh one another's sins, and coarser and finer are but human words; but faults in the higher nature may be less venal than those in the lower, and to the eye of Him who is Love, a sin against Love may seem a hundred times more base. No form of vice, not worldliness, not greed of gold, not drunkenness itself, does more to un-Christianize society than evil temper. For embittering life, for breaking up communities, for destroying the most sacred relationships, for devastating homes, for withering up men and women, for taking the bloom of childhood, in short,

For Sheer Gratuitous Misery-Producing Power

this influence stands alone.

Look at the Elder Brother—moral, hard-working, patient, dutiful—let him get all credit for his virtues—look at this man, this baby, sulking outside his own father's door. "He was angry," we read, "and would not go in." Look at the effect upon the father, upon the servants, upon the happiness of the guests. Judge of the effect upon the Prodigal—and how many prodigals are kept out of the Kingdom of God by the unlovely character of those who profess to be inside. Analyze, as a study in Temper, the thunder-cloud itself as it gathers upon the Elder Brother's brow. What is it made of? Jealousy, anger, pride, uncharity, cruelty, self-righteousness, touchiness, doggedness, sullenness—these are the ingredients of this dark and loveless soul. In varying proportions, also, these are the ingredients of all ill temper. Judge if such sins of the disposition are not worse to live in, and for others to live with, than the sins of the body. Did Christ indeed not answer the question Himself when He said, "I say unto you that the publicans and the harlots go into the Kingdom of Heaven before you"? There is really no place in heaven for a disposition like this. A man with such a mood could only make heaven miserable for all the people in it. Except, therefore, such a man be

Born Again

he cannot, simply cannot, enter the kingdom of heaven.

You will see then why Temper is significant. It is not in what it is alone, but in what it reveals. This is why I speak of it with such unusual plainness. It is a test for love, a symptom, a revelation of an unloving nature at bottom. It is the intermittent fever which bespeaks unintermittent disease within; the occasional bubble escaping to the surface which betrays some rottenness underneath; a sample of the most hidden products of the soul dropped involuntarily when off one's guard; in a word, the lightning form of a hundred hideous and un-Christian sins. A want of patience, a want of kindness, a want of generosity, a want of courtesy, a want of unselfishness, are all instantaneously symbolized in one flash of Temper.

Hence it is not enough to deal with the Temper. We must go to the source, and change the inmost nature, and the angry humors will die away of themselves. Souls are made sweet not by taking the acid fluids out, but by putting something in—a great Love, a new Spirit, the Spirit of Christ. Christ, the Spirit of Christ, interpenetrating ours, sweetens, purifies, transforms all. This only can eradicate what is wrong, work a chemical change, renovate and regenerate, and rehabilitate the inner man. Will-power does not change men. Time does not change men.

Christ Does

Therefore, "Let that mind be in you which was also in Christ Jesus."

Some of us have not much time to lose. Remember, once more, that this is a matter of life or death. I cannot help speaking urgently, for myself, for yourselves. "Whoso shall offend one of these little ones, which believe in me, it were better for him that a millstone were hanged about his neck, and that he were drowned in the depth of the sea." That is to say, it is the deliberate verdict of the Lord Jesus that it is better not to live than not to love. It is better not to live than not to love.

Guilelessness and Sincerity may be dismissed almost without a word. Guilelessness is the grace for suspicious people. The possession of it is

The Greatest Secret of Personal Influence

You will find, if you think for a moment, that the people who influence you are people who believe in you. In an atmosphere of suspicion men shrivel up; but in that atmosphere they expand, and find encouragement and educative fellowship.

It is a wonderful thing that here and there in this hard, uncharitable world there should still be left a few rare souls who think no evil. This is the great unworldliness. Love "thinketh no evil," imputes no motive, sees the bright side, puts the best construction on every action. What a delightful state of mind to live in! What a stimulus and benediction even to meet with it for a day! To be trusted is to be saved. And if we try to influence or elevate others, we shall soon see that success is in proportion to their belief of our belief in them. The respect of another is the first restoration of the self-respect a man has lost; our ideal of what he is becomes to him the hope and pattern of what he may become.

"Love rejoiceth not in unrighteousness, but rejoiceth with the truth." I have called this Sincerity from the words rendered in the Authorized Version by "rejoiceth in the truth." And, certainly, were this the real translation, nothing could be more just; for he who loves will love Truth not less than men. He will rejoice in the Truth—rejoice not in what he has been taught to believe; not in this church's doctrine or in that; not in this ism or in that ism; but "in the Truth." He will accept only what is real; he will strive to get at facts; he will search for Truth with a humble and unbiased mind, and cherish whatever he finds at any sacrifice. But the more literal translation of the Revised Version calls for just such a sacrifice for truth's sake here. For what Paul really meant is, as we there read, "Rejoiceth not in unrighteousness, but rejoiceth with the truth," a quality which probably no one English word—and certainly not Sincerity—adequately defines. It includes, perhaps more strictly, the self-restraint which refuses to make capital out of others' faults; the charity which delights not in exposing the weakness of others, but "covereth all things"; the sincerity of purpose which endeavors to see things as they are, and rejoices to find them better than suspicion feared or calumny denounced.

So much for the analysis of Love. Now the business of our lives is to have these things fitted into our characters. That is the supreme work to which we need to address ourselves in this world, to learn Love. Is life not full of opportunities for learning Love? Every man and woman every day has a thousand of them. The world is not a playground; it is a schoolroom. Life is not a holiday, but an education. And

The One Eternal Lesson

for us all is how better we can love.

What makes a man a good cricketer? Practice. What makes a man a good artist, a good sculptor, a good musician? Practice. What makes a man a good linguist, a good stenographer? Practice. What makes a man a good man? Practice. Nothing else. There is nothing capricious about religion. We do not get the soul in different ways, under different laws, from those in which we get the body and the mind. If a man does not exercise his arm he develops no biceps muscle; and if a man does not exercise his soul, he acquires no muscle in his soul, no strength of character, no vigor of moral fibre, no beauty of spiritual growth. Love is not a thing of enthusiastic emotion. It is a rich, strong, manly, vigorous expression of the whole round Christian character—the Christlike nature in its fullest development. And the constituents of this great character are only to be built up by

Ceaseless Practise

What was Christ doing in the carpenter's shop? Practising. Though perfect, we read that He learned obedience, and grew in wisdom and in favour with God. Do not quarrel, therefore, with your lot in life. Do not complain of its never-ceasing cares, its petty environment, the vexations you have to stand, the small and sordid souls you have to live and work with. Above all, do not resent temptation; do not be perplexed because it seems to thicken round you more and more, and ceases neither for effort nor for agony nor prayer. That is your practice. That is the practice which God appoints you; and it is having its work in making you patient, and humble, and generous, and unselfish, and kind, and courteous. Do not grudge the hand that is moulding the still too shapeless image within you. It is growing more beautiful, though you see it not; and every touch of temptation may add to its perfection. Therefore keep in the midst of life. Do not isolate yourself. Be among men and among things, and among troubles, and difficulties, and obstacles. You remember Goethe's words: "Talent develops itself in solitude; character in the stream of life." Talent develops itself in solitude—the talent of prayer, of faith, of meditation, of seeing the unseen; character grows in the stream of the world's life. That chiefly is where men are to learn love.

How? Now, how? To make it easier, I have named a few of the elements of love. But these are only elements. Love itself can never be defined. Light is a something more than the sum of its ingredients—a glowing, dazzling, tremulous ether. And love is something more than all its elements—a palpitating, quivering, sensitive, living thing. By synthesis of all the colors, men can make whiteness, they cannot make light. By synthesis of all the virtues, men can make virtue, they cannot make love. How then are we to have this transcendent living whole conveyed into our souls? We brace our wills to secure it. We try to copy those who have it. We lay down rules about it. We watch. We pray. But these things alone will not bring love into our nature. Love is an effect. And only as we fulfill the right condition can we have the effect produced. Shall I tell you what the cause is?

If you turn to the Revised Version of the First Epistle of John you find these words: "We love because He first loved us." "We love," not "We love Him." That is the way the old version has it, and it is quite wrong. "We love—because He first loved us." Look at that word "because." It is the cause of which I have spoken. "Because He first loved us," the effect follows that we love, we love Him, we love all men. We cannot help it. Because He loved us, we love, we love everybody. Our heart is slowly changed. Contemplate the love of Christ, and you will love. Stand before that mirror, reflect Christ's character, and you will be changed into the same image from tenderness to tenderness. There is no other way. You cannot love to order. You can only look at the lovely object, and fall in love with it, and grow into likeness to it. And so look at this Perfect Character, this Perfect Life. Look at

The Great Sacrifice

as He laid down Himself, all through life, and upon the Cross of Calvary; and you must love Him. And loving Him, you must become like Him. Love begets love. It is a process of induction. Put a piece of iron in the presence of an electrified body, and that piece of iron for a time becomes electrified. It is changed into a temporary magnet in the mere presence of a permanent magnet, and as long as you leave the two side by side, they are both magnets alike. Remain side by side with Him who loved us, and

Gave Himself for Us

and you, too, will become a permanent magnet, a permanently attractive force; and like Him you will draw all men unto you, like Him you will be drawn unto all men. That is the inevitable effect of Love. Any man who fulfills that cause must have that effect produced in him.

Try to give up the idea that religion comes to us by chance, or by mystery, or by caprice. It comes to us by natural law, or by supernatural law, for all law is Divine.

Edward Irving went to see a dying boy once, and when he entered the room he just put his hand on the sufferer's head, and said, "My boy, God loves you," and went away. The boy started from his bed, and called out to the people in the house,

"God loves me! God loves me!"

One word! It changed that boy. The sense that God loved him overpowered him, melted him down, and began the creating of a new heart in him. And that is how the love of God melts down the unlovely heart in man, and begets in him the new creature, who is patient and humble and gentle and unselfish. And there is no other way to get it. There is no mystery about it. We love others, we love everybody, we love our enemies, because He first loved us.

III. The Defence

Now I have a closing sentence or two to add about Paul's reason for singling out love as the supreme possession.

It is a very remarkable reason. In a single word it is this: it lasts. "Love," urges Paul, "never faileth." Then he begins again one of his marvelous lists of the great things of the day, and exposes them one by one. He runs over the things that men thought were going to last, and shows that they are all fleeting, temporary, passing away.

"Whether there be prophecies, they shall be done away." It was the mother's ambition for her boy in those days that he should become a prophet. For hundreds of years God had never spoken by means of any prophet, and at that time the prophet was greater than the king. Men waited wistfully for another messenger to come, and hung upon his lips when he appeared, as upon the very voice of God. Paul says, "Whether there be prophecies, they shall fail." The Bible is full of prophecies. One by one they have "failed"; that is, having been fulfilled, their work is finished; they have nothing more to do now in the world except to feed a devout man's faith.

Then Paul talks about tongues. That was another thing that was greatly coveted. "Whether there be tongues, they shall cease." As we all know, many many centuries have passed since tongues have been known in this world. They have ceased. Take it in any sense you like. Take it, for illustration merely, as languages in general—a sense which was not in Paul's mind at all, and which though it cannot give us the specific lesson, will point the general truth. Consider the words in which these chapters were written—Greek. It has gone. Take the Latin—the other great tongue of those days. It ceased long ago. Look at the Indian language. It is ceasing. The language of Wales, of Ireland, of the Scottish Highlands is dying before our eyes. The most popular book in the English tongue at the present time, except the Bible, is one of Dickens' works, his Pickwick Papers. It is largely written in the language of London street-life; and experts assure us that in fifty years it will be unintelligible to the average English reader.

Then Paul goes farther, and with even greater boldness adds, "Whether there be knowledge, it shall be done away." The wisdom of the ancients, where is it? It is wholly gone. A schoolboy to-day knows more than Sir Isaac Newton knew; his knowledge has vanished away. You put yesterday's newspaper in the fire: its knowledge has vanished away. You buy the old editions of the great encyclopædias for a few cents: their knowledge has vanished away. Look how the coach has been superseded by the use of steam. Look how electricity has superseded that, and swept a hundred almost new inventions into oblivion. One of the greatest living authorities, Sir William Thompson, said in Scotland, at a meeting at which I was present, "The steam-engine is passing away." "Whether there be knowledge, it shall vanish away." At every workshop you will see, in the back yard, a heap of old iron, a few wheels, a few levers, a few cranks, broken and eaten with rust. Twenty years ago that was the pride of the city. Men flocked in from the country to see the great invention; now it is superseded, its day is done. And all the boasted science and philosophy of this day will soon be old.

In my time, in the university of Edinburgh, the greatest figure in the faculty was Sir James Simpson, the discoverer of chloroform. Recently his successor and nephew, Professor Simpson, was asked by the librarian of the University to go to the library and pick out the books on his subject (midwifery) that were no longer needed. His reply to the librarian was this:

"Take every text-book that is more than ten years old and put it down in the cellar."

Sir James Simpson was a great authority only a few years ago: men came from all parts of the earth to consult him; and almost the whole teaching of that time is consigned by the science of to-day to oblivion. And in every branch of science it is the same. "Now we know in part. We see through a glass darkly." Knowledge does not last.

Can you tell me anything that is going to last? Many things Paul did not condescend to name. He did not mention money, fortune, fame; but he picked out the great things of his time, the things the best men thought had something in them, and brushed them peremptorily aside. Paul had no charge against these things in themselves. All he said about them was that they would not last. They were great things, but not supreme things. There were things beyond them. What we are stretches past what we do, beyond what we possess. Many things that men denounce as sins are not sins; but they are temporary. And that is a favourite argument of the New Testament. John says of the world, not that it is wrong, but simply that it "passeth away." There is a great deal in the world that is delightful and beautiful; there is a great deal in it that is great and engrossing; but

It Will Not Last

All that is in the world, the lust of the eye, the lust of the flesh, and the pride of life, are but for a little while. Love not the world therefore. Nothing that it contains is worth the life and consecration of an immortal soul. The immortal soul must give itself to something that is immortal. And the only immortal things are these: "Now abideth faith, hope, love, but the greatest of these is love."

Some think the time may come when two of these three things will also pass away—faith into sight, hope into fruition. Paul does not say so. We know but little now about the conditions of the life that is to come. But what is certain is that Love must last. God, the Eternal God, is Love. Covet, therefore, that everlasting gift, that one thing which it is certain is going to stand, that one coinage which will be current in the Universe when all the other coinages of all the nations of the world shall be useless and unhonored. You will give yourselves to many things, give yourself first to Love. Hold things in their proportion. Hold things in their proportion. Let at least the first great object of our lives be to achieve the character defended in these words, the character—and it is the character of Christ—which is built round Love.

I have said this thing is eternal. Did you ever notice how continually John associates love and faith with eternal life? I was not told when I was a boy that "God so loved the world that He gave His only-begotten Son, that whosoever believeth in Him should have everlasting life." What I was told, I remember, was, that God so loved the world that, if I trusted in Him, I was to have a thing called peace, or I was to have rest, or I was to have joy, or I was to have safety. But I had to find out for myself that whosoever trusteth in Him—that is, whosoever loveth Him, for trust is only the avenue to Love—hath

Everlasting Life

The Gospel offers a man a life. Never offer a man a thimbleful of Gospel. Do not offer them merely joy, or merely peace, or merely rest, or merely safety; tell them how Christ came to give men a more abundant life than they have, a life abundant in love, and therefore abundant in salvation for themselves, and large in enterprise for the alleviation and redemption of the world. Then only can the Gospel take hold of the whole of a man, body, soul and spirit, and give to each part of his nature its exercise and reward. Many of the current Gospels are addressed only to a part of man's nature. They offer peace, not life; faith, not Love; justification, not regeneration. And men slip back again from such religion because it has never really held them. Their nature was not all in it. It offered no deeper and gladder life-current than the life that was lived before. Surely it stands to reason that only a fuller love can compete with the love of the world.

To love abundantly is to live abundantly, and to love forever is to live forever. Hence, eternal life is inextricably bound up with love. We want to live forever for the same reason that we want to live to-morrow. Why do we want to live to-morrow? Is it because there is some one who loves you, and whom you want to see to-morrow, and be with, and love back? There is no other reason why we should live on than that we love and are beloved. It is when a man has no one to love him that he commits suicide. So long as he has friends, those who love him and whom he loves, he will live, because to live is to love. Be it but the love of a dog, it will keep him in life; but let that go, he has no contact with life, no reason to live. He dies by his own hand.

Eternal life also is to know God, and God is love. This is Christ's own definition. Ponder it. "This is life eternal, that they might know Thee the only true God, and Jesus Christ whom Thou hast sent." Love must be eternal. It is what God is. On the last analysis, then, love is life. Love never faileth, and life never faileth, so long as there is love. That is the philosophy of what Paul is showing us; the reason why in the nature of things Love should be the supreme thing—because it is going to last; because in the nature of things it is an Eternal Life. It is a thing that we are living now, not that we get when we die; that we shall have a poor chance of getting when we die unless we are living now.

No Worse Fate

can befall a man in this world than to live and grow old alone, unloving and unloved. To be lost is to live in an unregenerate condition, loveless and unloved; and to be saved is to love; and he that dwelleth in love dwelleth already in God. For God is Love.

Now I have all but finished. How many of you will join me in reading this chapter once a week for the next three months? A man did that once and it changed his whole life. Will you do it? It is for the greatest thing in the world. You might begin by reading it every day, especially the verses which describe the perfect character. "Love suffereth long, and is kind; love envieth not; love vaunteth not itself." Get these ingredients into your life. Then everything that you do is eternal. It is worth doing. It is worth giving time to. No man can become a saint in his sleep; and to fulfill the condition required demands a certain amount of prayer and meditation and time, just as improvement in any direction, bodily or mental, requires preparation and care. Address yourselves to that one thing; at any cost have this transcendent character exchanged for yours.

You will find as you look back upon your life that the moments that stand out, the moments when you have really lived, are the moments when you have done things in a spirit of love. As memory scans the past, above and beyond all the transitory pleasures of life, there leap forward those supreme hours when you have been enabled to do unnoticed kindnesses to those round about you, things too trifling to speak about, but which you feel have entered into your eternal life. I have seen almost all the beautiful things God has made; I have enjoyed almost every pleasure that He has planned for man; and yet as I look back I see standing out above all the life that has gone four or five short experiences, when the love of God reflected itself in some poor imitation, some small act of love of mine, and these seem to be the things which alone of all one's life abide. Everything else in all our lives is transitory. Every other good is visionary. But the acts of love which no man knows about, or can ever know about—they never fail.

In the Book of Matthew, where the Judgment Day is depicted for us in the imagery of One seated upon a throne and dividing the sheep from the goats, the test of a man then is not, "How have I believed?" but "How have I loved?" The test of religion, the final test of religion, is not religiousness, but Love. I say the final test of religion at that great Day is not religiousness, but Love; not what I have done, not what I have believed, not what I have achieved, but how I have discharged the common charities of life. Sins of commission in that awful indictment are not even referred to. By what we have not done, by sins of omission, we are judged. It could not be otherwise. For the withholding of love is the negation of the spirit of Christ, the proof that we never knew Him, that for us He lived in vain. It means that He suggested nothing in all our thoughts, that He inspired nothing in all our lives, that we were not once near enough to Him, to be seized with the spell of His compassion for the world. It means that—

"I lived for myself,

I thought for myself,

For myself, and none beside—

Just as if Jesus had never lived,

As if He had never died."

Thank God the Christianity of today is coming nearer the world's need. Live to help that on. Thank God men know better, by a hair's breadth, what religion is, what God is, who Christ is, where Christ is. Who is Christ? He who fed the hungry, clothed the naked, visited the sick. And where is Christ? Where? —"Whoso shall receive a little child in My name receiveth Me." And who are Christ's? "Every one that loveth is born of God."

Index

7 Decades

Verdict on Jesus through the years

1950

1971

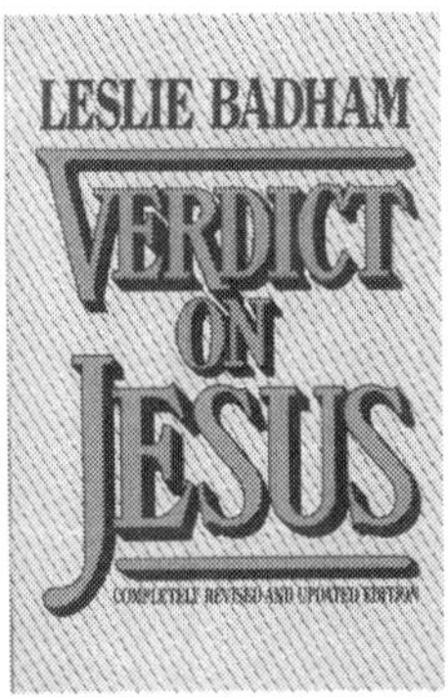

1983

1995

2010

2020

Leslie Badham

Author of Verdict on Jesus

Top left: Leslie Badham with Effie, his fiancée, at her graduation from the LSE in 1935

Top right: Leslie and Effie Badham with their children David, Christine, Clare and Paul in 1963

Middle: Leslie Badham with Queen Elizabeth at Windsor Parish Church in 1965

Bottom left: Leslie Badham RAF Chaplain 1940-45

Visit the Verdict on Jesus Website

www.verdictonjesus.com

The Verdict on Jesus website features short, educational videos for individuals and groups studying the life of Jesus. Videos include

- 'Historically Reliable Evidence of Jesus'
- 'Philosophy of Religion & Belief in God'
- 'Jesus in the World's Religions'
- 'Was Jesus a Liberal?'

...and many more!

You'll also find essays on historical Jesus research and more information about the authors and the Newson Trust.

Printed in Great Britain
by Amazon

59750488R00194